MARTIN LUTHER

HIS CHALLENGE THEN AND NOW

First published in 2017
by **COLUMBA PRESS**
23 Merrion Square North
Dublin 2, Ireland
www.columba.ie

ISBN: 978-1-78218-328-0

Set in Linux Libertine 10/14
Cover and book design by Alba Esteban | Columba Press
Printed by Jellyfish Solutions

MARTIN LUTHER

HIS CHALLENGE THEN AND NOW

P. Fintan Lyons O.S.B.

columba press

Remembering
Right Reverend Noel Willoughby
Michael Hurley SJ

CONTENTS

FOREWORD

Over the centuries since his death there have been innumerable biographies of Luther, and the present five-hundredth anniversary of his symbolic gesture of protest has led to some new attempts to take the measure of the man. Reformation studies by authors of Lutheran background accord him a monumental stature, while he sometimes figures mainly as a foundational figure in a developing story told by authors of Anglican and Reformed backgrounds. A recent Lutheran biographer, Scott Hendrix, speaks of the dilemma an author faces: 'We cannot tell the story of his life separately from that of the early Reformation, but neither can we allow the Reformation to overwhelm the person'.[1] The fifth centenary has led to some new or new editions of biographies, including a comprehensively researched new biography by Lyndal Roper in 2016[2] and one by Peter Stanford in 2017[3]. Many Luther studies in the past were from a confessional standpoint; authors from a Reformation tradition have seen Luther as a needed prophetic figure, while those in the Catholic tradition have acknowledged the need for reform, but have been inclined to believe that without Luther the barque of Peter would somehow have righted itself. Catholic writers have tended instinctively to place Luther in the history of theology, while those of other traditions have understandably spoken of the ecclesiastical abuses of the time. Owen Chadwick's *The Reformation* opens with the words, 'At the beginning of the sixteenth century everyone that mattered in the Western church was crying out for reformation'[4] and he instances examples of multiple and non-residential benefices, concluding elegantly, 'What one honest man believed to be an abuse, another honest man defended'.[5] Personally, I have found it quite challenging, yet ultimately rewarding, to explain the significance of the small Saxon town of Wittenberg in Germany on the map of medieval Europe to students from other continents – to make Luther and the Reformation somehow 'relevant' in the context of the history of Christianity and clarify how his challenge to the church of the time was perceived and what it had been. The project that will occupy me here, after providing a basic biography, is to record my perception of what Luther's challenge to the church in his day essentially was, to show his relevance to the efforts of the Catholic Church to continue in the path of renewal undertaken at the Second Vatican Council and, finally, to show how his theology can today address a secular world which has Christian, including Reformation, roots. The task arising from a historical survey is then to assess how he may still pose a challenge to the Catholic Church and I would hope that this study could be of assistance to the other churches as they engage in a similar task of renewal and witness.

Given that Luther said he would use his power as a baptised Christian to excommunicate the pope and cardinals if the Bull of condemnation against him proved genuine (which he knew it was),[6] could there be any common ground between him and the papal church then or now? It is a fact, however, that Luther was concerned about how the true church must be characterised and when he was reacting to the radical reformers who denied infant baptism, which they considered the mark of the papal church, he defended it saying: 'indeed everything that is Christian and good is to be found there' (though he would go on to speak of the antichrist presiding over it).[7] This statement was made in 1528. This was the more mature Luther, who had gone through the process of separating himself from Rome but was now realising that the church was not something confined to theory but a community with visible aspects, including sacramental rites.

Over the whole history of his thinking, even at its most polemical, Luther raised issues which still need to be taken seriously and in a contextualised rather than an isolated way. For the account of Luther's career I have relied on existing scholarly resources, the later phase of the Reformation being my own area of special interest, but the study of his relevance to contemporary issues is one to which I have tried to make my own contribution. This text began as an article but developed into a book, because articles I had read by others or written myself could never in the space allotted account for all the theological, social and especially the political factors needed to contextualise the Luther phenomenon.

INTRODUCTION

The year beginning 31 October 2016 was chosen to mark the fifth centenary of the Protestant Reformation because of Martin Luther's posting of his theses against indulgences on that date in 1517, and that puts him squarely at the heart of this commemoration. As Roper says, 'there is no doubting the significance of the theses themselves: the Reformation was sparked by a single text'.[1] He was indeed the dominant figure at the beginning, but even within his lifetime the movement became a multi-faceted one with other leaders and other centres of action. Luther himself was left out of negotiations, while the next couple of generations saw the emergence of separate denominations. Schleiermacher in the nineteenth century believed the Reformation still went on. It is worth considering then how relevant Luther is to the story of this huge event in the history of Christianity and whether this relevance continues today. There had been movements of a similar type earlier than the sixteenth century: the Waldensians in Italy in the twelfth, the Lollards in England in the fourteenth and especially the Hussites in Bohemia in the fifteenth.

Luther's relevance to religious history begins with the fact that in his attempt to remedy what he saw to be corruption in the church he unintentionally unleashed forces which ruptured a monolithic Christian society, leaving it divided and prone to continual fissiparous forces.[2] In some ways he is still relevant, if only because the issues with which he attempted to deal have never fully gone away and the contemporary project to bring Christianity back to a recognisable state of unity will require re-visiting many of the issues on which he challenged his contemporaries, and not just the ecclesiastical authorities, because religion and politics affected each other very much.

His relevance to the religious and cultural issues of today can be distinguished from the historical question of what were the immediate effects of his career. He accepted at the end of his life that only limited success had attended his efforts, yet the change that took place in Christendom after Luther was obviously real. But it is hard to estimate how much of it was actually due to Luther or his immediate successors in the Reformation movement. Wilhelm Dilthey (1883-1911) saw the beginning of a new social order stemming from the writings of Luther, a society marked by the recognition of the autocracy of the human person, an appreciation of the secular world and the fostering a new kind of personal religion free from the influence of repressive institutions. Much interest has also focused on the kind of society, its moral values and economic outlook, which existed in the period following the second stage of the Reformation, that influenced by Calvin. In the late nineteenth century, Max Weber (1864-1920) advanced the theory that capitalism flourished because of the Protestant ethic that emerged from Calvinism in the sixteenth and seventeenth centuries. Ernst Troeltsch (1865-1923) agreed with Weber about later Protestantism, but Troeltsch held against Dilthey that Luther's Reformation remained pre-modern, creating a religion that was still church-dominated, in which life was still ruled by supernatural revelation, but based now on the Bible rather than papal hegemony and subservient to the princely, or later state, authorities. All these attempts to identify the influence of the Reformation on society have had their critics; it has been noted that capitalism already operated in the society into which Luther was born and it was also the system that obtained in Renaissance Italy. The Medici family, which gave the church Pope Leo X, Luther's protagonist, were financiers with branches in various parts of Europe.

By the beginning of the sixteenth century, the prohibition of usury in Christian tradition was breaking down as low-interest lending to people in need became part of normal living and Luther would come to accept the practice as part of his distinction between the two kingdoms, the realms of church and state, or more exactly, the two sets of relationships within which the Christian lived, usually described as the two kingdoms. On the one hand, the law of the gospel required forbearance, forgiveness, refusal to exploit another's condition; on the other, the common life of mankind required regulation by just laws to ensure justice was available to all. While he had no systematic teaching on these matters,[3] in later centuries Luther came to be criticised for apparently granting to the state an autonomy which could leave the community passive in face of the state's control of culture and this was held to explain the failure of Lutherans, as Troeltsch might have predicted, to adopt a critical attitude towards the policies of Germany's National Socialist government before and during World War II. Such criticism hardly took sufficient account of the emergence of the Confessing Church, the movement against Nazism in which Dietrich Bonhoeffer (1906-1945), who was committed to Luther's theology rather than liberal versions of it, played a prominent part.

What Luther's movement brought to early modern society in Germany was an emphasis not just on the national culture and economy but also on the local community and, as will be seen, this included promotion of family life even though he denied marriage was a sacrament. As Bainton comments: 'The influence of the man on his people was deepest in the home'.[4] The Bible in his vernacular translation took a prominent place in the family, bridging the gap between home and church and giving literacy a boost. In fact, he is credited with contributing considerably to the emergence of the German vernacular and its literary riches. His contributions to hymnody further enriched the culture which went on to produce the monumental figure of J. S. Bach in less than two hundred years. This was quite an impressive legacy to leave behind for someone who even as a national figure and religious leader took pride in claiming that he was of farming stock, going back to his grandfather and great-grandfather.[5]

To speculate on what would not have happened without Luther may be a futile exercise, nor is it clear, according to a historian of the entire Reformation period, Carlos Eire, whether the 'Reformations' which did occur changed the world for the better or for the worse – a legitimate question, he maintains, that most historians prefer to avoid. He formulates an answer, as will be seen at the end of this study.[6] It does seem clear, however, that even without the upheaval of the Reformation the church's structures and administrative control would have been put under enormous strain as a new world opened up through revolutionary developments, technical and social, at the end of the fifteenth century. It is interesting that contemporaneously with Luther's promotion of Augustine's Neoplatonist theology, though from a different perspective, the inchoate scientific mentality was beginning to replace the Aristotelian philosophy of nature with a return to more Platonist ideas, as a foundation for science and technology. Not that the world of commerce and politics reflected on these deeper principles; rather it was a case of the new technologies such as astronomical and navigational equipment favouring voyages of exploration and the expansionist policies of old Europe's states. This resulted in rapid growth in trading activity, a new commercially focused society.

Medieval thinking in religion as in much else would have found itself less and less relevant in this new situation, while on the other hand it is clear that the theology and the ecclesio-political structures actually generated by the Reformation movement had significant effects on European culture. It is true that the early Reformation churches were inward-looking rather than missionary-minded, so there is certainly a question as to whether what Luther inaugurated left Christianity less adapted to the task of bringing the gospel message to this new world, new in culture and new in geographical extent. At first sight, negative effects of the Reformation are apparent. The wars now described as the wars of religion, which devastated much of old Europe in the century after Luther's death and sparked off a secularisation process in European culture so evident today, could hardly have happened, at least not under a religious banner, if Christianity had remained united. Missionary activity, when it began to emerge in the Protestant world, embodied the contradictions which have hindered all missionary progress ever since. But would the health of Western Christianity have declined even more from its fragile state in the sixteenth century and would the divided witness of West and East have continued to be an obstacle when facing the spread of Islam? These are fascinating questions, but impossible to answer.

A study of the phenomenon of Luther, and his effects on church and society, leads in the end to recognising that issues which existed then are endemic to Christianity in every century. In a quick survey there seem to be various interrelated issues which came to the surface in a notable way because of Luther's stance but were always present, and apparently still are, in the life of the church and its relationship to society: ecclesiological issues in the sense of the Church's self-under-standing but also broader ones concerning religion in a secular society. The final chapter will deal with the question of Luther's challenge when these issues are debated with a view to finding contemporary solutions. Here, a brief introduction will be given to the material to be discussed.

The internal issues come most readily to mind because in his day Luther began as a religious and a theology professor, the sort of person who would be expected to make an insightful contribution to the church's well-being by pointing to necessary theological and pastoral reforms. In modern times, this was the agenda for Vatican II and various gifted theologians made their contribution to the council's thinking. The council's theology endeavoured to be creative by privileging mystery over institutionalism with its attendant drawbacks and adopted a 'People of God' perspective. The church can learn from how Luther had to cope with the unexpected consequences of his focusing on the individual rather than the institution and the divisions which soon appeared. Luther's concentration on the individual act of faith, through making justification by faith the main principle of his theology, brought a subjective dimension of religion to the forefront in a way that made a sense of corporate belonging more difficult to retain. Contemporary theology's aspiration to enfranchise fully the individual believer raises questions about the psychological as well spiritual state and indeed educational status of the believer. Much has been written about Luther's attempts to deal with an anarchic movement claiming to be guided by the Spirit and about his own personality. The charismatic movement's rise in the church after the council was rather less problematic, but the question remains whether the need was recognised in the council and afterwards for a pneumatological Christology which would have enabled the charismatic movement to prosper.

One of the most important insights of Vatican II theology was the foundational nature of Revelation (as seen in the importance of the relevant Constitution). The consequent policy of emphasis on scripture in the life of the church can gain from confronting Luther's all-encompassing theology of the word, which led him to express both the nature of the church and of the mass in terms of the word. In fact, his theology has been seen as a way forward to ecumenical consensus on the eucharist and the whole sacramental system by Karl Rahner in his writings, for example, 'The Word and the Eucharist'.[7] John Zizioulas' theology of the church as a community gathered by the Spirit is encapsulated in the title of his book *Being as Communion* and is different from Luther's theology of the church as creature of the word. But his theology of the eucharist is very close to that of Luther when he says: 'the eucharist is not a "sacrament", something parallel to the divine word: it is the eschatologisation of the historical word, the voice of the historical Christ, the voice of the Holy scripture, which comes to us no longer as "doctrine" through history, but as life and *being* through the *eschata*'.[8] The key to finding convergence between Luther's theology and that of the Catholic tradition will be identified as eschatology in the final, analytical section of this study.

Luther limited the number of sacraments to those only for which he believed there was a mandate from Christ, baptism and eucharist, though he availed himself all his life of a rite of penance and he had a high regard for what he called the estate of marriage. His theology of the sacraments was based on his sense of the importance of materiality in the realm of grace – so he was very much at odds with Zwingli, as will be seen later. Today's Catholic sacramental theology recognises the importance of the basic elements of bread, wine, water and oil for the symbolic understanding of the economy of grace and this shared perspective offers much to the process of convergence.

An issue which has come more into focus with the papacy of Pope Francis is the relationship between central authority and the local church. This question was of course at the heart of the Reformation movement and at the time involved the question also of the relationship between a council of the church and the papacy. Expanding the present-day discussion to include this perspective could be helpful, especially when synods are regularly held and local episcopal conferences are brought into the reckoning. The ambiguities of Luther's attitudes in this regard could profitably be borne in mind.

Turning to the external issues, the context in which Luther's movement grew was highly political in the sense that alliance with rulers or military force at times determined its growth or threatened its existence. In relation to social justice, his tendency to favour the rulers against the demands of the peasants at the time of the Peasants' War of 1525 came from his dissociation of religion from social issues, which today seems simplistic, and yet the distinctions he made echo in some way the ideals expressed in the Sermon on the Mount. Today, church-state relationships encounter added difficulties because of ethical issues unknown in Luther's time and require even more discernment than his perspective could provide. From the history of the Reformation, the lesson can be learned that neither patronage nor hostility advances the church's position and that the relationship between church and state depends on many factors, in particular the extent of nationalism. In Germany, the strong sense of being German led to a 'Germexit' in relation to Rome (as happened in England under Henry VIII). There was also a degree of populism, whipped up by Luther's publications, but also by the rapid growth of pamphleteering in the early sixteenth century, of the *Flugschriften* or short, cheaply produced pamphlets (a phenomenon corresponding to the similar growth and influence of the social media today).[9] How the social media and populism affect not just the Catholic Church but religion generally should not be underestimated.

The problems besetting the well-being of Christianity as a cultural phenomenon, as giving a 'tone' to society, can be seen reflected in the story of Luther and a society which became Lutheran in tone. It can be helpful to take account of the many-sided cultural, economic and political contexts in which his theology developed and the interaction between them. Five hundred years later, it is both important and challenging to understand the world in which Luther grew up, one which looked back on centuries of an unchanging culture steeped in Christian tradition, but was now undergoing sudden change at the level of thought and social and political structures, much like what has happened in the Western world in recent times.

Up to Luther's time, as it happens, the world's primitive technology had remained unchanged for many centuries; the sun in its regular cycle ruled all of life, as in a fundamental sense it always will while the earth lasts. It was the ultimate source for the energy provided by the physical effort of animals and humans and the food from which that energy came. Fire was important for its ability to change an energy source into more usable ones. But it could not be turned into light except in the simple form of torches, giving people only limited control over daily life in relation to work, education and leisure.

The economy of a world unaccustomed to technological discovery was jolted and forever altered in the late fifteenth century by the discovery of printing, a technology derived from weaving and multiplying the results of the physical effort previously put into manuscript production. That this benefited the Reformation is clear – though it also benefited its opponents in the dispute – but its effects on the culture generally were enormous because of the spread it brought to existing knowledge and new thinking, hitherto the preserve of the few. New thinking developed in economics, science, technology, politics and of course theology.

Printing was a hugely important factor in the emergence of the era known as modernity. An interesting example relating printing and modernity – and by chance in the context of the Swiss Reformation – can be found in the story of church life in the town of Zürich in the early stages of the Reformation there. The priest Huldrych Zwingli was administrator at the Great Minster – an important church, with its own chapter. In his preaching he drew attention to the contrast between law and gospel; the church laid down many laws whereas the gospel conferred freedom on Christians, freedom to judge for themselves. A crisis arose on March 5th 1522, Ash Wednesday, and was recorded in a contemporary chronicle:

> Elsi Flammer, maidservant of the printer in the Niederdorf, said she had by her master's orders, cooked some sausages on Ash Wednesday, and that the People's Priest of Einsiedeln, Bartholomew Pur and Michael Hirt had eaten of them.[10]

The printer, Froschauer, was subsequently hauled before the town council, where in his defence he said:

> Prudent, gracious, pious and dear Lords, as it has come to your knowledge that I have eaten flesh in my house, I plead guilty, and in the following manner: I have so much work on hand, and it is costing me so much in body, goods and work, that I have to get on and work at it day and night, holy day and work-a-day, so that I may get it ready for the Frankfurt Fair.[12]

The work in hand was the Epistles of St Paul, presumably in the interests of the new reform movement or, more accurately perhaps, arising from the humanist movement's drive to make the scriptures available, but the defence the printer gave provides a very early glimpse of the culture we have come to call modernity. The scientific revolution that formed that culture fully had yet to come, but the relationship between man and the world is already altering here, forty years after the invention of printing. The machine is beginning to impose its rhythms on human life and Froschauer feels its pressure. Modernity's philosophy will in time subscribe to the idea of an unending cycle of production and consumerism affecting all of religion.

Part 1

A BASIC BIOGRAPHY OF LUTHER

CHAPTER ONE

Luther's early years

Luther was born into a society that was feeling the effects of technological progress on the economy by way of the growth of industry and of the capitalism which made it possible. The mining industry forms the background to his story. Born on November 10th 1483 at Eisleben in the south-west of Saxony, he was baptised the next day on the feast of St Martin of Tours, hence his Christian name of Martin. The family moved the following year to Mansfeld some twenty kilometres away, where his father, Hans Luder (as the family was then called), got involved in copper mining, possibly even as part-owner of a mine, and by the beginning of the sixteenth century had become a mining inspector as well as operating seven smelters in a joint venture with others. Industry was built on borrowed capital and as it prospered brought more money into circulation and even into ordinary workers' pockets. The economy would gradually create a new culture deeply dedicated to material progress, but religious observance continued to reflect older priorities.

It was a climate where the canonical idea of an 'indulgence', which for several centuries already had involved payment of money, could flourish. The concept derived from church teaching that even after sin had been forgiven there remained punishment for sin to be endured either in this life or in a place of purgation in the next life, purgatory, before the forgiven sinner would be purified sufficiently to come into God's presence in heaven. The arrangement came about at the time of the first crusade to liberate the Holy Land in 1095, when Pope Urban II granted all engaged in it full remission of post-forgiveness penance because of the danger of dying abroad. While this was meant to be a magnanimous gesture on the pope's part, the hardship, the time spent away from home and the financial cost were also recognised as an effective expression of penitence in this arrangement. Penance could then be costed, so there was a logic to the practice that emerged of a donation in response to its remission. The granting of indulgences was always a papal prerogative and entailed the rather mysterious corollary that papal jurisdiction somehow extended to the next life. Originally granted rarely and as a great privilege, indulgences became more frequent and were granted under less strict conditions as the centuries passed, giving rise to what has been described as 'a clear case of inflation' and inevitable devaluation even though the spiritual treasure which provided the backing for this economy, the forgiveness Christ merited for humankind by his passion, was limitless.[1]

When crusades proved no longer feasible, an indulgence could be gained by a more realistic and more affordable local pilgrimage such as that to Trier, the shrine of the Holy Robe of Christ, or by the recitation of certain prayers or giving money to charity. Hans Luder, for example, had the resources to combine with other men of Mansfeld to apply to the bishop to have an indulgence attached to the local church. This was because the concept of pilgrimage also allowed, as in the Mansfeld case, that the local church could be a pilgrimage site through enshrining relics of saints, from some faraway place usually, and there was great competition among dioceses, religious orders and princely patrons to acquire relics. The pilgrimage itself was the original foundation for an indulgence, but what was in the holy place was clearly intrinsic to its spiritual value. For centuries before the first indulgences the concept of the relic had been established and grown in importance; pilgrimages were established to where relics were to be found. The practice of pilgrimage was an expression of a cult of the martyrs whose relics were preserved and was inspired by a belief in the resurrection of the dead. These dead heroic witnesses of the faith would one day reclaim their bodies and in the meantime their relics were a channel through which supernatural power was available for the needs of ordinary life. The cult of the martyrs became a cult of relics. For those given to superstition, they were often the main channel of grace, competing with the sacraments themselves. There is even evidence of the reserved eucharist, the body and blood of Christ, being placed in the same category as 'other' relics and placed with them in an altar.[2]

Given their importance, a good collection of relics brought spiritual prestige to a church or monastery and brought with it pilgrimages and the money pilgrims spent. This even gave rise not only to trading in relics but the practice of stealing them, called *sacra furta* to distinguish it from mere theft and give it respectability. Its vindication was often based on an alleged request from the saint to be moved to the place where the relics were now to be found. As will be seen later, in a situation that was to become notorious, Luther's patron and protector, Friedrich of Saxony (1463-1525) was a collector of relics and even went on pilgrimage to the Holy Land in 1493 to acquire more, all being then housed in the Castle Church of Wittenberg and displayed for pilgrims on the feast of All Saints, November 1st.

A significant development occurred when it became possible to acquire an indulgence on behalf of another, an expression generally of filial piety. Since from earliest times the practice had existed of making an offering for a mass celebrated for the dead, the granting of an indulgence in favour of the deceased came naturally to be associated with making an offering.

This was the background to Luther's early years. Life was hard for both agricultural peasants and the industrial workers of the towns. As with the country dwellers, in addition to domestic work the wives played a significant part as ancillary workers along with their husbands at the mines. Families were large and infant mortality was high. Luther may have had an older brother who died, leaving him the eldest of a family consisting eventually of four boys and four girls. He spoke in later years of the frequency with which he was punished in school and remembered some harsh punishments at home both by his mother and father. Biographers have devoted much attention to the relationship between him and his father and its relevance to Luther's later development as a rebel against the ecclesiastical establishment, because he refers to this relationship in his account of his development; attention will be given to this aspect of his career later. While it seems not to have been an emotionally satisfactory relationship and one not free of violence at home. Life in the town itself would appear to have included frequent cases of ill-will and violence between residents, fuelled by drink at a time when beer was the commonly substituted alternative to poor quality drinking water. But religion with its suasions, prohibitions and consolations acted as a control on community life and religious practice was not without its feasts as well as its fasts. Death was a commonly present reality, but so was the reality of heaven and the saints. It is difficult today to appreciate how important the duality and mutual presence of heaven and earth were in people's perceptions. With it came awareness of saints but also of malign spirits – part of a pagan heritage in a pre-scientific age. Luther never ceased during his life to refer to the devil and his tricks, while his momentous decision at the age of twenty-two to become a friar came in the form of a promise to St Anne.

That is to anticipate, however. At about fourteen, he left Mansfeld to go to school seventy kilometres to the north in the cathedral town of Magdeburg where he lodged with an official of the archbishop, probably because this man was of a mining family. Here his education continued as in the Latin school in Mansfeld; Latin, 'the language of the church, of law, diplomacy, international relations, scholarship and travel' dominated the curriculum.[3] However, after one year his parents moved him to the town of his mother's family, Eisenach, at the time a less prestigious town than Magdeburg and twice as far away to the south, though compared with the mining town of Mansfeld it was a more cultured environment with many religious houses. In fact, Eisenach became a town with remarkable associations, partly because Luther spent formative years there and was later to spend a year in the Wartburg Castle overlooking the town when he was in protective custody while under the ban of the empire. But long before Luther, the Wartburg was the residence of one of the most remarkable women of the Middle Ages, St Elizabeth, the Hungarian princess who married the Thuringian King Ludwig and who after his death during a crusade lived a remarkable life of dedication to the needs of the poor, dying there in a house of the Franciscans at the early age of 24 in 1231. Luther came to know about St Elizabeth and revered her memory all his life, even calling his first daughter Elizabeth. The town also has a connection with J.S. Bach, who was born there nearly two hundred years after Luther's schooldays. Though Bach had to move at the age of ten to his brother's house in another village because of both parents' death, the town has continued to have a strong connection with Bach; it has the world's first Bach Museum, for example. Luther stayed there until he went to university in Erfurt at the age of seventeen and seems to have been happy as 'he always spoke later of his "good city of Eisenach" ... His school curriculum had at its centre the speaking, writing and versifying of Latin'.[4]

At Erfurt University, the curriculum was that which first emerged in the schools at Paris in the twelfth century: for the bachelor's degree the *trivium* of language, logic and philosophy and for the master's the *quadrivium* of geometry, music, arithmetic and astronomy. Luther got his bachelor's degree in 1502 and his master's in 1505. His qualifications included *Baccalareus Biblicus,* which entitled him to give introductory lectures on the Bible; *Formatus,* which signified a working knowledge of scholastic terminology, and *Sententiarius,* which authorised him to lecture on the first two books of Peter Lombard's *Sentences,* the standard medieval compendium of doctrine.[5] The teaching of philosophy at Erfurt, as in other universities of the time, centred on the texts of Aristotle, a practice standard for centuries, since the beginning of what was called scholasticism, the study of philosophy and theology based on his writings. This philosophy was used to formulate theological theses by scholars such as Thomas Aquinas. Luther studied Aristotle's philosophy but it is not known how familiar he became with the theology of Aquinas in his theology studies, as these were centred on Peter Lombard's *Sentences,* which precede Aquinas and include Augustine in their sources. (Aquinas

himself commented on the *Sentences* as part of his formation.) Luther did become familiar with Aquinas at some stage as he spoke disparagingly of him in his *Table Talk* in 1538, describing him as 'the most loquacious' of all the scholastics.[6] But he was also introduced to the more recent thinking of the later scholastics such as William of Ockham (1285-1347), whose philosophy had attracted the name Nominalism. Nominalism denied one of the most basic tenets of the philosophy of the earlier scholastics such as Thomas Aquinas (and also the earlier Augustine) by maintaining that individual things could be known as individual things without the concept of a universal nature residing in them being a necessary stage in the knowing process. This had serious implications for such issues as how God's existence could be known and was a factor in the emergence of the importance of the Bible as a way of knowing God.

While Luther would later reject all scholasticism, all theology based on philosophy, he continued to regard Ockham as his master in dialectical skills, as a philosopher but not as a theologian. As will be seen later, he would come to see all of scholastic theology as infected with Pelagianism, the heresy which attributed the ability to contribute to one's salvation by human effort unaided by grace.

Another important, even outstanding, feature of Erfurt was the influence there of the new movement, humanism, which was greatly attached to classical learning, the return to the sources through study of the languages – Greek and Latin – of the ancients. Aristotle was taught using original texts, though probably in Latin translation. Luther would later become proficient in Greek under the tutelage of Philip Melanchthon, Professor of Greek at Wittenberg and several years his junior.

All of this was in the future for the young master of arts, who as planned by his father now turned to the study of law. It would be of considerable importance to his father in his business to have him back home as a lawyer. But this was not to be. Having graduated in February 1505 he had to wait for the start of the law term in May and some biographers have identified this period of inactivity as one in which he suffered from mood swings. Apparently he wandered about sadly and was deeply affected by the death of a fellow student.[7] It seems to have begun the cycle of depression and elation, 'desolation and ecstacy', as one commentator put it,[8] that affected him for the rest of his life. The assessment of his psychological state is bound up with that of his spiritual development and centres on his experience of *Anfechtung* (literally, attack), which preoccupied him at a crucial time in his spiritual and theological development, as will be seen later.

Commentators have noted that while he did begin the law term in due course, he left it after four weeks and went home to Mansfeld. Why he did so is not known, nor what discussions may have taken place there, but the event proved a prelude to a series of radical experiences which followed. On his way home, he accidentally severed an artery in his leg with his sword and narrowly avoided bleeding to death. On his way back from Mansfeld a few weeks later, a thunderstorm with lightning strikes quite near him caused him to panic and call on St Anne, the patron saint of the mining industry, to save him, promising as he did so to become a religious. Afterwards, according to what he said in his *Table Talk* in 1539, he had second thoughts and many tried to persuade him to change his mind, but he persevered and invited his best friends to a party the night before he entered the Augustinians at Erfurt. He told them they would see him no more and they escorted him with tears to the cloister.

Several questions arise here. The most easily answered is why he entered the Augustinians, though there were five other religious communities in Erfurt. The Observant Augustinians were a stricter branch of the order which had its origins in the thirteenth century when some religious communities came together to adopt the rule of St Augustine. In the fifteenth century a reform movement brought about a stricter more monastic way of life in some branches of the order, to distinguish their way of life from that of the mendicant orders, the Franciscans and Dominicans. They were then termed 'monks' as they followed the traditional monastic regime, though they had priors rather than abbots as leaders and, significantly, retained the mendicants' identifying characteristic of mendicancy, of soliciting alms publicly. Though Luther applied the term 'monk' to himself and others, they should technically have been called 'friars' because of the importance of mendicancy and the fact that their structures of government (a centralised order and provincial chapters etc. imposed by the papacy) reflected those of the mendicant orders. The Erfurt Observant priory engaged in intellectual work, had a good library and had some members on the staff of the university, so it would be attractive to an intelligent young man who probably knew some of them. At that time, it is likely that any of the religious communities would have accepted him without much in the way of preliminary discussions. That would be true of the Augustinians also and especially because he was a student at Erfurt University.

The more difficult questions concern the nature and motivation of his decision. Coming about two weeks after the storm incident, by modern standards entering would seem very precipitous, while his perseverance in his decision in face of some self-doubt – whatever about the counsel of his friends – would have suggested the need for a longer time of reflection. There may, however, have been some thoughts in his mind about such a vocation over the period of his university studies at least, while some biographers hold that he was moved by his religious outlook over a longer period. This would have been one of fearful reflection on the danger of losing his soul, given the great emphasis on the four last things of death, judgment, hell and heaven in preaching, in church art and in the minds of the populace. Death from the frequent outbreaks of plague was a constant reality. The fear of judgment could also have been particularly strong in Luther's case; certainly it was to become his great preoccupation after some years of religious life, as will be seen later, and to commit to the demands of religious life could well have seemed the safest course of action. It was a courageous choice in fact, as it meant turning away from a prestigious and rewarding career as a lawyer, thereby incurring his father's wrath; it was quite a number of years before his father became reconciled to his decision. Indeed it was really only when he reversed it by leaving the habit behind and entering marriage that Hans was satisfied; Luther began the process of reconciliation when he made a letter to his father the preface to his tract on monastic vows in 1521.

Enough is known about religious life at the time of his entry and especially about that of the Observant Augustinians to make it certain that his life as a novice would involve much austerity in terms of food, clothing, living conditions and discipline, as well as long hours of prayer and study. From his own account and from the facts of his progress, it is clear that he was very successful as a young religious.

Having entered the community on July 17th 1505, he was ordained a priest on May 2nd 1507, in his twenty-fourth year. This would be considered quite young, though not unknown, by today's standards, but the period of preparation would be considered impossibly short, considering the preparatory studies now canonically required. It was not unusual at the time, however, as the main requirement (apart from the necessary religious motivation and some theological formation) was sufficient knowledge of Latin to be able to perform the sacramental duties. The reality, however, was that both in terms of suitability and ability, there were shortcomings in the application of the criteria to the priesthood of the time and this was perhaps the most fundamental reason for the calls for reform on the part of critics such as Erasmus. By the standards prevailing, Luther was perfectly qualified for this important step in his life as a religious.

His ability could not have been doubted but questions could have been raised regarding his suitability for such rapid progression to a status where emotional stability would be of crucial importance in his role as a dispenser of the mysteries (to use a Pauline term) and guide of souls at important stages in the lives of the faithful. His testing in that regard occurred on the day of his *Primitz*, the celebration of the first mass, which could be delayed as it was in Luther's case, for several weeks. This was to allow his parents to attend and the date was actually set to suit his father, who came with a party of about twenty on horseback and with a gift for the community of twenty gulden – a standard practice expressing the joy of the family and as a contribution to the cost of the festivities. All of this indicated goodwill on the part of Hans; in the only account extant, there is no mention of Luther's mother.

The first test for Luther came in the course of the celebration of the mass. As he began the prayer asking God the Father to receive the offerings and change them into the body and blood of Christ, *Te igitur clementissime Pater* ... a prayer then said in a very low voice to emphasise its sacred character, he hesitated. In his own account he recalled his experience:

> At these words I was utterly stupefied and terror-stricken. I thought to myself, 'With what tongue shall I address such majesty, seeing that all men ought to tremble in the presence of even an earthly prince? Who am I, that I should lift up my eyes or raise my hands to the divine majesty. The angels surround him. At his nod the earth trembles. And shall I, a miserable little pygmy, say "I want this, I ask for that?" For I am dust and ashes and full of sin and I am speaking to the living, eternal and the true God.'[9]

The different versions of the event given later by Luther himself have allowed biographers to use imagination in describing it. In the 1961 play, *Luther,* by John Osborne, this scene at his first mass is performed off-stage, but it is presented in very dramatic form in the film version in 1974.

What he said about his experience is not surprising, because of psychological and spiritual unpreparedness on his part – psychological because of Luther's particular temperament, spiritual because a longer and more adequate theological and spiritual preparation would have been needed. His theological formation as a member of the Augustinian community included the study of the theology of Gabriel Biel (1420-1495), one of the foremost theologians of the time and the one who coined the phrase typical of Nominalism: 'do what is in you' (*fac quod in te est*) indicating belief that God gives the grace necessary for salvation to those who already strive for it. This theology Luther accepted at the time but subsequently rejected (for the first time publicly in an internal discussion among faculty members in Wittenberg in 1516).[10] He spoke in later years of how much he had appreciated Biel originally and this appreciation would have included the study by Biel which was a standard part of preparation for the priesthood, *Sacri Canonis Missae Expositio.*

In it Biel discussed the central part of the mass in eighty-nine chapters. He was concerned with justifying the practice of the time, the long established custom of offering masses for deceased individuals and individual intentions, and thus had to allow that a mass celebrated had limited value from the point of view of graces received compared with the sacrifice of Calvary; otherwise one mass would suffice to redeem the world and liberate all souls from purgatory. Consequently, he saw the mass as a commemorative representation of the historical sacrifice of Christ and had the difficulty of how to relate the two. He followed the approach which had obtained for several centuries in 'expositions' of the canon, of interpreting it allegorically. That meant refraining from interpreting the texts theologically, implicitly accepting the mass was a sacrifice but not investigating that interpretation and concentrating on the actions and vestments instead. Biel's way of presenting the mass as sacrifice was to consider that the two separate consecrations of the bread and wine represented the sacrificial death of Christ through the separation of his body and blood. This was the standard Nominalist approach. 'In this way, the whole mass became a dramatic re-enactment of the sacrifice of Calvary.'[11] Visualising the mass in relation to Calvary, the vestments of the priest were considered symbols of the passion of Christ; the cincture a symbol of his captivity, the alb the garment he wore on the way to Calvary, the chasuble embroidered with a cross a symbol of the cross he carried, the steps up to the altar representing the ascent of Calvary. For the faithful of the time, this dramatic representation could be powerfully emotive, but in reality was symbolism of a superficial kind compared with that intrinsic to the liturgy of the Orthodox Church and obtaining today in Catholic liturgical theology.

One of the inherent difficulties was that allegory meant there was no real connection between the symbolic and what it represented, and therefore, for example, no real connection between the priest and Christ. Luther felt the burden of this when he considered that he was addressing God in his own personal capacity or dignity, something that is evident in the passage cited above, and he realised how unworthy he was to do so. He referred to this realisation that all seemed to depend on his personal worth when he recalled his first mass many years later: he almost died because he felt that he had no real faith: 'I reflected only on the dignity of my person, that I wasn't a sinner and feared that I would omit something'.[12]

A psychological difficulty arose at the breakfast following the mass, as this was the first time he was with his father since he departed for the cloister. His father must be considered to have shown goodwill, but in his presence Luther was inevitably uneasy. After his ordeal of addressing God the Father, he may now have looked for some words of reassurance from his earthly father. The events which followed are described in a different sequence in the accounts Luther gave of the occasion many years later, but it is clear that there was an altercation between father and son, the sort of thing that can arise unexpectedly and against the participants' own wishes in a situation which is highly charged with emotion. It is likely that Luther took the initiative of suggesting to his father that everything had turned out well, despite past disappointment on his part. He was justifying his decision to enter the cloister and referred to the vow he had taken on the day of the storm. This brought an unfortunate reaction from his father, who retorted that he hoped it had not been an illusion of the devil. As Todd remarks, 'it was typically ham-handed, this poking rough-and-ready German fun at his son'.[13] It was the wrong thing to say to a man who so often felt besieged by the devil and had just gone through moments of self-doubt and even of panic. The situation worsened when Luther presented the life of the cloister as one of quiet – a safe haven from such temptations – which caused Hans to take the high moral ground and remind him of the commandment to honour one's parents.

Luther was fortunate that in the aftermath to this unhappy occasion, he soon found a spiritual father in his religious life. He came to be favoured by the Vicar General of the Augustinians in Germany, Johann Von Staupitz (1460-1524), who steered him to doctoral studies. The background to this decision seems to have included a relationship between the two which could be described as that of spiritual direction, as the most recent and well documented biography by Lyndal Roper makes Staupitz out as Luther's director and confessor,[14] as does Roland Bainton in his general history of the Reformation,[15] though an earlier work, John M. Todd's biography, gives as his 'probable' director John von Grefenstein and relates an unattributed conversation between these two concerning Luther's frequent desire to confess.[16] If the former account is correct, Staupitz had a complicated task in dealing with Luther both as someone under his authority and also a soul he directed. In fact, what would today be seen as a conflict between the external and internal forums would be today considered unacceptable. The confidentiality proper to a relationship in the internal forum can allow issues to be dealt with satisfactorily before the authorities in the external forum have to make decisions about the status and future of someone subject to them. In his case, Staupitz seems to have acted to solve what he saw as Luther's problem of preoccupation with self, or scrupulosity. While that would be a reasonable approach on the part of a seasoned theologian and spiritual guide, what all studies of Luther have shown is that his problems of conscience had a basis also in his theological perspective, where 'conscience' had broader connotations, as will be seen later. Luther was apparently very troubled because of what he called his *Anfechtungen*, a word which be translated as temptations but could also have the sense of 'attacks', indicating assaults by the devil. This struggle with him was in Luther's world view part of the conflict between God and the devil – as Heiko Oberman's well-known study, *Luther: Man between God and the Devil*, puts it. Luther seems to have been more aware of the devil than others even in a period where the existence of the devil loomed large in people's consciousness.

He was also influenced by both Augustine's theology of predestination and the Nominalist philosophy of his studies in which the idea of covenant between God and man raised the possibility that reliance on God's goodwill might be misplaced. To this aspect of Luther's theological and spiritual development it will be necessary to return when dealing with his subsequent career. Staupitz, whose attitude to these traditions seems to have been more liberal, thought to solve the problem by directing him to engage more intensely in academic study. That could explain the conversation of 1517 between them reported in his *Table Talk* in 1531; he recalled their conversation under a pear tree when Staupitz challenged him with the assertion that undertaking these studies would give him a real job to do, or depending on how the German he interpolates into the Latin text is translated, would give him much trouble. Luther remarks that at the time he did not understand the significance of the challenge but four years later realised it referred to his future conflict with the papacy.[17]

As a member of the Augustinian community he began his academic career in Erfurt University and caused resentment in the community and the university when after some time he prepared his doctoral dissertation for the University of Wittenberg rather than Erfurt. This was because Staupitz had been dean of the Theology Faculty since 1502 and wished him to come there and eventually succeed him. Luther was conferred with the doctorate 'in Biblical Studies' (*In Biblia*) in Wittenberg University in October 1512, by Andreas Karlstadt (1487-1541), who was three years younger than Luther, but senior to him academically as he had become dean of the faculty of theology when Staupitz left that same year. The graduation fee was paid by the Elector Friedrich on condition that Luther would accept a permanent post in the university which Friedrich had founded and wished to develop as an alternative to Erfurt. In order to understand Luther and his world, it is important to note that Friedrich, before he died, could not recall ever having met Luther and probably never did because of the social structures of the time. At a crucial moment in Luther's career to be discussed later, his appearance at the Diet of

Worms in 1521, the elector communicated with him from his own quarters through Spalatin, his secretary. Nevertheless, October 1512 was the beginning of his loyal support for Luther, which would cause Friedrich trouble in the years ahead, but also give him a pivotal role in relations with the papacy and in the election of a new emperor. How politics and theology were intertwined is one of the most important aspects of Luther's story.

CHAPTER TWO

The well-being of Christendom

The intertwining of politics and theology had acquired a new complexity centuries before Luther. A medieval maxim held that *sacerdotium, imperium* and *studium* came together 'as the three mysterious powers or virtues by whose harmonious co-operation the life and health of Christendom are sustained'.[1] In addition to the church and the secular authorities as the controlling powers of the Christian society, a new influential factor had emerged. This third factor, the *studium*, had to some extent its source in the monastic schools of learning but principally in the universities, which from simple origins in the twelfth century schools in Paris and Bologna became institutions in society. Their presence and influence would in time be marked by buildings proclaiming a status akin to that hitherto associated with the religious and secular estates.[2] Wittenberg University, founded in1502, should be seen in this context.

The inclusion of the universities among the three mysterious powers gives prominence to the role of ideas and raises the question of how influential ideas can be. In relation to the Reformation, one historian has pointed to the danger of giving too much importance to ideas, or at least to the areas where they are considered to have been influential. Carlos M.N. Eire gives the example of the study by Karl Holl in 1911, *The Cultural Significance of the Reformation*, the central proposition of which was that 'Luther threw two major ideas as active forces into the stream of culture',[3] namely, a new concept of personality and a new concept of community. For Holl, Luther's theology of justification by faith led to the emergence of the independence of the individual and a culture imbued with a deep sense of responsibility. Eire holds that Holl was applying Luther's paradoxical theology in a simplistic way to the culture of what he described as 'the German people', while neglecting other forces affecting the actual culture – and coming to extremely erroneous conclusions in the process, for example, that the disposition of the people made it impossible for them to favour expansionist politics, or that imperialism could never possess the German people. Holl died in 1926. The idea of the three mysterious powers and their interplay is precisely what is needed to avoid what Eire describes as Holl's gross error in predicting the behaviour of the actual German nation on the basis of an unhistorical abstraction.

The existence of the 'three mysterious powers' raised a question for the doctrine of the 'two swords' which went back to the middle of the first millennium and was epitomised in a statement by Pope Gelasius, who in 494 wrote to the Emperor Anastasius: 'There are two powers, august Emperor, by which this world is chiefly ruled, namely, the sacred authority of the priests and the royal power. Of these, that of the priests is the more weighty'. The new academic presence in the early second millennium at first augmented 'sacred authority', through the rediscovery in the eleventh and twelfth centuries of canon law manuscripts from Carolingian times, originally gathered by monks into disorganised collections but later codified famously in Bologna by the monk Gratian in his *Concordance of Discordant Canons* (1140) – better known as the *Decretum*. In addition there were collections of papal decretal letters, the one prepared by Raymond of Pennafort in 1234 becoming a second element of canon law alongside Gratian's collection.

The realisation that each *ordo* or category of the church's life, from popes to bishops and dioceses as well as religious communities, should be regulated and supported by appropriate laws and privileges came logically to be of particular advantage to the supreme authority, the papacy. It was a formidable body of law, superior to that of any of the European powers of the time and administered by a *curia* of professionals, all clerics. It moved the balance between *sacerdotium* and *imperium* in the direction of the first of these. The fact that a series of

popes well versed in law, in particular Innocent III (r.1198-1216), occupied the papal throne greatly strengthened the power of the pope.
Innocent, in a sermon on the anniversary of his consecration as pope,
quoted and applied to himself a text from the Prophet Jeremiah:

> I have set you over nations and over kingdoms, to pluck up
> and to break down, to destroy and to overthrow, to build and
> to plant.... Others are called to the role of caring, but only
> Peter is raised to the fullness of power.[4]

His famous conclusion was that he was 'established in the middle
between God and man, lower than God but higher than man; less
than God but greater than man; (one) who judges all, and is judged
by none'. Pope Boniface VIII (r.1294-1303), a century after Innocent,
did not realise how unstable this power balance really was, possibly
because though a trained canon lawyer and even a diplomat he 'was
rude and ill-tempered'.[5] In his Bull, *Unam sanctam* of 1302, he restated
the old two swords principle in obscure but stark terms:

> The former (the sword) is to be administered for the church
> but the latter by the church; the former in the hands of the
> priest; the latter by the hands of kings and soldiers, but at the
> will and sufferance of the priest.[6]

How comprehensive a claim he was making is open to question, as
Jedin[7] points out that in a consistorial address at that time Boniface
said that he did not wish to usurp the jurisdiction of the king. Nevertheless, the bull concluded with the statement that it was necessary
for the salvation of every man that he be subject to the Roman pontiff.
This statement was itself a quotation from Thomas Aquinas, but was
taken out of its context of a treatise on the schism between East and
West, and overall the tenor of the Bull aligned itself with Innocent
III's claims, repeating his statement that the highest spiritual power
can be judged by no one except God. As Knowles remarked: 'there
can be little doubt that Boniface himself meant it to be an assertion
of the paramountcy, if not the monopoly, of power enjoyed in the

temporal and spiritual spheres by the pope'.[8] Whatever the nature of it, the claim seems to have been graphically illustrated by Boniface's habit of having statues of himself in prominent places.

A king having the power of a physical sword in hand might not be persuaded by that, however, and the unfortunate Boniface came out the loser in a dispute with Philip IV of France over taxation issues and the immunity of the clergy from prosecution.[9] There were some dirty tricks involved – forged papal letters insulting the French – but physical force as well: a French force, with the connivance of some cardinals belonging to an opposing faction, captured Boniface at his place of residence, Anagni, and imprisoned him. He died a year later.

This did not bring an end to the papal administration, but the French influence continued to prove disruptive in papal affairs and led to successive popes residing at Avignon in France for most of the fourteenth century. (This exile from Rome came to be known as the Babylonian captivity, recalling the fate of the Jewish people in the Old Testament, and would provide Luther with a neat and evocative title for his tract on the church in 1520.) Away from Rome and its curial organisation, the papal bureaucracy in Avignon developed its own administrative and financial system and attempted to continue the policy of dominating the state, though it was weakened by being away from its natural seat of power. Clement V (r.1305-1314), the pope who began the Avignon exile, was under the influence of the French king, Philip IV, but endeavoured to exert his dominance elsewhere. A challenge arose when he became entangled in a row with the Republic of Venice, which had taken over Ferrara, a papal fief. In 1309 he moved decisively against Venice by excommunicating the doge and the signoria and putting the whole Republic under interdict. He called for a crusade against it, an unheard of way of taking up the crusader's cross. This was a devastating blow for a people who had always been loyal to Rome in a country where cities' loyalties were more fickle and they took it very seriously, extricating themselves only by undertaking to pay a huge fine of ninety thousand florins after some four years of being deprived of the sacraments.[10]

This was an example of how the Avignon papacy had become prey to financial abuses and received criticism for such excesses as the luxurious environment of the great palace built there. Calls for reform came naturally from Italy, from Petrarch, for example, and there were impassioned pleas from the mystic, St Catherine of Siena. Her influence seems to have been particularly important in the decision by Pope Gregory XI (r.1370-1378) to return to Rome. But this move to a city now impoverished brought its own problems and led to the disaster of the Western Schism (1378-1414), involving three claimants to the papacy at one stage, until the situation was resolved at the Council of Constance (1414-1418).

The background to this council involved the development of a theory of the role of church councils in church government and therefore called conciliarism, by scholars such as Jean Gerson (1363-1429), Chancellor of the University of Paris. These were men well versed in canon law and who from the *Decree* of Gratian knew that the position espoused by Innocent III of being 'below God but above men' had to be restricted in practice. Their thinking had to take account of canonical legislation built on a foundation of authority descending from a supreme head, but also had to reckon with a populist view such as that proposed by Marsilius of Padua (1290-1343), a philosopher and earlier rector of Paris University. In a political treatise entitled *Defender of Peace*, he overturned the old priority by attributing all power to the people, who as citizens delegated power upwards to the king and as the body of the faithful conferred it on the pope. For Gerson and other like-minded leaders of opinion the solution to the schism was to promote the concept of a church council which could recognise or depose papal claimants. In an early controversy with authority, Luther would also come to adopt this approach.

Here the influence of the *studium*, the universities, was felt in a search for a new equilibrium. The wellbeing of Christendom now depended on harmony between the church, secular authority and the university. The previous duality of *sacerdotium* and *imperium* was envisaged by a writer such as Giles of Rome (whose writing influenced

Unam sanctam) as corresponding to the relationship between soul and body, with the soul governing the body. This principle with its Platonist overtones came into question both as a result of the decline of papal power after Boniface and the growth in university studies of Aristotle's politics and ethics at the expense of Platonism.

The conciliar movement reached its climax with the decree *Sacrosancta* of the Council of Constance in 1415, which asserted that as a lawfully constituted general council it 'has its authority immediately from Christ; and that all men ... including the pope himself are bound to obey it in matters concerning faith, the abolition of schism, and the reformation of the church of God in its head and members'.[11] This precedent will prove important to Luther. The movement effectively collapsed, however, as a result of shrewd moves by Pope Eugenius IV (r.1431-1447) in 1439, but the legacy remained of a decree which had placed limits on papal authority as well as of a council at Basel in 1435 which had restricted papal rights to revenues. This council had also made conciliatory moves towards moderate Hussites, the followers of John Hus, who had been condemned and burned as a heretic by the Council of Constance. The Hussite affair was to become part of the disputes in which Luther would be involved with the church authorities.

The pre-Reformation church

But by the middle of the fifteenth century the papal administration was back functioning with juridical sophistication reminiscent of the days of Innocent III. Indeed, part of the new assertion of status was in the form of a physical building; Eugenius IV wished to restore the old St Peter's, going back to the Emperor Constantine, and his successor set about replacing it. By the beginning of the sixteenth century it was pulled down and Pope Julius II (r.1503- 1513) began the construction of what eventually became the present St Peter's, with financial consequences that would become part of Luther's story. The popes of the fifteenth and into the sixteenth century had to balance the need to accept that reforms were needed at the highest level with their determination to assert supreme authority. Pope Leo X, who would become Luther's principal target, asserted the supremacy of the papacy over church councils in a Bull, *Pastor aeternus* of 1516, several years before he became aware of Luther and his challenge to that authority.

What Luther and others did not realise was that the administration had a long history of dealing with problems and was not easily intimidated. It is true that some canonists did emphasise the authority of the pope to the extent that the normative authority of scripture was obscured, though because of the inconsistency of their assertions, according to George Tavard,

> they did not entirely make scripture a creature of the pope. Yet the trend of their thought is clear and the emphasis they laid on an arbitrary authority naturally implied a toning down of the relevance of the written word of God. The basic dilemma of the fifteenth century resides in this struggle between the traditional and theological conception of scripture as the backbone of the church's authority and the canonistic pressure for a sharper and sharper affirmation and practice of the primacy of the pope.[12]

As regards the role of scripture, there were traditions of biblical exegesis going back several centuries in the religious orders and with them Luther would have to engage when he began to teach. The exegetes most often mentioned from those centuries are Nicholas of Lyra (1270-130), a Franciscan, and Jacques Lefèvre d'Etaples (1455-1536), a diocesan priest who lived at the French Benedictine Abbey of Saint Germain des Prés. Their methods were in strong contrast: Lyra was a strong proponent of the literal sense of scripture, while Lefèvre carried spiritual interpretation to extreme – accusing Lyra of being a 'Judaizer' who aligned himself more with Jewish than with Christian tradition.[13] As will be seen, Luther chose Lefèvre's approach but his debt to Lyra also needs to be acknowledged.

Another important aspect of the church's life in the period preceding Luther, and which would influence him in his struggle to develop his own theology, was the spirituality of the fourteenth century mystical tradition which arose as a reaction to late medieval scholastic theology and was developed particularly by the Dominican Meister Eckhart (1260-1328) and his fellow Dominican and successor in mystical teaching, Johannes Tauler (1300-1361). It was a spirituality of union with God through a complete assimilation of the creature to the creator. The creature is a pure nothing whose nothingness is filled with God through a birth of God in the soul. There is a complicated link between this tradition and the scholastic tradition it sought to replace; the late scholasticism of thinkers such as William of Ockham was characterised by a reduced claim to know God through natural theology, an inability to prove God's existence through reasoning from nature, thereby driving the thirsting soul to seek direct contact with God by contemplation. Thus the scholastic tradition itself paved the way for a spirituality in which union with God required complete detachment from self, a state described by Tauler as abandonment, *Gelassenheit*, a term which would later become a source of division between Luther and both his mentor Staupitz and his colleague Karlstadt. Despite the passivity of the mystical state there remained nonetheless in this mystical approach a Nominalist heritage of practical piety which would form part of Luther's religious training. The role of mysticism combined with practices of piety affected the development of the spirituality of Luther and his contemporaries and brought to the surface issues of personal psychology which in turn affected the development of theological positions.

That Luther would be open to the mystical approach could be expected not only because he was under the influence of Staupitz, who was well versed in the writings of Eckhart and Tauler, but also because his own studies in scholastic theology had generated in him by 1515 a highly critical approach to scholasticism, especially to Aristotle. In early 1517, under the influence of Karlstadt, who was engaged in a similar transition, Luther published theses for academic discussion, *Disputation against Scholastic Theology*.

At the time the best known articulation of mystical theology was the treatise known as *German Theology,* an edition of which Luther published in 1518, shortly after his campaign against indulgences and his striving for a new approach to theology had begun. When defending his attack on indulgences Luther was still enamoured with this mystical tradition, finding 'more good theology in Tauler than in all the scholastic theologians combined'.[14] But the elements of this tradition that appealed to him were not really specifically mystical, it was rather the rejection of the scholastic method in favour of a more personal approach to religion and he would in due course reject mysticism as being ultimately an example of reliance on works to gain God's favour.

The movement known as humanism was another feature of the culture in which Luther spent his formative years. In origin an ill-defined movement to promote rhetorical eloquence, it soon developed a fashion for writing in classical Latin style and re-discovering Greek literature in its original texts. It has been described as a 'republic of letters from Hungary in the East to England and Spain in the West, from the Baltic in the North to Florence or Rome or Naples in the South',[15] transcending national boundaries by its literary culture and critical attitude. The humanists combined a desire for textual purity with an aspiration towards upright living. It was a movement in love with all things human, anticipating Pope's eighteenth century comment that 'the proper study of mankind is man'. A great attraction of the classics was that they seemed to show an attitude to life which anticipated that of the humanists. Being 'concerned with ethics and morality on the one hand and source texts on the other, [the humanists] at some point expressed opinions on religious questions'.[16] The anti-papal writings of the recent centuries provided a stimulus for humanist literature; religious orders as well as the clergy became an obvious target for literature calling for reform.

Desiderius Erasmus (1466-1536) was an exalted figure among them. His early work, *The Handbook of the Militant Christian* (1503) began with the simple sentence: 'We must be watchful in life' and went on to suggest that prayer, an understanding of the scriptures – aided by familiarity with classical literature – and self-knowledge were the means to avoid the snares of evil and live a good Christian life. He felt the need to go back from the sophistries (*sophisticas artutias*)[17] of the theology of the day and return to its source and simplicity. His satirical work, *In Praise of Folly* (1511), did not spare clergy or religious and his *Complaint of Peace* (1517) singled out the 'warlike' Pope Julius II.[18] He stood out among the humanists for the fact that most of his writings were devoted not to the classics but to the Christian life and especially to the New Testament. According to Bainton,

> His ideal, like that of Luther, was to revive the Christian consciousness of Europe through the dissemination of the sacred writings, and to that end Erasmus first made available in print the New Testament in the original Greek.[19]

Clearly, his writings would be of interest to the young Luther, a member of the Observant or reforming branch of the Augustinians, a critic of scholastic philosophy, but as yet loyal to Rome (though his later reminiscences often cast his 1510 visit to the city in a different light).

However, well in advance of his acerbic debate with Erasmus on the freedom of the will in 1524, he was already adopting a critical stance towards him in 1516 when he asked Georg Spalatin (1484-1545), the influential court chaplain and librarian of the Elector Friedrich, to point out respectfully in a letter to Erasmus that his understanding of the Old Testament was flawed because he favoured Jerome more than Augustine. He commented critically again in 1517 in a letter to a friend, Johann Lang, lecturer at Erfurt and humanist scholar. He said he was reading Erasmus and was pleased that he exposed the ignorance of the clergy and monks, but his estimation of him was decreasing. 'He does not treat sufficiently of Christ and God's grace; human things (*Menschliche*) carry more weight with him than godly things.'[20] It is clear from the letter that Luther was in fact already distrustful of any contribution of human nature to salvation and gives an indication of where he and Erasmus will differ fundamentally by 1524: Erasmus will assert the value of the human when defending the freedom of the will.

While Luther's priorities were different from those of the humanists, it would not be accurate to say that he was interested in substance and they in style. Of the humanists, Dickens said: 'The *studia humanitatis* meant vastly more than the tricks of Ciceronian Latin'.[21] Luther did benefit from the humanist movement through immersion in the classical languages and even studied Hebrew, all of which would be of singular importance later for his work in translating the Bible. He gained too as his movement began by joining in the humanist programme of publishing tracts and even pamphlets to further the cause. Luther the academic scholar, accustomed to the idea of discussion of theses within university circles, copied the tactics of the humanists when he began to go public through adopting a populist style that was direct, coarse and often apocalyptic. They were a limited social group because of their intellectualism, while Luther became more successful than they in reaching the ordinary people, creating in this way a populist movement.

This was tantamount to supporting German nationalism at a time when the sense of a united Europe was declining through the rise of distinctive national vernaculars and competitive trading – trade routes from the Far East were beginning to favour some more than others. The Holy Roman Empire had its political centre in Germany, but its spiritual centre in Rome as emperors since Charlemagne were crowned there and, even after the decline which set in with Boniface VIII, recognised in Rome a kind of titular headship. But resentment was growing over the amount of money that flowed to Rome in tribute because of the ecclesiastical primacy. Both England and France had legislated against the untrammelled flow of revenues to Rome; in England the *Statute of Praemunire* in 1392 was one such measure, while in France in 1438 the *Pragmatic Sanction of Bourges* forbade, among other things, the payment to Rome of *annates,* the first year's revenue of a bishop. As will be seen, various payments to Rome became an issue in Germany just as Luther came on the scene.

CHAPTER THREE

The beginning of conflict

Growing nationalism and resentment against Rome over money matters were causing tension in the relationship between Rome and the
German estates. In this situation, Luther with his radical new theology in the University of Wittenberg was one player who might have
a contribution to make to the continual balancing of forces needed
to sustain a stable and dynamic Christian society. As it turned out,
his particular contribution to the *studium* in the course of his teaching at Wittenberg got to the heart of the matter and did have an ex-
traordinary effect on the other two, the church and the empire. His
increasingly high profile may be presented as the result of a brilliant
theological discovery undermining so much of the theological orthodoxy of the time, but it may also be explained in part as the result
of his privileged position under the secular protection of the elector
of Saxony, Duke Friedrich, and the growing reputation of Friedrich's
University of Wittenberg, in which Luther was a star professor. There
was also the relative freedom from close supervision by diocesan
authorities which his status as a friar in the important Augustinian
religious order gave him. The story of Luther needs to be told in the
context of the political and ecclesiastical as well as the theological
situation of his time and on a larger scale than his location in Saxony,
because of the inter-connection of the various duchies and their role
in the empire, especially in the election of a new emperor. From early
in the sixteenth century, the ailing Maximilian was preoccupied with
the issue of his successor.

It would then be overly simple to consider the significance of Luther by concentrating on what was to become his well-known principles of scripture as the sole religious authority, or his making 'justi-

fication by faith' the principle by which his theology would stand or fall, as if these were to be the sole criteria by which his place in the history of Christianity should be assessed. A broader canvas has to be painted, though with Luther depicted as a very significant figure. Theological issues have always needed contextualisation.

Luther came on the scene at a time when political stability was an issue because of the impending election and because of the ambition of Prince Albrecht of Brandenburg. Albrecht was Archbishop of Magdeburg from 1513, administrator of the diocese of Halberstadt and aspired to be Archbishop of Mainz as well, so to become one of the electors of the new emperor. The story of his financial affairs in the course of achieving his aim is well known. The dispensation from the Holy See needed in order to hold these multiple benefices was expensive and in consequence he borrowed from Jakob Fugger's Bank at Augsburg. Pope Leo X agreed to the preaching of an indulgence, half of the income from which would enable Albrecht to service his debt, while half of it went to Rome for the re-building of St Peter's. Whatever may be said about the theology of indulgences, the preaching of this new one to a theologically ill-informed populace was open to financial exploitation, especially because the archbishop's urgent need for cash meant that the campaign was presented simply as fundraising for the new St Peter's, with no mention of the Fugger Bank.

It was also to be carried out by an experienced indulgence preacher, a Dominican friar, Johann Tetzel (1465-1519). Albrecht instructed him to emphasise that a plenary indulgence could be gained for the souls of dear dead relatives and friends by making an offering of a quarter of a florin. This extension of the remission from one's own debt of penance to include application to the souls in purgatory made the indulgence much more popular and had in fact been introduced some fifty years earlier by Pope Sixtus IV (r.1471-1484). Bainton quotes what purports to be the text of Tetzel's standard sermon, with a conclusion in the form of a doggerel verse which has achieved notoriety: 'As soon as the coin in the coffer rings/The soul from purgatory springs'. In German it rhymes very well.[1]

Tetzel began to preach the indulgence in 1516, going from town to town in solemn procession; 'a cross bearing the papal arms preceded him and the pope's Bull of Indulgence was borne aloft on a gold-embroidered velvet cushion'.[2] Indulgences were gained customarily by visiting a shrine containing relics and Albrecht had in fact a large collection in the church at Halle, but in this case people were spared that trouble and the indulgences were, so to speak, being brought to them. Tetzel's progress began in Albrecht's Brandenburg which bordered on Saxony, but he was not allowed by Friedrich to cross the border, for the very good reason that Friedrich's own collection of relics, with indulgences attached for those who venerated them, was a source of income for the upkeep of the Castle Church in Wittenberg and the remuneration of the many clergy – up to twenty-five at one time – who ministered there, engaged principally in offering masses for the dead.

The sources give various numbers for the size of Friedrich's collection, from about 16,000 to 20,000, and it is known that the centrepiece was a reliquary containing what was said to be a thorn from the Saviour's crown of thorns. The indulgences which could be gained by those rightly disposed who venerated individual relics, with indulgences of hundreds of days attached, could cumulatively amount to millions of days, which would be beyond people's comprehension. But there were probably some relics in the collection to which a plenary indulgence was attached, meaning that all the penance in the form of temporal punishment due to sin was remitted.

However, on this special occasion people from Wittenberg crossed the border to Tetzel in nearby Jüterborg, as Luther noted later. He had been concerned about the morality of the indulgence system for some time and had preached a sermon raising questions about indulgences in January of 1517 in the presence of the elector, the nobility and the faculty of the university. This could hardly have pleased the elector. Luther admitted in 1541 that he had incurred the displeasure of the elector on that occasion, 'Friedrich had taken it badly, because he was very fond of his religious foundation'.[3] The occasion was the anniversary of the dedication of the Castle Church. On such an occasion a special indulgence was granted and Luther had the task of preaching about it. 'This sermon reveals a Luther only beginning to question indulgences, often unsure of his own position. It seems to be his first public criticism of indulgences outside the classroom.'[4] The sermon emphasises the importance of repentance as will be the case in the *Ninety-Five Theses* nine months later and has an even stronger statement than will be found there: 'You see, therefore, how dangerous a thing the preaching of indulgences is, which teaches a mutilated grace, namely, to flee satisfaction and punishment'.[5]

Nine months elapsed before he followed up with an academic publication. It would be perfectly understandable that a theologian like him, who had raised questions before a congregation that included his peers, would be stimulated to initiate a discussion of indulgences by posting academic theses for debate, a standard university practice. Despite the tradition that he nailed his *Ninety-Five Theses* to the door of the Castle Church, he never referred directly to having done so, but he did send letters to the relevant bishops, Albrecht of Mainz and Hieronymus of Brandenburg, enclosing copies of the theses and warning Albrecht in a covering letter: 'What a horror, what a danger for a bishop to permit the loud noise of indulgences among his people, while the gospel is silenced'.[6] The source for the traditional account of the nailing of the theses to the chapel door was his friend Melanchthon, writing an introduction to his works many years later, but there has been a discovery of a note by Luther's secretary in his later years, apparently confirming the tradition. But neither man was in Wittenberg at the time.[7]

The date on which he seems likely to have publicised his protest in some way was October 31st 1517, the eve of All Saints, the day on which the elector displayed his great collection of relics in the Castle Church. In the theses (see Appendix 1), Luther did not dispute the validity of indulgences or the existence of purgatory, but, as in the January sermon, the nub of his argument was the importance of repentance as part of the process of receiving an indulgence. He had taken careful note of the translation of Mk 1:14 in the New Testament by Erasmus; instead of the Vulgate's 'Do penance', Erasmus in the *Novum instrumentum omne* had translated the Greek as 'Be ye penitent'. In his 1527 edition he made it 'Change your minds'. In the second instance the emphasis on interiority was even more obvious.

Accordingly, the first thesis was: 'Our Lord and Master Jesus Christ, when He said *Penitentiam agite*, willed that the whole life of believers should be repentance'. Thesis No. 12 then makes a historical point: 'In former times the canonical penalties were imposed not after, but before absolution, as tests of true contrition'. He was implying that repentance was no longer necessarily proven when the rite of penance ceased to be public and the order was reversed. The call for interiority is still consistent with penitential acts, however, unlike his later position in which all question of merit will be repudiated. He even proposes: 'It seems unproved, either by reason or scripture, that [the souls in purgatory] are outside the state of merit, that is to say, of increasing love'. This may of course be simply a thesis to be discussed and his personal view may already be moving away from this possibility.

He makes a distinction between the 'treasures of the church' and the 'merits of christ' which will come to the fore in his debate the following year with Cardinal Thomas de Vio (1469-1534). (The cardinal is better known as Cajetan, in accordance with Italian custom, as he was a native of Gaeta.) Luther will at that point imply that there are no treasures of the church to be drawn on for indulgences, but that all is grace – there are no human resources which can contribute to salvation. But now in Thesis 60 he holds that the keys of the church, given by Christ's merit, are a treasure which can be dispensed. 'For it is clear that for the remission of penalties and of reserved cases, the power of the pope is of itself sufficient' (No. 61). Nonetheless, towards the end, he becomes more skeptical of papal power. Citing the 'shrewd questionings of the laity', he asks in No. 82,

> Why does not the pope empty purgatory, for the sake of holy love and of the dire need of the souls that are there, if he redeems an infinite number of souls for the sake of miserable

money with which to build a church? ... Why does not the pope, whose wealth is today greater than the riches of the richest, build just this one church of St Peter with his own money, rather than with the money of poor believers?

The *Ninety-Five Theses* was a document inviting discussion, though the proposed seminar never happened. However, though it was in Latin, it was very quickly circulated in Germany – it spoke to people's grievances about how money they could ill afford was so much tied in with their attempts to live religious lives. Suddenly this whole economy was being questioned and undermined. The Latin text was apparently translated surreptitiously and given to publishers who spread it throughout Germany. Yet his *Sermon on Indulgences and Grace* of the following March, which was more uncompromising in its criticism of indulgences and in German from the outset, very quickly surpassed it in circulation, being reprinted fourteen times in its first year, 1518.

All of this had more consequences than being hailed as a hero, even the most popular person in northern Germany according to some accounts. Tetzel wrote against him and Albrecht of Mainz wrote a letter of complaint to the pope on the basis of the report of theologians of the University of Mainz, which judged that Luther's writings denied papal authority. The Dominican theologians in the curia could not be expected to rush to the defence of an Augustinian when the matter was raised there. Luther's superiors thought it wise to have a theological seminar in which he might be brought to alter his position and so a disputation was arranged for Heidelberg.[8] In the course of it, his theology was judged to be more radical than criticism of indulgences. By questioning the pope's sanctioning of indulgences, he appeared to be denying his supreme authority. After some time, a summons came to him from the curia to come to Rome and caused Luther to believe that he was now in danger of being tried for heresy. But a respectful letter he wrote to the pope in response to the call contained the question, 'What am I to do? I cannot recant'.[9] He feels besieged by his critics and defends himself by the fact that his employment by the Elector Friedrich in his university is an indication of his integrity, but he goes on to offer himself in submission to the pope's judgment: 'Make me alive or kill me, accept or recant, agree to or reject. Whatever you decide is acceptable to me'.[10]

What began as a subject for debate within the academy was now influencing public opinion throughout a large portion of Germany; an adventitious approach to long-established pastoral practice was creating divisions in the religious culture and beginning to make its economic effects felt, with inevitable consequences for politics. It would not be an exaggeration to say that the equilibrium of Christendom was under threat. It was already a time of uncertainty in political governance, as happens when a highly patriarchal society is faced with a dynastic transition. Emperor Maximilian was determined to have his grandson Charles, the teenager recently crowned king of Spain, elected as his successor while he himself was still living. For this he needed the votes of the majority of the seven electors – four secular and three ecclesiastical. He also needed Pope Leo's agreement, because to carry the title of emperor the chosen one needed to be crowned by the pope. Leo, however, was not in favour of Charles as he would be the ruler of territory in southern Italy as King of Spain and thus the Papal States could be held in a pincer grip between north and south. The other candidate in the election was Francis I of France, on whom Leo was not keen either, as he held territory in northern Italy, but who had the support already of four of the electors. Support in this case came about as a result of financial payments – bribes – and the vote of one elector was enough to change the balance. Maximilian therefore had to borrow heavily to bring this about and even succeeded in winning the support of Albrecht, the new Archbishop of Mainz, despite Albrecht's close financial connection with the pope. Maximilian's attempt to achieve unanimity in the election was endangered however by the independent stance of Duke Friedrich, Luther's overlord, a man, it was said, who could not be bought.

Thus there was a complicated political background to Luther's emergence as a public figure, in addition to deep-seated theological suspicions and even the religious order rivalry he generated. The Emperor Maximilian was enraged by his theological revolt and was also influenced by the need to win the pope's favour in regard to the upcoming election when he wrote in August 1518 to the curia requesting Luther's excommunication. However, it was hazardous to adopt such an attitude to Luther because of the need to keep Friedrich disposed to favour the election of Charles. Maximilian was sensitive as well to the complaint that so much money was flowing out of Germany to Rome – particularly because of the indulgence campaign – while Rome was requesting further financial aid for a new crusade, money the German estates were reluctant to contribute.

The interview with Cajetan

These were issues for the imperial diet which had been meeting since the spring of 1518, with the Papal Legate, Cardinal Cajetan, in attendance. The diet would have the responsibility of implementing the drastic consequences of Luther's excommunication should it be imposed. Cajetan had the difficult task of trying to win support for the crusade and at the same time block the election of Charles. In this situation, the position of Friedrich, the uncommitted elector, was crucial. With Maximilian successful in winning over four electors (even Albrecht of Mainz), Cajetan knew that Friedrich had to be treated carefully and that his desire to protect the reputation of his University of Wittenberg, along with its best known professor, would have to be respected.

For his part, Friedrich was a devout man who was concerned for theological orthodoxy and consequently had to take the summons to Rome seriously. A meeting between him and the cardinal achieved the desired result for both; Friedrich was relieved that Cajetan was willing to arrange that the summons to Rome be changed to one to Augsburg where he would meet and question Luther in the fatherly way the elector suggested. The fact that Cajetan was a Dominican and a superb Thomist theologian did not seem to have arisen in the discussions brokered by the elector's secretary, Spalatin, who also hinted that all going well Luther might be offered a bishopric. Upon being informed, the curia arranged that Friedrich should be conferred with the Golden Rose, the Holy See's recognition of the virtue of a Christian prince – as well as having his natural children legitimised.

Luther was greatly relieved that the summons to Rome, with two days left before he would be considered contumacious, was now changed to a summons to meet Cajetan at Augsburg. What he did not realise was that the arrangement was one of political expediency and Cajetan would not be in a mood for a theological debate. The meeting between the two was to be in private, being held after the end of the imperial diet. Cajetan could hardly be in the best of moods having had to listen to the refusal of the German estates to take part in a crusade against the Turks and their complaint about the large amounts of money going from Germany to Rome because of the *annates* and indulgence payments: 'German money, causing nature itself to wonder (*berwunderung*), flies over the Alps'.[11] He had now to prolong his stay in Augsburg and deal with someone who had campaigned against indulgences and been accused of heresy, but was also under the protection of one of the German princes more loyal to the Holy See.

His protracted wait was caused in the first instance by Luther's hesitation about turning up. He had heard of plots against his life and one of the Mansfeld Counts, also called Albrecht, warned him not to leave Wittenberg.[12] He was also distrustful of the Italian cardinal, but Spalatin and Friedrich, in Augsburg, were of the opposite view. The further wait came from Luther's decision to travel the three hundred miles on foot, accompanied only by a confrère. Roper describes the countryside through which they travelled:

> His route was punctuated by the imperial towns, with their big half-timbered houses, imposing town halls, guild houses and workshops where craftsmen produced outstanding metalware, fabrics and scientific instruments.[13]

On October 7th they arrived in the impressive city of Augsburg, home of the Fugger family, whose palace consisted of an opulent set of buildings, in one of which Cardinal Cajetan was lodged. (To their credit, the Fugger family had also set up a social housing project, a set of one-up-one-down dwellings for the poor, located in a suburb.)[14] Luther was housed in a cell in the Carmelite convent, there being no Augustinian community in Augsburg. After three days, he wrote to Spalatin who had already left Augsburg with his lord, Friedrich, for Wittenberg. The letter reveals his sense of isolation as he awaits the arrival of Staupitz, though he had dined with the distinguished humanist, Dr Peutinger, the evening before. He was living in hope and fear and had been visited by an official of the cardinal who advised him not to engage in a tournament, but simply to retract his errors. The conversation did not go well and Luther claimed to have sent him away. He believed the cardinal was inwardly very hostile to him, however he might appear outwardly. He concluded: 'In sum, the Roman church (if it is appropriate to call it that) is in insatiable need of gold, and devouring it thirsts for more.'[15]

The meeting at Augsburg has been well documented, quite apart from the fact that Luther wrote several letters during it and on the second of the three sessions had brought a notary, as it was now clear that what Cajetan was committed to was not a debate but a demand for a simple retraction of his errors. He wrote a second time to Spalatin on October 14th, saying that the cardinal had promised to be lenient, paternal, but in fact was proving inflexible and had called in Staupitz after his arrival, asking him to put pressure on Luther to retract. He now had no faith in the cardinal.[16] The cardinal, following his brief, had asked Luther to retract and Luther replied that he had not come to Augsburg to do that when he might just as easily have done it at home in Wittenberg; he would like to be instructed as to his errors. There followed an argument about the merits of Christ and how these had become the treasures of the church, Cajetan quoting the Bull *Unigenitus* of Clement VI of 1343 and Luther challenging his interpretation of the text. The exchanges between them, which included Cajetan's assertion that the pope was the interpreter of scripture, led Luther finally to the fateful statement that the pope in his interpretation of scripture abused it. In the appeal to a council, which he published the week after the meeting, he said he felt he had not received justice, because 'I teach nothing but scripture'.[17] It was a claim that would grow into a conviction of certain knowledge of the meaning of scripture, which would enable him to appeal to 'conscience' when challenged to recant, as he would be at Worms, three years later.

On the same day, after his interview with Cajetan, he wrote a long memorandum to the cardinal setting out his position point by point. He was not unaware of the Bull *Unigenitus* of Clement VI on indulgences and held with the interpretation he had already given. In any case, a pope could be in error as Gal 2:11-14 demonstrated, when Paul corrected Peter. He quoted a work of Palormitanus to the effect that not only is a general council superior to the pope but so also is any layman, if better informed.[18] However, three days later he wrote a letter of apology to Cajetan for the strong language he had used in relation to the pope.[19] But in a letter of the 18th after the final interview he adopted a different attitude: the cardinal knew that he had come out of obedience, through many 'dangers, in ill-health and poverty' but he could not afford to stay on waiting to hear from him, nor had he the necessary money. In any case he had been told not to return unless he would recant, but he should not have cause to do so as he had submitted his case to the judgment of the church. What more could he do? He had been advised to appeal from the pope badly informed to the pope better informed – a point he would make a week later in a letter to the pope. In a snub to Cajetan, he suggested that it should be a case of the church deciding to condemn him or not; Cajetan accepting that judgment rather than Cajetan deciding and the church accepting his judgment.[20]

The meeting had ended badly; Luther seemed unaware of the political ramifications, while Cajetan ignored them and left Luther to face the consequences, upset probably by Luther's point-scoring and the fact that his instructions had been not to debate but to demand a retraction. Luther for his part thought he had won a debate. A few

days after the meeting, he composed an appeal to the pope, notice-
ably lacking in tact as he addressed him as an equal (despite protesta-
tions of obedience), appealing from Leo badly informed to Leo better
informed and this was posted on the door of the cathedral, while his
friends, fearing for his safety, arranged for him to climb over Augsburg's city wall at night. This left Cajetan in the position of having to
refer the case back to Rome. He sent his report to Friedrich saying he
should either send Luther bound to Rome or else banish him from his
territories. Back at Wittenberg on October 31st 1518 – a year to the
day since the affair began – Luther had a record of his meeting with
Cajetan printed, thus hardening the lines of dispute and leaving Friedrich in a difficult position. He did try a defensive strategy by writing
to Cajetan saying that there were learned men in the universities who
held that Luther's teaching had not been shown to be heretical and
that he would send him to Rome or banish him only after he had been
convicted of heresy.

CHAPTER FOUR

The debate at Leipzig

The political situation now caused the Luther affair to be put on hold.[1] The ongoing problem of the election of an emperor led Leo to continue his strategic approach to Friedrich. In the months after Augsburg, Luther corresponded with the elector and with his secretary Spalatin out of concern for his safety. He was reassured by the entry of the University of Wittenberg into the affair with a request to Friedrich to obtain from Rome a precise account of what they objected to in one of its professors. Luther was safe but uneasy and still trying to defend his position. He looked to the prince's council for permission to print both his *Appeal to a Council,* which he had written while still in Augsburg, and his *Proceedings at Augsburg.* He was refused, but had them printed anyway, which he then realised was a mistake because Rome had assigned an assistant, in practice a replacement, for Cajetan, Karl Von Miltitz (1490-1529), who had been secretary to Leo and was considered suitable for his mission as he was of a Saxon family. Though not well informed theologically, Miltitz had diplomatic skills and his aim in a discussion at the Castle of Altenburg to which he invited Luther in early January 1519 was to smooth out disagreement between him and Rome by telling Luther that Tetzel, the preacher of the notorious indulgence, was more at fault than he. Miltitz persuaded him to draft a letter to the pope, to assure him that he never wished to blame papal authority or that of the church for the indulgence scandal and wished only that money would cease to corrupt the church. Miltitz asked for and got his agreement to desist from writing about indulgences (something he was requiring of Tetzel also) and, thus satisfied, brought all involved to dinner in the castle.[2] But political events ensured that the only real outcome of this meeting would be that a year later, through Miltitz's persuasion, Luther prefaced his *Freedom of a Christian* (1520) with that letter to the pope praising him and warning him of insidious forces within the Roman curia.

On January 12th 1519, Maximilian died and the manoeuvring over the election intensified. A messenger was sent to Cajetan with instructions and money, making it clear that a German prince was now favoured over Francis I of France and that the Elector Friedrich might be in the best position to gain the support of all. This would render Cajetan's earlier demand to Friedrich to send Luther to Rome no longer of interest. But by the end of January, the curia had changed its stance. Maximilian's agreement of the previous year with four electors made Charles too powerful for Friedrich to take on, so now the policy was to favour Francis in the hope that competition between him and Charles would at the last minute open the way to Friedrich to succeed. Promises of cardinals' hats were made to the ecclesiastical electors and money from both Francis and Charles poured in and was pocketed, but the electors adopted the strategy of putting off a decision as long as they could. Friedrich showed himself as incorruptible as in the previous year. His position was therefore all the more crucial and, as Miltitz had reported that Luther seemed now more amenable it was decided to make an advance to the elector by adopting a positive attitude to him in his support for Luther.[3] This strategy required a letter from Leo to Luther himself. In a brief of March 29th 1519, Leo extended to him a fatherly invitation 'to set forth at once for Rome, there to make the retraction which he postponed when before the Legate'.[4] As Leo had issued a brief to Cajetan on August 23rd 1518 that he was to summon Luther to Augsburg as a notorious heretic, he was here either badly informed or disingenuous. Leo's view may have been that if things were as Miltitz suggested there would be no reason for him to be doubtful about Friedrich and his policy of protecting Luther. The letter containing this Brief was sent to Friedrich as Imperial Vicar. He realised that Luther, who in his *Appeal* had declared the pope to be antichrist, would never consent to go to Rome and the letter was never given to him.

That same summer, 1519, brought some clarification of Luther's theological position by an event that had been in the offing since the previous spring and was to prove a turning point in Luther's journey as a theologian and leader of the new movement. John Eck (1486-1543), the pro-Chancellor of Ingolstadt University, was an acquaintance and possibly a friend at that time of Luther. His intellectual formation had been similar to Luther's; he had read the scholastic theology of the time and then studied Augustine. More than Luther, he was attracted to humanist scholarship and had introduced reforms in the theology faculty at Ingolstadt. For whatever motive, and it may have included an ambition to make a name for himself or receive ecclesiastical preferment, he had published a refutation of the *Ninety-Five Theses* not long after they had become widely diffused in Germany. Luther's colleague, Karlstadt, published a reply in late spring 1518, before a protest arrived from Eck to the effect that his document was meant to be for private discussion. With Luther's affairs being on hold for some time, this new controversy was played out by correspondence, but when Eck met Luther during the Augsburg meeting with Cajetan he pressed for a debate with Luther himself in public. It took from October 1518 to June 1519 to bring it about, ostensibly with Karlstadt because of its origin, but in practice with Luther, as Eck wanted. Eck had in the meantime published a set of twelve theses showing his conviction that the central issue to be debated was papal authority.

Friedrich's cousin, Duke Georg of Saxony (1471-1549), was known to be critical of indulgences and was happy to provide a venue for the debate at Leipzig, despite the local bishop's prohibition. Leipzig was located on a trade route between Eck's area and Wittenberg; it was a seemingly neutral venue and the nearest large town to Wittenberg. The timing, if not the venue, proved to be to Luther's disadvantage as the meeting took place in summer, drawing large crowds, Eck arrived there on the eve of the Corpus Christi procession and took part in it with local dignitaries, thus emphasising Catholic tradition.[5] Luther, Karlstadt and Melancthon arrived the next day, June 24th, escorted by armed students, creating or at least anticipating a hostile environment. There was a comic incident in the midst of the opposing theatrical displays – Eck's Catholic pageantry and the Lutheran party's ostentatiously high profile, manifested by the escort and the piles of books with which Karlstadt had loaded their wagon. As they were about to enter the city gate the overloaded wagon got stuck in the mud and an axle broke.

The debate was to prove a significant milestone in the emergence of a Lutheran community. It was scheduled for the *aula* of the university, but so great was the crowd that Duke Georg allowed it to be held in the auditorium of Leipzig Castle after mass in St Thomas Church. It began with the singing of the *Veni Creator* in the auditorium and an address in Latin of two hours from the professor of Greek at the university on the proper decorum for conducting an academic debate. Formalities of various kinds were to mark the proceedings throughout and contributed to the event lasting for nearly three weeks, from June 27th to July 15th. It was in fact the location that brought an otherwise interminable wrangle to an end: Georg needed the hall for a ball.

The debate between Eck and Karlstadt began with arguments over procedures – whether there should be stenographers, whether books should be allowed; the erudite Eck, who had no need of them said no, but Karlstadt insisted and proceeded to bore the audience by reading from them at length. The contest focused on the question of the freedom or otherwise of the will, an issue that would later become central to Erasmus' critique of Luther and a factor in bringing about a fundamental division between the new and old theologies.

After a week, Luther's turn came and, as Eck had rightly guessed, he wished to discuss the antiquity of the papal primacy and whether it was of divine or human origin. Luther interpreted the scripture text always appealed to in support of papal primacy, Mt 16:18, 'On this rock I will build my church', to refer to Christ himself as the 'rock'. This was a major assault on traditional orthodoxy and he followed it with an account of church history designed to prove that not all churches had always been subject to the pope (he referred in particular to the Greek Church). While his approach could reasonably be described as partisan and he used obscure sources, he did have a point when it came to the historical argument, as historians today, whether Catholic of Protestant, recognise that little can be established with certainty about the first generations of the church in Rome.[6] In his double argument, from scripture and history, his aim was to prove that the papacy was of human origin. When Duke Georg interjected: 'What does it matter whether the pope is by divine right or human, he is the pope just the same', Luther made the mistake of agreeing, saying that by denying the divine right of the papacy he was not proposing a denial of obedience. Eck saw at once the subversive nature of this assertion; the requirement of obedience to the pope was always seen to arise from his divinely appointed authority. Luther proceeded to damage his case further by minimising the pope's office, saying that it did not matter whether there were ten or a thousand popes, the unity of Christendom could be preserved, to which Eck responded by pointing to the de facto dissensions between the various nations.

Both contestants were on shaky ground in basing their positions on history. Luther had prepared by consulting little known authors, such as the papal historian and humanist, Bartolomeo Platina[7] while Eck turned to the *Isidorian Decretals* which had included supposed letters from Popes Anacletus and Clement of the first century, to the effect that the primacy derived not from the apostles but from the Lord himself. Luther responded that he would never believe that the 'holy pope and martyr' (Clement) had ever made such a claim. His instinct was right; the *Decretals* had already been shown to be false by two humanist scholars and cardinals, John of Torquemada (1468) and Nicholas of Cusa (1464). Both declared the earlier documents to be forgeries, especially those purporting to be by Clement and Anacletus.

Debate about more recent history provided a trap into which Luther was lured by Eck. The host, Duke Georg, belonged to a family that had gained the duchy from the emperor of the time for fighting against Hussite raiders who, after the death of Hus at Constance, had invaded and ravaged Saxon lands. Eck led Luther towards a discussion of Hus by first claiming he was adopting the errors of the Englishman John Wycliffe (1330-1384), who in the fourteenth century translated the Bible into English as part of a campaign to assert its authority over that of the pope, and had gone on to adopt the views of Marsilius of Padova on the authority of the secular over the ecclesiastical authorities (Caesaropapalism). It was true that Wycliffe's movement had influenced John Hus, so Eck could then add that Luther was therefore also accepting the errors of Hus himself, who had claimed that neither Peter nor his successors were head of the church.

Amazingly, it would seem to the modern reader, Luther took time during the lunch break, which came just then, to go to the university library and read the Acts of the Council of Constance which had condemned Hus, where he found among the reproved articles a sentence about the unity of the church which he recognised as being derived directly from St Augustine. On the resumption, he claimed to have found many articles which could not be condemned. He settled on a condemned article which had stated that it was not necessary to believe that the Roman Church was superior to all others and declared that innumerable Greeks had been saved though they never heard of this supposed superiority. Therefore, either some articles were interpolated or else, if as Eck claimed they were part of the council's teaching, then councils could err and had in fact erred and had contradicted each other, as in the case of the recent Council of the Lateran (1512-16), which had reversed the decision of Constance that a council is above the pope. 'A simple layman armed with scripture is to be believed above a pope or a council without (scripture).'[8] This was the response Eck needed to clinch his argument: Luther not only denied papal authority but also the reliability of a council of the church – the institution he had appealed to after Augsburg. It meant that each man was his own authority; his interpretation of scripture – which Luther had said interpreted itself – was normative. Eck described Luther's stance as the 'Bohemian virus, to attach more weight to one's own interpretation of scripture than to that of the popes and councils, the doctors and the universities'.[9]

They went on to debate purgatory, a logical development considering that it figures in some thirteen of the *Ninety-Five Theses*. Luther did not deny its existence, but instead the effectiveness of prayer for those held there. He did so by questioning the authority of the text in 2 Macc used traditionally to pray and make offerings for the dead, because it belonged to the apocryphal books of the Bible. At that time, this was simply to question the authority of scripture because the book belonged to the official canon of scripture. Surprisingly, when they went on to discuss indulgences, there was scarcely any debate. Eck himself was a critic of the whole economy of indulgences; his difference with Luther continued to be his charge that Luther was setting himself up as an authority over against tradition and papal authority and the authority of scripture itself. At the end of the eighteen-day debate, Luther now appeared to be a supporter of some at least of the beliefs of the executed heretic, John Hus, and a critic of the authority of councils, of papal authority and even of that of scripture. On what authority he believed anything to be true seemed to be his own inner conviction and this position he was prepared to defend even to the shedding of his blood.[10] Even though he had yet to publish works such as *The Babylonian Captivity of the Church* and *An Address to the German Nobility*, which would set out his theology in some detail, Leipzig was very significant event in his career as a reformer.

The election of Charles V

It was now mid-July 1519 and another significant event had just taken place, the election on June 28th of the new emperor, who was not unsurprisingly Charles, king of Spain, now Emperor Charles V. In the immediate lead up to the election, Friedrich remained in a powerful position. Leo continued his diplomatic campaign and things moved rather quickly with the election due at the meeting of the diet in the last days of June. In a letter which Miltitz was to deliver eight days before the election Friedrich was urged to exert himself to strive for the election of the King of France and if that proved impossible he should himself accept the imperial crown. But on May 4th, Leo sent Cajetan a letter which gave him power to declare Francis I elected even if he had only three votes. Then on May 29th he acknowledged that Francis had no chance of being elected in a straight vote. In a move which may have come from the curia rather than Leo, papal representatives in Germany received an instruction that they were to insist with Friedrich that he vote for Francis or else manoeuvre to obtain the crown for himself. But Friedrich was unmoved. Considering that it was useless, as Leo wrote to Cajetan, to beat his head against a wall, Leo decided on June 17th to sign a treaty with the Spanish ambassador.[11] But before news of this reached Germany, Friedrich was again being urged, this time by Miltitz, to vote for Francis or effectively for himself. Part of the deal was that a cardinal's hat was offered for one of his friends. 'In Rome at this time Luther was considered the friend of the elector.'[12] Jedin comments on this development:

> Out of concern for the papal State and the position of the Medici in Italy, then, the pope behaved as though Luther and his protectors had not been declared heretics. He dropped the proceedings for almost a year and gave the Lutheran movement time to strike deeper roots; he held back the bull of excommunication and instead offered the imperial crown and the red hat.

This is the shocking conclusion reached by a historian through considering the phenomenon of Luther in the context of the politics of his time. His theological stance, from that perspective, does not seem to have been of much account. Charles had been elected emperor while he was still in Spain; in 1520, after some months back in his native Netherlands, he arrived in Germany and was crowned in October at Aachen – Charlemagne's ancient seat – by two of the electors, the Archbishop of Trier and the Cardinal Archbishop Albrecht of Mainz, thus sealing the intertwining of church and state. No longer was it a crowning by the pope, but it was at least by a cardinal, who as such now formed part of the curia and could represent the pope. The marginalisation of Luther was part of the putting aside of all theological contribution to the balancing of powers in the society of the time, as church and state reached an accommodation with regard to their respective spheres of influence, one, however, that would be short-lived.

CHAPTER FIVE

Luther's theology

For a crucial period from January 1519, when Miltitz met with Luther, to the spring of the following year, the Lutheran movement had time to grow, when in the interests of politics the church chose to ignore it. The new emperor, Charles, was occupied in the Netherlands and had yet to take account of the effect Luther was having on society in Germany. This respite allowed Luther to continue his teaching career, which had begun in Wittenberg University in 1511. Having the degree *Baccalaureus Biblicus*, he taught scripture from 1513 to 1518, dealing with the Psalms, Romans, Galatians and Hebrews. It became clear over those years that his approach to theology was innovative, even revolutionary, in relation to the orthodoxy of late medieval Europe.[1] His entry to the public square in 1517 through the posting of the *Ninety-Five Theses* gave some indication of how his thinking had developed, in the sense at least of indicating, by the document's tenor, unease with the pastoral application of the orthodox theology. But from the notes still extant of his lectures on the Psalms it seems that there was deeper questioning involved over the period 1512-1517. What was happening was influenced by his personality, his studies and teaching in the preceding few years and the fundamental conclusion he had reached about his relationship with God.

This period has been much studied; the importance of his personal psychology, his relationship with his father in particular, his religious and academic training, including the influence of members of his religious order and the currents of theological thinking, all these contributed to his coming to what was for him a momentous conclusion about his relationship with God. It is from his study and teaching of scripture that he came to his fundamental insight about a central topic in them, especially in Romans: God's justice or righteousness, and how the human person, by nature a sinner, can satisfy God's justice, can be justified before God. Luther's sense of his own sinfulness had grown strongly over the years of his youth and early manhood, causing him great anxiety, even depression. In accord with the spirituality of the time and of the religious life especially, he had tried more and more to merit God's forgiveness by prayer and ascetical practices. This spirituality he would come to excoriate as 'works righteousness'. When exactly this occurred is uncertain as his own recollection of the event towards the end of his life appears to date it somewhat later than is likely.

Two contrasting theological traditions were in the background at that time and both affected his spiritual and theological progress. The more prominent one in theological schools, including Erfurt where he had his basic theological formation, was called the *via moderna*.[2] It emphasised the importance of personal effort to become pleasing to God through growth in merit, in effect, working towards one's salvation using spiritual resources such as prayer and sacraments and meritorious activities such as pilgrimages. This approach lacked the intellectual rigour of earlier thinkers such as Thomas Aquinas and allowed in the end a materialistic conception of the whole economy of salvation. The sacraments had the objective effect of conferring grace on the recipient simply by being performed – *ex opere operato* was the Latin shorthand way of expressing it – and only minimal attention was given to the issue of the faith needed for the sacrament to be effective. Inevitably this theology came in time to be criticised as seeming to restrict God's freedom in relation to the dispensing of grace. A break in the chain of cause and effect was posited by the Franciscan, Duns Scotus (1266-1308), who allowed only that a totally free God gave grace on the occasion of sacraments being conferred, thus raising the question of whether God could be relied upon to do so. The non-philosophical solution to this dilemma was to invoke the biblical but also medieval commercial idea of a covenant between God and humanity, according to which each would fulfill the obligations agreed upon – commerce entered through the assumption that humanity was capable of making its contribution. The charge could be made that this was a revival of the fifth-century heresy of Pelagianism, which attributed the ability to contribute to one's salvation by human effort unaided by grace (as mentioned earlier). But the *via moderna* implicitly assumed the correctness of St Anselm's twelfth-century theory of the salvation of the human race through the mediatorship of Christ, who being God and man could satisfy the requirements of God's justice on behalf of all humankind. Luther was trained in this later scholasticism. It will emerge that he had difficulty with this idea of a covenant and its requirements; this will only be resolved for him by his discovery of the true nature of God's justice, which did away with what he had perceived to be his obligations.

The other theological tradition, which ultimately was the fundamental influence on Luther's understanding of humanity's relationship with God, came about as a reaction to this positive appraisal of the human capacity to act in a way pleasing to God on the basis of inner ability, doing what was in one, as the Latin tag, *fac quod in te est,* put it. It was a revival of Augustine's conception of the human person as totally dependent on grace in order to act justly. This theology has been labelled *via antiqua.* Augustine's interpretation of Rom 5:12 on the basis of the Vulgate translation, which states that 'in Adam all have sinned', had led him to emphasise the inevitable sinfulness of human activity because of the corruption inherited by generation. Augustine was undoubtedly pessimistic about human nature because of what he considered an inherent orientation towards rebellion against God though he did recognise that the sinner could in some sense cooperate with God's grace to bring about a transformation making him just in God's sight. Luther however became convinced that in fact he could never meet the conditions of the covenant. There was no way God would accept his efforts as sufficient to merit salvation.

According to his account in a preface to his collected works in 1545, he had been meditating on the text of Rom 1:17, 'The righteousness of God is revealed in [the gospel]', while in this desperate state. Suddenly he came to understand that righteousness was to be understood not as a righteousness in which God punishes sinners, something active, but as a passive righteousness 'by which the merciful God justifies us by faith'. His attention had focused with huge revelatory results on the end of the sentence: 'the righteousness of God is revealed through faith' while the verse ends: 'The one who is righteous will live through faith', which could also be translated: 'One who is righteous through faith will live'. This made him feel as if he had been reborn. In the preface,[3] he dated this event to 1519, but scholars generally agree that it must have occurred about 1515. Whenever it came, Luther regarded his new understanding of God's righteousness as a gift liberating him from his previous constant efforts to live according to the demands of life as an Augustinian friar in order to merit salvation. This brought a new perspective not only on the theology of the time but clearly also on his way of living and on the traditional pious practices of the day. However, it was at the level of theology rather than practice that his new approach became evident. The *Disputation Against Scholastic Theology* he organised among the faculty of Wittenberg on September 4th 1517 was more radical than the famous event of the posting of the *Ninety-Fives Theses* against indulgences nearly two months later. And in the months following the indulgence controversy it was still the issue of theological dispute that occupied his energies. He got an opportunity to promote his new anti-philosophical theology at the meeting of the Augustinian order in Heidelberg in April 1518. He made no mention of indulgences but his condemnation of a theology which exalted 'works' and did not recognise human incapacity to merit went beyond what he had said in the *Ninety-Five Theses*. He also quoted Augustine on lack of free will, on total corruption.

Apart from academic discussion, he was also moving away from traditional orthodoxy in his approach to pastoral life, which continued to occupy much of his time. He preached a sermon in 1519 which showed how his new understanding of his relationship with God was affecting his pastoral practice. It anticipates his treatment of the sacraments which was to come in the 1520 tract, *The Babylonian Captivity of the Church,* in that it consists of a major repudiation of the use of the sacrament of penance as it was then constituted. In *A Sermon on the Sacrament of Penance,*[4] he attacked the approach to the sacrament which included the requirement that penitents have full knowledge of their sins and express true repentance. It involved detailed examination of the penitent by priests through the almost universal practice of using manuals containing very detailed lists of possible sins. He was conscious of how tortured he had felt in the past when endeavouring to satisfy all the requirements for a valid confession, but after his realisation that the great truth was God's loving forgiveness rather than any human attempt to satisfy God's justice, he felt liberated. To people concerned with whether they were sufficiently penitent, he could now say that they should accept that their contrition could never be adequate and cast themselves on God's mercy, never doubting this certainty. Some months later, in the Spring of 1520, he followed up the sermon with a tract, *Confitendi Ratio,* containing a detailed critique of how the sacrament was celebrated, though his denial of the sacramental status of the rite had yet to come.

The issue which proved most challenging in the *Ninety-Five Theses* had been one relating not to an alternative theology but one relating to the ecclesiastical administration instead. It was the reason for the reaction against him at Rome, where the official papal theologian, Silvester Prierias, a Dominican, produced his *Dialogue Against the Arrogant Theses of Martin Luther Concerning the Power of the Pope* in December 1517. The title says it all. This element of Luther's thought, doubt about the pope's authority, was seen to be the problem and was soon to become the fundamental issue between him and ecclesiastical authority, partly perhaps because of the intemperate nature of Prierias' diatribe.

Though for some time he would not be quite consistent in his attitude to the pope and his authority and distinguished between pope and curia, Luther's attitude was quickly hardening. Repeated calls for him to retract his views from his own religious authorities and from the papal legate Cajetan at their meeting in Augsburg, already mentioned, brought him to a position – implicit at least in the *Ninety-Five Theses* – that for him scripture was the only authority and its interpretation was self-evident, leaving no room for the traditional papal role of supreme authority. This may seem a case of a theologian coming into conflict with the ecclesiastical institution, but as seen already the political undercurrents were powerful. Not only political, however, but individual and collective forces brought about the confrontation.

On the individual level, there was the factor of Luther's personality. A highly regarded study of Luther by Heiko Oberman in 1982 was entitled *Luther: Man between God and the Devil.*[5] This presents Luther as a man driven by a sense of a cosmological struggle between God and the devil, where the devil and the papacy become conflated and this certainly was the case for Luther by the end of his life. The first major psychoanalytical study was by a Danish psychiatrist, Paul Reiter, and in two volumes (1937-41).[6] Reiter held that Luther had a basic tendency to depression and an anxiety neurosis that was related to his father fixation. Erik Erikson's well-known 1958 psycho-biographical study, *Young Man Luther,*[7] continued in that line and endeavoured to find in Luther's personal history an explanation for his rebellion against church authority linked with his relationship with his father. This psychological approach, following on centuries of theological biographies, itself needed to be balanced by subsequent studies which endeavoured to take account of both the theological and psychological aspects of their subject. A good example is found in Roper:

> [Luther's] relentless sense of the drama of his relations with his own father led him to the most profound understanding of God.... If he is less able to transmit a sense of God's fatherly care for the believer, he certainly conveys the awesome distance that lies between God and human beings.[8]

It will be necessary to return to this aspect of Luther's theology and personality in the final section of this study. The views from different angles do help towards an understanding of why Luther in the years 1518 to 1521, at least, appears such a driven figure, at times fearing martyrdom and at other times joking about and caricaturing his adversaries.

The official response

He was also a man in actual danger in the aftermath of the Leipzig debate, as Rome after the imperial election returned to consideration of his case. It should be dealt with before Charles V arrived in Germany, so meetings of the curia in relation to the Luther affair began in spring 1520. In an early approach to the case, an attempt was made to suppress Luther by having the general of the Augustinians write to Staupitz, as vicar in Germany, asking him to silence Luther. Torn between conflicting loyalties, Staupitz released Luther from his vows, was himself required by the curia to abjure any errors and resigned his post. (Two years later he became a Benedictine in Salzburg and died there as abbot in 1524.) A curial cardinal wrote with the same request to Friedrich, who replied that after Leipzig he had referred the case to the Archbishop of Trier. In the aftermath also of Leipzig, Eck made his way to Rome to make his contribution to the curia's deliberations – arriving halfway through and not altogether welcome on the part of Cajetan, it appears.[9] Eck had arrived with a new book he had written on papal primacy and claimed to be the only one who had sufficient information to catch all of Luther's errors.[10]

At Leipzig the universities had been called in to adjudicate, but Erfurt had declined and Paris had not responded. Though their views had not been solicited, Cologne and Louvain had sent their judgments and Eck brought these with him to Rome. Both were severely condemnatory of Luther's views on human depravity, penance, purgatory and indulgences. But Louvain was oddly silent on the attack on the papacy while Cologne, a largely Dominican institution, drew attention to heretical notions with regard to the fundamental doctrine of papal primacy. Between May and June there were four meetings of the cardinals' consistory which included heads of the religious orders and 'consultants' like Eck and Prierias, the papal theologian. Lively discussion showed up diverse views on how to proceed, canonists having one approach and another on the part of those who considered the question of expediency of any publication, given the divided situation in Germany. All this left Cajetan, the most accomplished theologian, dissatisfied that his request to have Luther's writings carefully examined by a specialist group was not accepted. The deliberations and resulting document have been criticised for lack of knowledge as to what Luther actually had written and for failing to refute Luther by specific reference to the Bible and to the Fathers.

Early in the proceedings Leo himself left for his hunting lodge at Magliana, today a village just off the motorway from Rome to Da Vinci Airport. Summer was after all not the time of year for tackling a serious case of dissent from church teaching. When the document condemning forty-one errors in Luther's teaching was finalised it was sent to Leo for promulgation and became the Bull *Exsurge Domine* of June 24ᵗʰ 1520. This document has received more attention and humorous comment for the circumstances of its publication than for the seriousness of its content, beginning as it does with the call: 'Arise, O Lord, and judge your cause. A wild boar has invaded your vineyard', both sentences being quotations from the psalms. The text focuses on the loyalty the German nation 'which has always been eager to repress heresy', recalling the war against the Hussites, and then condemns the forty-one theses listed by the commission. Luther is alluded to by name and the efforts made already to reconcile him to the church are listed, but he is now declared a heretic. Nevertheless, sentence of excommunication will not be pronounced at once; sixty days are given for him to recant in a ceremony in Rome (and also in several German cathedrals).[11] To initiate the process of publication, Luther's books were burned in Piazza Navona and the task of publication in Germany assigned to the redoubtable Eck and also to a new Papal Legate, Girolamo Aleandro (1480-1542), a learned academic and an acquaintance of Erasmus – he had been rector in Paris. He would prove to be very energetic in his campaign against Luther.

There was now the difficulty of publishing the Bull in Germany. Eck was able to have it published in a few German towns but the University of Leipzig, which had welcomed him a year previously, would have nothing to do with it. Duke Georg commanded it to be displayed publicly, but this led to it being desecrated by supporters of Luther. From Leipzig, Eck sent the Bull to the University of Wittenberg, where it was received in early October, but the rector evaded the task of enforcing the decree by claiming that Eck had not transmitted the Bull in due form. In various other towns, Eck had no success and only with difficulty succeeded in imposing it in his own University of Ingolstadt. Aleandro arrived in Cologne on October 29th but Friedrich, who was marooned there by gout, refused to receive him. However, he managed to present the Bull and a letter from Leo to Friedrich while the latter was actually attending mass some days later. The attempt to burn Luther's books was frustrated by students who somehow rescued them, while the archbishop and chapter boycotted the event.

The months which followed proved to be of particular importance in the Luther affair, as in Germany support for him grew, especially from two knights, Ulrich von Hutten and Franz von Sickingen, who considered that he could be of use in their campaign to advance German nationalism. Through their influence, popular enthusiasm grew and he seemed to respond to this by consolidating his theological stance in several treatises. In particular, he exploited the situation by publishing his *To the Christian Nobility of the German Nation*. By the nobility he meant the ruling class from the emperor down. Written in German, this tract represents a new and audacious approach to his campaign for reform.

Hitherto he was content to dispute theologically in Latin – as at Leipzig, for example. He was content to do so knowing that he had the protection of the Elector Friedrich when danger threatened, as it seemed to in Leipzig and even before that in Augsburg. Now he calls on not simply 'nobles' but all Germans to rally to the cause of reform. He does so by using a clever image. Papal power was buttressed by three walls: that the church had its own spiritual law; that the papacy alone had the right to interpret scripture; and that only the pope could call a council of the church. His attack on the concept of the church's spiritual law was a logical consequence of the fact that his appeal was to the laity. Hitherto, clergy had enjoyed in many ways exemption from secular law; removing this buttress put everyone on the same level and gave the laity the right to take whatever moves were necessary to reform the church. In relation to the other two, in the Leipzig debate with Eck it was already part of Luther's thinking that a lay person had as much right as the pope to interpret scripture and after his meeting with Cajetan at Augsburg he had himself appealed for the calling of a council. The first attack was the most fundamental in many ways as it effectively struck at the concept of a hierarchical church based on the idea of the sacrament of order and the jurisdiction going with it. (This understanding of the church would be dealt with in the tract that was soon to follow, *The Babylonian Captivity of the Church*.) While the address to the nation was in German and in popular language, there were many quotations from scripture and references to church history, so that more than rudimentary education would have been needed to access the line of reasoning fully. He availed of one of the most useful arguments in relation to lay invocation of a council by referring to that at Nicaea in 325: 'the most celebrated council of all, that of Nicaea, was neither called nor confirmed by the Bishop of Rome, but by the Emperor Constantine'.[12]

Here was an example of the third player (the theologian) endeavouring to influence the second (secular powers) in order to bring about reform in the first (the church) for the well-being of Christendom. In the section called *Twenty-Seven Articles Respecting The Reformation Of The Christian Estate* in Part 2 of the treatise, he gives his views in detail on the relation between the church and the secular powers: the pope should have no power over the Emperor, except to anoint and crown him at the altar, as a bishop crowns a king (No. 9).

In the section headed 'Of the matters to be considered in the councils', he excoriates not only the Roman curia but the papacy itself as a historical institution, without referring to the actual incumbent, Leo X:

> It is a distressing and terrible thing to see that the head of Christendom, who boasts of being the vicar of Christ and the successor of St Peter, lives in a worldly pomp that no king or emperor can equal, so that in him that calls himself most holy and most spiritual there is more worldliness than in the world itself.

He judges 'the popes' to be corrupt:

> This wantonness and lying reservation of the popes has brought about an unutterable state of things at Rome. There is a buying and a selling, a changing, blustering and bargaining, cheating and lying, robbing and stealing, debauchery and villainy, and all kinds of contempt of God, that antichrist himself could not rule worse.

He goes on in No. 14 to assert the right of the theologian to instruct the church authorities, even on such a sensitive matter as the celibacy of the clergy:

> [The] minister should not be forced to live without a lawful wife, but should be allowed to have one, as St Paul writes, saying that 'a bishop then must be blameless, the husband of one wife ... having his children in subjection with all gravity' (1 Tim 3).

He will return to this issue when the initial reform in Wittenberg, in his absence, prompts his own colleague, Karlstadt, to renounce celibacy and celebrate his own marriage ostentatiously.

His awareness of the antichrist had already surfaced in an interesting way in his Lecture on Ps 69 (68) in about 1514.[13] He quoted Sermon 33 of St Bernard of Clairvaux (1090-1153) on the Song of Songs, in which Bernard spoke of the ages of the world, his own age being the age of the antichrist. Previous ages had been that of persecution of the church followed by that of heresy, but his age was the age in which the enemies were within: 'All are her children, at the same time, all are her adversaries ... They are Christ's ministers, but they serve antichrist'. He went on to identify these enemies as the prelates of his day with 'gold mountings on bridles, saddles and spurs'.[14] Bernard concluded with a prayer that God would slay this antichrist and it is interesting to note that he did not believe that the visible reign of the antichrist was actually at hand, because he recounted in a letter (*Epistola* 59) a visit he had made to St Norbert who was convinced that this was the case, 'I did not feel compelled to agree with him'.[15] Luther identified with the critical attitude of Bernard but may not have been aware of Bernard's reservations concerning the day of the antichrist. In his interview by Cajetan in 1518, he was more concerned with the issue of the authority of the pope and this was true also in his debate with Eck in 1519, when he was content to argue that the papacy was not of divine origin, but was to be obeyed nonetheless. Now, however, he is referring to the 'popes', or papacy, in terms of being the antichrist and this is a significant development. The papacy itself is identified with the antichrist, he is going beyond the practice of several centuries of hurling abuse at an individual by labelling that person 'an antichrist' and not simply an opponent or even enemy. The gospel injunction to love even one's enemies no longer applies; hatred of the devil or antichrist was the response and now Luther would be permitted to adopt this attitude to the papacy. The full implications of his attitude to the papacy will be considered in the chapter on his challenge to the church of his day.

CHAPTER SIX

The publications of 1520

Luther completed his next attack on papal authority, *The Babylonian Captivity of the Church*[1] in early October. As the title implied, Rome was Babylon and the pope the antichrist. This is one of the best known of his works, as it sets out the theology of the sacraments with which his name is always associated. 'At the outset, I must deny that there are seven sacraments, and hold for the present to but three – baptism, penance and the bread'. Later in the text he will say that penance cannot be proved from the scriptures. The text actually begins with an expression of regret that he had written a little book on indulgences because at that time he was still under the Roman tyranny. Now he simply makes a throwaway remark: indulgences are 'impostures of the Roman flatterers'.[2]

He then revisits the issue of communion under both kinds, which had caused his opponents to call him a Hussite, and concludes 'that it is wicked and despotic to deny both kinds to the laity'. He dismisses the by then standard teaching on the eucharist, which followed St Thomas Aquinas by focusing on the concept of the change of the substance of bread and wine in the eucharist, with the accidents remaining.

> When I learned later what church it was that had decreed this – namely, the church of Thomas, i.e., of Aristotle – I waxed bolder, and after floating in a sea of doubt, at last found rest for my conscience in the view that it is real bread and real wine, in which Christ's real flesh and blood are present, not otherwise and not less really than they assume to be the case under their accidents.[3]

He makes a valid and interesting point when he says that 'the church had the true faith for more than twelve hundred years, during which time the holy Fathers never once mentioned this transubstantiation'. Transubstantiation was a 'monstrous word for a monstrous idea'.[4] This is the first of several publications in which he takes the position which is often called 'consubstantiation' (though he does not use the term).

In a tract of the previous year, *The Sacrament of the Holy and True Body of Christ and the Brotherhoods*, he had used the traditional language: 'the bread is changed into his true natural body',[5] so the 'sea of doubt' may have been a reality for him. There was an innate conservatism in Luther, possibly deriving in part from the moulding of his personality by formation in a community of strict observance, where rituals would be used to reinforce reverence. This will result in his hesitations in regard to how the rite of mass should be reformed when he turns to that issue three years later. In the *Captivity* tract he is concerned with inner meaning and turns to the theology of the mass, repudiating the official belief that 'mass is a good work and a sacrifice' and asserting instead that 'the mass, or sacrament of the altar, is Christ's testament which he left behind him at his death, to be distributed among his believers ... a testament [being] a promise which implies the death of him who makes it'.[6] It is worth noting that he talks in terms of alternatives; as the mass is not a sacrifice he is committed to describing it simply as a sacrament, hence his comments that the mass cannot be a sacrifice because '[t]he same thing cannot be received and offered at the same time'.[7] Seeing it in terms of something 'received', like baptism, his focus is on the individual. What is received is the forgiveness of sins. In discussing his reform of the liturgy, it will be necessary to return to the question of individual rather than corporate participation.

Turning to baptism, he expresses gratitude that it has remained as instituted: 'He desired that by it little children, incapable of greed and superstition, might be initiated and sanctified in the simple faith of his word. Even today baptism's chief blessing is for them'.[8] The true nature of baptism makes the traditional rite of the sacrament of penance redundant, again because of the divine promise:

> Just as the truth of this divine promise, once pronounced over us, continues to death, so our faith in the same ought never to cease, but to be nourished and strengthened until death, by the continual remembrance of this promise made to us in baptism. Therefore, when we rise from sins, or repent, we are only returning to the power and the faith of baptism from which we fell, and find our way back to the promise then made to us, from which we departed when we sinned.

In consequence, the baptised person is assured of salvation – as long as they continue in the faith: '[e]ven if he would, he could not lose his salvation, however much he sin, unless he refused to believe'.[9]

Though denying the sacramentality of the rite of penance, he acknowledges its pastoral usefulness:

> Of private confession, which is now observed, I am heartily in favour, even though, it cannot be proved from the scriptures; it is useful and necessary, nor would I have it abolished – no, I rejoice that it exists in the church of Christ, for it is a cure without an equal for distressed consciences. For when we have laid bare our conscience to our brother and privately made known to him the evil that lurked within, we receive from our brother's lips the word of comfort spoken by God himself; and, if we accept it in faith, we find peace in the mercy of God speaking to us through our brother.[10]

Here he seems to be speaking from 'within' the church and not consciously setting up a new community and it is worthy of note that in the *Babylonian Captivity* there is a statement by way of comment on 'an anonymous friar of Cremona' who had written against his teaching on the distribution of the eucharist under both kinds:

> He is a simple and unlearned man, who is endeavouring to recall me to the Holy See, from which I am not conscious of

having ever withdrawn, nor has any one proved that I have.'[11]

Having received a copy of the Bull *Exsurge* in October, in November he published *Against the Execrable Bull of the Antichrist*, averring that as it condemned manifestly Christian articles it must have come from the antichrist. But he went on to identify the hand of Eck, with whom he had debated at Leipzig, and whom he described in very unflattering terms. Two weeks later he produced a tract, *On the Freedom of the Christian Man*, in which he set out his basic theology of justification. The scope of Luther's theological investigations in this one year of 1520 is quite impressive. Broadly speaking, the appeal to the German nation could be described as a pastoral document, the *Babylonian Captivity* clearly had to do with the theology of the church, while the tract on freedom was about salvation. This last work is in the end the one which sets his theology apart from that of the church of the time and brought about the principal repudiation of him by the Council of Trent over twenty five years later.

The tract on freedom, *On the Freedom of the Christian Man*,[12] dated November, was introduced by an 'Open Letter to Pope Leo X', ostensibly because of the promise he had given to Miltitz the previous year. It is especially interesting from the point of view of how it fits in, if at all, with the treatises of that year in regard to Luther's attitude to the papacy. The letter is dated September 6th 1520, while the *To the Christian Nobility of the German Nation* dates from August and the *Babylonian Captivity* from October 6th. The August document, as indicated above, contains an attack on the papacy and not simply the curia, but the letter to Leo adopts an entirely different attitude, addressing him in most respectful terms and carefully distinguishing between him and the curia – logically, therefore, between the papacy and the curia. Though at the time of writing to Leo he had not yet received a copy, he was probably well aware of the contents of the Bull at this stage and may well have become concerned about his safety. The tone is defensive, blaming Eck for all the problems that had arisen, 'seizing me for one little word which I had let slip concerning the primacy of the Roman church'.[13] Miltitz, in contrast, he singles out for praise for the peace arrangements he had made. Then, 'prostrate' before Leo, he asks him to intervene in the case, while declaring his determination not to recant and acknowledging 'no fixed rules for the interpretation of the word of God'. He knows he is 'presumptuous in trying to instruct so exalted a person' and recommends to him the well known book, *On Consideration,* which St Bernard had sent to his former disciple, Pope Eugenius. He professes sympathy for Leo 'driven and buffeted about in Rome' and, disingenuously, given the content, offers him the little gift of his treatise *On the Freedom of the Christian Man,* a text which in fact did not appear until November. It was written in German and was not polemical, unlike the address to the nobles. It has been described as a 'comforting devotional tract'.[14]

On the basis of the title, one can say that the subject of the treatise is the freedom which faith brings:

> the Christian man is the most free lord of all. Yet faith which unites with Christ makes the Christian like Christ who came in the form of a servant. This polarity arises from the fact that man is composed of a twofold nature, the flesh lusting against the spirit, and the spirit against the flesh (Gal 17). 'What can it profit the soul that the body should be in good condition, free, and full of life? Again, what harm can ill-health, bondage, hunger, thirst, or any other outward evil, do to the soul.[15]

Here, Luther takes the simplistic approach of identifying 'flesh' with the body and so his conclusion that it will profit nothing for 'justification and liberty of the soul' that someone's body 'should be adorned with sacred vestments, or dwell in holy places, or be occupied in sacred offices, or pray, fast and abstain from certain meats' is not necessarily true. If these are works of the flesh in the Pauline sense, that is, not under the auspices of the Christian spirit, that will be the case, but things done 'in the body' cannot as such be denied spiritual significance. Still Luther recognises that 'it will not at all injure the soul that the body should be clothed in profane raiment, should dwell in profane places, should eat and drink in the ordinary fashion'.

Having the word is what counts: by it the soul 'is rich and wants for nothing; since that is the word of life, of truth, of light, of peace, of justification, of salvation, of joy, of liberty, of wisdom, of virtue, of grace, of glory, and of every good thing'. And that word of God cannot be received by any works, but by faith alone. 'Hence it is clear that, as the soul needs the word alone for life and justification, so it is justified by faith alone and not by any works.' As the touch of Christ brings life, so 'absorption of the word' communicates to the soul all that belongs to the word. Luther then introduces the concept of righteousness and says that to attribute this to God is 'to be ourselves true and righteous'.

He then reflects on the union between Christ and the soul, which he compares to marriage and the complete sharing it involves. On this he bases his assertion that

> all we who believe in Christ are kings and priests in Christ.... Consequently, by the words, 'priest', 'clergy', 'spiritual person', 'ecclesiastic,' an injustice has been done, since they have been transferred from the remaining body of Christians to those few, who are now, by a hurtful custom, called ecclesiastics. For holy scripture makes no distinction between them.[16]

In the *Babylonian Captivity*, he had denied the sacramentality of the priesthood and here he takes the further step of denying any distinction between clergy and laity. At the same time, he does not deny the necessity of ministry to be performed by men specially delegated to do so: 'the minister of Christ must be prudent and faithful in so ruling and teaching the people of Christ in all these matters that no root of bitterness may spring up among them, and thus many be defiled, as Paul warned the Hebrews'. Nor does he deny the usefulness of 'ceremonies'. They belong to a disciplinary regime.

> By the use of these still, he remains in this mortal life upon earth, in which it is necessary that he should rule his own

body, and have intercourse with men. Here then works begin; here he must not take his ease; here he must give heed to exercise his body by fastings, watchings, labour, and other moderate discipline, so that it may be subdued to the spirit, and obey and conform itself to the inner man and faith.[17]

This is in contrast with the foolish who turn the liberty of faith into licence.

It is worth noting that Luther here anticipates the problem he will encounter with his own associate Karlstadt. Karlstadt's spirituality of *gelassenheit* included not simply abandonment of oneself to God but a detachment from and neglect of the ordinary ways of religious observance. 'They think that everything is now lawful for them, and do not choose to show themselves free men and Christians in any other way than by their contempt and reprehension of ceremonies, of traditions of human laws.'

It is interesting too that Luther's position is not to be contrasted too radically with the medieval tradition regarding the relationship between faith and love, as he says: 'Here is the truly Christian life; here is faith really working by love; when a man applies himself with joy and love to the works of that freest servitude, in which he serves others voluntarily and for nought; himself abundantly satisfied in the fullness and riches of his own faith'. How important 'ceremonies' are in Luther's scheme is best shown by the imagery he uses towards the close of the tract:

[C]eremonies are to be no otherwise looked upon than builders and workmen look upon those preparations for building or working which are not made with any view of being permanent or anything in themselves, but only because without them there could be no building and no work. When the structure is completed, they are laid aside.[18]

The building he wishes to construct remains faith.

Historians of the Reformation have seen in this last of the 1520 publications the point at which a final division occurs between Luther and the medieval Catholic tradition, for which the concept of merit was fundamental. 'Works', such as the fastings, watchings, labour, of which Luther speaks disparagingly, if done in faith and love, contribute to the Christian's growth in grace. 'Ceremonies' such as the sacramental rites are not merely scaffolding but part of the building up of the merit of the Christian's life in Christ.

The days were going by and Luther continued his daily teaching at Wittenberg. They ran out on December 10th 1520 – sixty days after Luther was deemed to have received the Bull – and Luther's reaction was to stage a public burning of the Bull. To modern ears, burning books would seem a futile gesture, but at the time (apart from the fact that books were scarce and expensive) a public burning was part of the judicial process and quite significant as a form of condemnation of their content and of their author and an advance warning of what was promised concerning the author's fate. Part of the programme of publishing the Bull had been the burning of Luther's books in Cologne and Mainz, not without opposition as already noted, and the Wittenberg bonfire was in retaliation. It was a carefully managed event, with a formal announcement nailed beforehand to the door of the parish church by Melanchthon, inviting all who 'were lovers of evangelical truth' to gather at the allocated place at nine o'clock in the morning on the 10th.[19] The place chosen was where the hospital rags were burned.

Luther came after his morning lecture accompanied by his students and cast on to the flames not only the Bull but also the Papal *Decretals* and the book of canon law, thus indicating that he was repudiating not only the recent judgment but the whole tradition built up since the heyday of canonist popes such as Innocent III, whose reign almost a century before Boniface VIII marked the apogee of papal power. In his defence of the burning, Luther said that the canon law was burnt because it made 'the pope a god on earth'.[20] It was now three months since he had written his open and apparently respectful letter to Leo X and despite the reservations he had expressed about the authorship of the Bull in November, he was now consigning to

the flames a document with Leo's Medici family coat of arms prominently displayed on the title page. The distinction between the papacy, or the 'Romanists', and the person of Leo (if it ever meant much to
him) was becoming less and less real. The burning of his books as part
of the publication of Leo's Bull against him seems to have introduced
a personal element into the affair. According to one biographer he
addressed the pope in the person of his ambassador the Bull: 'because
you have brought down the truth of God, he also brings you down
into this fire today'.[21] His defiant stance was well understood and en-
thusiastically supported by the students, who after he and the other
professors had gone back to the university prolonged what was now
a charade by processing around the town in an imitation of the student initiation ritual. They cut up a copy of the Bull, placed parts in a
barrel which they drove about on a wagon. They read from the works
of Eck and another opponent of Luther before burning the books and
the barrel and in the afternoon wandered about the town blowing
trumpets and singing funeral masses for the Bull. It was a further
demonstration of Luther's popularity but also of his effectiveness as a
teacher and propagandist for his new theology.

Apart from his support by the professors and students in Wittenberg, his many publications were widely distributed within a few
years and made him perhaps the best known and most popular person in Germany. As noted earlier, it was also a period of widespread
pamphleteering – a pamphlet war – with humanist writers leading
the charge against the papacy creating, as one commentator on public
opinion at that time put it, a Rome that Luther loved to hate.[22]

CHAPTER SEVEN

The Diet of Worms 1521

With the expiry of the ultimatum, the political situation became relevant in a new way. Friedrich's officials sought to have the case transferred to Germany to be tried by the emperor. While in The Netherlands in 1520, before his coronation as emperor, Charles, the emperor-elect, received the Papal Legate, Aleandro, who raised the question of Luther with him. He was not disposed to deal with a matter already decided upon through the issuing of the Bull *Exsurge*, but after his coronation at Aachen went to visit Friedrich,[1] still resting at Cologne. Aleandro got in first, urging Friedrich not to involve the emperor. Friedrich decided to call in Erasmus, whom all considered a supporter of reform but a moderate one. Erasmus pondered and then would only say that Luther had gone a little too far.[2] After the meeting with the elector, Spalatin persuaded Erasmus to write down some points in Luther's favour. In his *Axiomata,* Erasmus identified a love of power ('tyranny') and dislike of learning as the source of the conflict, claiming that people of pure faith and morals were least offended by Luther's writings. Some people were taking advantage of the pope's good nature while he preferred the glory of Christ to his own and wanted only the salvation of souls. It would be good for the dignity and interest of the pope if the affair were to be settled by wise men, free of suspicion. The Bull itself was barbarous and unworthy of a 'mild' Vicar of Christ. Only two universities had ruled against Luther and they did not agree as to their reasons. Luther's proposal to defend himself publicly seemed fair and he sought neither rank nor profit.[3]

Some points emerge clearly in the response of Erasmus: he speaks as a humanist who is in a sense above the fray and finds the Bull defective both as a theological assessment of Luther's position and of his motivation – though after a few years he will radically disagree with Luther's theology. He attributes goodwill to Luther, but also to Leo, whom he does not hesitate to praise.[4] But he almost immediately regretted his decision to come down off the fence, from his position as the one whom all respected as the proponent of reform while respecting the institution. But his document had been taken and printed and was even in the hands of the legate Aleandro.

Armed with these comments, Friedrich was in a better position to dislodge Charles from his declared and devout position that he could not interfere in a matter on which the pope had apparently spoken. At his election Charles had signed the constitution of the empire, which included among its provisions that no German of any rank should be taken for trial outside Germany. He was conscious of the fragility of the bonds holding so many estates together and now divided over the question of Luther. Despite the constant interventions of Aleandro, on November 4th he decided that Luther should have a hearing. Prompted by the University of Wittenberg, Friedrich suggested a hearing at the forthcoming Diet of Worms and Charles wrote to him on November 28th agreeing, saying that Friedrich should bring Luther to the diet, 'that he may be thoroughly investigated by competent persons'.[5] Some complicated manoeuvring and re-assessing of positions followed, as Aleandro objected to the invitation on the grounds that one who had been condemned by pope, cardinals and prelates should not be judged now by the laity. The emperor rescinded his decision on December 17th, for reasons unknown, but he may have been persuaded by Aleandro or irritated by news of the burning of the Bull at Wittenberg. He could have avoided the volte-face if he had waited a little because Friedrich turned down the invitation, uncertain as to what Charles really had in mind. In response to Friedrich's enquiry, Luther expressed willingness to go to the diet, saying: 'If Caesar calls me, God calls me'.[6] Aleandro proposed to Charles that he should issue an edict banning Luther without waiting for the diet to convene or approve, but Charles refused.

When Friedrich arrived for the diet on the feast of the Epiphany, he rode into Worms dressed as one of the three kings. He brought gifts for the emperor, who thereupon rescinded his recent decision and promised to take responsibility for Luther's case. The sensitive issue of before whom and what kind of hearing Luther would have was not specified. During the diet sessions which followed, Aleandro made two unsuccessful attempts to have the edict of condemnation issued without hearing Luther. Meanwhile tensions between the local Germans and Charles' Spanish troops were growing; attempts were made to sequester Luther's publications and pamphlets, while posters circulated in the city depicting the various personalities in scurrilous or positive terms. Aleandro feared for his life.[7] Tension grew in the diet itself, with Friedrich and Albrecht having to be separated on the floor of the diet by Cardinal Lang. The nub of the matter was what conflicts, even insurrection, might arise in a divided Germany if Luther was not given a hearing. 'More than half of the delegates, including some bishops and most secular rulers, had not publicly taken sides for or against Luther.'[8]

The diet was presented with a motion that Luther's books be banned without an invitation to him to appear, but rejected it. Unrest was growing among the peasants and Luther was perceived at that stage to be a supporter of their rights, so any move against him could spark off trouble. The diet demanded that he be brought under safe conduct and be examined by learned men. He should be brought to answer, not to argue. 'If he would renounce what he said against faith, other points could be discussed. If he refused, then the diet would support the edict.'[9]

Most of the members of the diet saw the issue in political terms, but Aleander and Catholic prelates like Albrecht and, significantly, Charles himself, quite genuinely did not. He was determined to show he was not soft on heresy, while recognising the political risks involved in dealing with Luther. He therefore expressed the invitation to appear at Worms in friendly terms; Aleandro took the German in which he addressed Luther to mean: 'Noble, devout, dear to us'.[10] He offered a safe conduct of twenty one days but did not specify what form the proceedings would take. Luther's advisers at Friedrich's court were hesitant; after all, Hus had accepted an invitation with safe conduct attached to attend the Council of Constance a century earlier and had been burned at the stake. Luther decided to accept but to an unidentified friend he wrote on March 24th: 'This shall be my recantation at Worms: "Previously I said the pope is the Vicar of Christ. I recant. Now I say the pope is the adversary of Christ and the apostle of the devil"'.[11] His mood therefore was confrontational, or, as Mullett observes: 'Luther seems to have been determined to turn his trial into an opportunity for a national clarion call'.[12] At this point there was an interesting twist in the affair. Glapion was the emperor's confessor and the leader of a moderate Catholic party; he had agreed with the attack on indulgences and found a wonderful Christian spirit in the *The Freedom of a Christian Man*, but he was appalled by the attack on the sacraments in *The Babylonian Captivity*. He hoped that Luther might be persuaded in private to repudiate the views he had expressed there, presumably in a fit of passion. Glapion's approach seemed to offer an attractive possibility of solution but he must not have taken account of much else that Luther had written and could not have known all he said in his letters and sermons. He put his proposal to Friedrich, who remained determined to have the diet deal with the matter, and then tried it on the famous knights Von Sickingen and Hutten. Hutten sent his chaplain to meet Luther on the way to Worms, but Luther refused to divert from his decision.

Luther set out for Worms on April 2nd in an open carriage, which had been provided by the Wittenberg goldsmith, accompanied by a group of friends and preceded by the imperial herald, who had come to summon him. He was escorted, according to some accounts, by more than a hundred armed men.[13] Unlike his earlier journey to Leipzig, this was something of a triumphal procession. Crowds greeted him along the way as 'a miracle man who was so brave as to oppose the pope and all the world who held the pope to be a god against Christ'.[14] At Erfurt, the rector of the university and sixty horsemen rode out to meet him. He was hesitant about staying in what had been his former community, as Erfurt was in the territory of the Elector Albrecht. But he was welcomed there by his friend, Prior Johann Lang, and in the cloister chapel preached a sermon in which he said that the devil had for long held the people in thrall.[15] The party arrived in Worms on April 16th 1521. A crowd of two thousand turned out to greet him and escort him to his lodgings in a house of the Order of St John, where an imperial official and two knights were also accommodated.

When escorted into the hall next afternoon, the contrast between his simple black-belted robe and the splendid apparel of the princes and prelates, bedecked with gold chains and jewels, was obvious. Only Aleandro was missing; his dignity would not allow the papal representative to be present when one excommunicated by the church was to be given a hearing by a lay tribunal. Facing Luther on a canopied throne was the young emperor in his magnificent robes. He was of noble lineage and was now ruler of the greatest empire since Charlemagne, while Luther was, as he always liked to insist, of peasant stock. The environment could not be other than intimidating as the fifteen hundred people present included Charles' Spanish entourage as well as the Germans princes and knights. He had been given only the barest briefing about questions he would be asked and to which he was to give a simple answer. The proceedings were to be in Latin and German – which was not much help to Charles, whose native language was French.

He was asked by an official of the Archbishop of Trier, coincidentally named John Eck, if the books laid out before him were his and if he would disavow them. To the first part he replied in the affirmative but to the second he replied that this was a matter affecting the salvation of souls, that Christ had said that whoever would deny him, he would deny before the Father, and so he asked for time to reflect, thereby increasing the tension. He was given twenty-four hours and told to be ready to reply next day without any written text. Next day, the hearing was delayed until late in the evening, the setting a room lit only by torches adding to the drama. The questions of yesterday were repeated and this time Luther responded in German by distinguishing between his three types of publication.[16] The first category dealt with faith and morals and had never, he said, provoked objection. The second category gave him the opportunity he sought to appeal to the Germans: 'The second category makes a case against the papacy, because it tortures consciences and squanders our people's resources. To retract these books would be to consent to this tyranny and approve its continuation'. He then named the third category as one 'directed against persons who defended the Roman tyranny'. He concluded by asking for a debate, to convince him of his errors by the writings of the prophets and the gospel. 'If I could be better instructed, none would be more eager than I to retract whatever errors there are. I would be the first to throw my books on the fire.' Towards the end, there was a note of warning: 'To reject the word of God for the sake of peace and quiet would be a terrible beginning to this imperial reign'. This was intended as much for the Germans as for Charles, who probably didn't understand the language – the famous quotation about his speaking German to his horse, if true, would belong to his later years. Luther then asked if he should repeat what he had said in Latin and did so.

As in the debate at Leipzig he was appealing to scripture, but here he was appealing also, in another sense, to Germany and deliberately giving priority to its language. The princes and prince bishops withdrew to consider the situation. For the bishops, there could be no discussion as the church had defined doctrines clearly enough. But the matter could not be allowed to end there; Luther must be required to say whether he retracted or not. So Eck returned to the questioning, prefacing it with a long speech in which he said that no one would discuss points of doctrine long since fixed by councils and that Luther had only to believe like everyone else. So, once again, did he wish to retract, yes or no? This time, Luther said in Latin that unless convinced by scripture (adding that he accepted neither pope nor councils by themselves) he could not or would not retract anything. Then he broke into German: 'I cannot. Do with me what you will. God help me'. According to the official transcript that is all he said. The version published subsequently at Wittenberg added the legendary saying: 'Here I stand; I can do no other'. Not wishing the proceedings to end at this highly charged moment with Luther somehow dominant, Eck resumed his examination, but the emperor signalled for guards to take Luther out. As he went there were conflicting reactions – Germans calling out and waving their arms in victory, the Spanish guards shouting '*Al fuego!*', while the Germans missed the meaning of this call for a heretic's burning.

Luther was content. He had appealed to conscience, saying 'My conscience is captive to the word of God' (*Victus sum scripturis a me adductis et capta conscientia in verbis Dei*).[17] It was not the first time he appealed to 'conscience' in face of authority's strictures. At Augsburg in 1518, he had already claimed special ability to interpret scripture, saying he only taught what was in scripture. His use of the word 'conscience' has been subjected to interesting scrutiny by Lyndal Roper in her 2016 biography.

> [Conscience] has a modern resonance, suggestive of freedom of thought and of the right of all individuals to decide for themselves. But this was not what Luther meant. The German term he used, *Gewissen,* is closely connected to words like 'knowing' and 'certainty'; in Latin, the root of *conscientia* – another word he used regularly – means 'with-knowing'.[18]

Roper gives the modern meaning of conscience as a part of the mind that imposes external norms and moral judgments, saying that this is not what Luther meant. For him, 'the word of God is absolutely clear and plain in its meaning' and 'conscience' is the individual's internal knowledge of the objective meaning of God's word. Hendrix has a similar view: '[H]is conscience "captive to the word of God" was not an internal moral meter that measured right and wrong, but loyalty to the highest authority on which one depended for the truth'.[19]

Roper continues: 'Moreover, for Luther the conscience is not just an intellectual faculty but is also linked to a complex palette of emotions'. At this point, her description of Luther's conscience begins to take on the characteristics of conscience as a moral faculty and brings to mind his relationship with Staupitz, who had to deal with Luther's burdened conscience, which had led him to confess frequently. This reference to his spiritual problems could confuse the issue unless one takes account of Luther's breakthrough in understanding of God's righteousness. His understanding, in effect, moved his conscience from that modern sense of moral imperative into that of certainty about the meaning of God's word.

What is of greater interest here, however, is the origin of this *conscientia* in Luther, something not discussed by Roper, but the nature of it seems to suggest that the Augustinian theory of knowledge may be at its root. It seems most likely that, being well formed in Augustine's theology, Luther's conviction concerning his grasp of, or his being grasped by, the word, his 'knowing-with' or *con-scientia*, came from subscribing to Augustinian illuminism, that is, that he believed he had certainty in relation to the word of scripture through having the indwelling Christ, the word. There are various places in St Augustine's writing where the illumination of the mind is described and, though Augustinian scholars differ as to the exact nature of the process involved, the same effectiveness is attributed to it as to grace in the moral order. (See Appendix 2.)

His conviction would be unassailed by external stimuli, namely, the teaching by external sources of authority, such as tradition, teaching of councils and especially the papal *magisterium*. In his *Assertio omnium articulorum per Bullam Leonis X* (1520), his response to the Bull *Exsurge Domine*, he contrasted contemporary practice with that of the early church, asking why the first or only place should not be given to the study of sacred letters in deciding questions, as in the early church – 'they did not read Augustine or Thomas'. In a case of conflicting views,

> scripture has to be the judge and this cannot be unless it is given the principal place in everything which is attributed to the Fathers, that is, that it is of itself certain, accessible

and clear, that it interprets itself (*sui ipsius interpres*), that it tests and judges and illuminates everything else as Ps 119 indicates.[20]

The reference appears to be to Ps 119:130, 'The unfolding of your word gives light; it teaches the simple'. The assertion that scripture interprets itself and the use of the word 'illuminates' support the idea that for Luther the external word of scripture was made clear in its meaning (interpreted itself) by an internal faculty of illumination because of the indwelling Christ. In his dispute with Erasmus concerning the 'freedom' or 'bondage' of the will, four years later, he made a distinction between the internal and external clarity of scripture.

> If you speak of the internal clarity, no man perceives an *iota* of what is in the scriptures unless he has the Spirit of God.... If on the other hand, you speak of external clarity, nothing at all is left ambiguous, but everything there is in the scriptures has been brought out by the word into the most definite light, and published to all the world.[21]

He deals with the external clarity further on, saying that it is established by the 'public ministry of the word ... and is chiefly the concern of leaders and preachers of the word'. He was confident that the internal illumination allowed him to oppose papal interpretation on the one hand and the Anabaptist (Müntzer, Karlstadt) understanding on the other; at Leipzig this had led Eck in exasperation to charge him with being his own interpreter.

Any threat to his position he came to see as the work of the devil and the devil's primeval rebellion against the creative word. When he was chided for setting himself up as autonomous interpreter of scripture, his conscience in the ordinary sense of the word – which caused him to be scrupulous in matters of religious observance – yielded its place to the stronger sense arising from this divine illumination.[22] There is an issue here, however, which will be discussed in some detail at the end of this study: the possibility that Luther's personality and even his state of mental health were such as to make him unwilling to question his convictions. How his theological insight and emotional drive interacted is one of the perplexing issues in Luther studies and has tended to polarise studies into abstract theological assessments on the one hand and psychoanalytical studies on the other.

Whatever its origin, his conviction must have sustained him as he was questioned at the diet. But there was also, whenever he glanced around him, a group of his fellow-countrymen to whom his stance mattered, not because they shared his intellectual conviction but because he had become the symbol of their nationalist ideology. Had he retracted, his words could have destabilised the uneasy truce between the German estates resentful of all foreign power and the Catholic emperor endeavouring to unite all his territories. By maintaining his stance, only he himself would suffer the consequences; he would remain a hero to many but, following the inevitable issue of an edict, he would come under the ban of the empire, liable to be hunted down and executed. The ecclesiastical consequences hardly meant much to him; he had been excommunicated in the Bull *Decet Romanum Pontificem* of January 3rd 1521. He had in any case consistently repudiated papal authority and explicitly done so in his *Against the Execrable Bull of the Antichrist* in late 1520, where he said that if the Bull *Exsurge* came from Leo (which he really knew it did), then he must regard the see of Rome as possessed by Satan and as the throne of antichrist and would no longer obey it or be bound by it.[23] If the three documents of 1520, despite Glapion's view, mark the point at which Luther's theology departs from the officially held doctrines, the stance he adopted at the Diet of Worms most clearly marks his separation from the communion of the Catholic Church.

As it turned out, being hustled away by the guards did not mark the end of Luther's involvement with the diet. The next day, the emperor called in the electors and a number of princes for a consultation about how next to proceed. As they looked for time to reflect, he took them by surprise by giving them his own view. In a paper he had written himself, he professed his Catholic faith, saying that he was a descendant of a long line of emperors, kings and archdukes who were all faithful to the church of Rome. He was resolved to follow their steps. 'A single friar whose view goes counter to all Christianity of the past thousand years and of the present must be wrong.'[24] Realising what was at stake, the young emperor pledged his lands, friends, his very life to combat heresy. He had delayed too long, but was now determined to proceed against Luther as a notorious heretic, while granting him a safe conduct, provided he did not preach or make a tumult on the way. Those present were shocked at the realisation of what this would in time mean, the burning of a heretic ordered by the supreme secular authority. The shock extended to the town and overnight a placard appeared in various places with the powerful symbol of the *Bundschuh*, the peasant's sandal-clog, which contrasted with the high boots of the nobles and proclaimed a revolt against the privileged establishment. A chilling notice read: 'Unhappy the people whose king is a child!'[25]

Among the electors, there was a discussion about whether Luther might be recalled for questioning. The emperor refused but the diet got its way and named a commission to implement it. In public and private sessions, the argument turned once more on the question of interpretation of scripture and whether he could in conscience – in the normal sense – retain his position against all authority. But this was precisely what could not convince Luther, who had, as already indicated, his own idea of 'conscience'. As one of his interlocutors, the humanist Johannes Cochlaeus observed, 'Luther's inner certainty depended on identifying his cause with Christ's: if you did not share Luther's views, there was no higher authority to which you could appeal'.[26]

This last effort of a couple of days failed and the emperor gave Luther notice that he must leave on 26th April. The journey back to Wittenberg was more leisurely than might be expected in the circumstances, with the Edict of Worms putting him to the ban about to be issued. If apprehended he was to be executed without further trial, yet there was time to stop and visit his father's relatives at Möhra, where despite the emperor's prohibition he preached in the open air to the local peasants. At Friedberg on 28th April he took time to write a long letter to the emperor in an attempt to vindicate himself. As a 'humble little monk' he pleaded with Charles to allow the examination of his books by independent, erudite judges, lay or ecclesiastical.[27] At Eisenach, where he had been to school, he again preached at the request of the priest, who had taken the precaution of having a notarised letter of protest against his doing so already prepared!

On the Wartburg

At Eisenach he was apprised of the plan for an apparent kidnapping. As the by now small group entered a forest in the afternoon, four horsemen appeared and with a show of violence took him from the cart; his companion, Amsdorf, panicked even though he had known of the arrangement but not when it might happen. When out of sight around a corner the men put him on a horse to begin a journey by a circuitous route until the party arrived late at night at Wartburg Castle, high above Eisenach and hidden in the woods. The men who in appearance kidnapped him were trusted servants of the Elector Friedrich, to whom the castle belonged. All was in readiness for his arrival; he was given a set of knight's clothing and told he was now Junker (Knight) Georg, though it would be some time before his tonsure disappeared and a beard grew. From the Wartburg on 14th May he wrote to Spalatin giving the details of his journey, including his 'kidnapping' and expressed surprise and pleasure at having been welcomed on the way by the Abbot of Hirsfeld, who accommodated him in the abbatial quarters and prevailed upon him to preach the next day, even though Luther protested that he might be breaching the terms of his safe conduct by doing so.[28] His sojourn in this isolated place, with only the castellan, Captain von Berlepsch, and two serving boys in attendance, was to last from May to March of the following year, 1522, apart from a couple of days in December when, heavily disguised, he visited Wittenberg.

Living in such an eyrie was conducive to soul-searching. Because of Luther's disposition it brought on the mood swings which had affected him since his student days. It was a time of loneliness, feelings of being cut off from his friends, of spiritual trials and physical maladies. He wrote to Melanchthon: 'I can tell you in this idleness there are a thousand battles with Satan. It is much easier to fight against the incarnate devil – that is, against men – than against spiritual wickedness in the heavenly places. Often I fall and am lifted again by God's right hand'.[29] This is yet another example of Luther's world view:

> Christ and the devil were equally real to him; one was the perpetual intercessor for Christianity, the other a menace to mankind until the end ... There is no way to grasp Luther's milieu of experience and faith unless one has an acute sense of his view of Christian existence between God and the devil: without a recognition of Satan's power, belief in Christ is reduced to an idea about Christ.[30]

For Luther, God's omnipotence was real, but as such hidden. In the incarnation God divested himself of omnipotence thus laying himself open to the devil's fury. The Christian living in and with Christ must expect to feel the same attacks and Luther mentions, almost casually, the many attacks he experienced and even how he ignored the devil's poltergeist activities. In popular accounts, there is the story, probably apocryphal, of his throwing an inkwell at his adversary – though there is said to be an ink stain on the wall of his room in the tower. The combat with the devil did have some kind of physical aspect, as he felt overcome by lassitude and temptations of a bodily nature. In a letter to Spalatin he revealed his thoughts:

> I sit here like a fool, hardened in leisure, pray little, do not sigh for the church of God, yet burn in a big fire of my untamed body. In short I should be ardent in spirit, but I am ardent in the flesh, in lust, leisure, laziness and sleepiness.[31]

There is an allusion here to Rom 12:11, as he contrasts his way of life with St Paul's call to his hearers to work for the Lord, ardent in spirit. He seems also to be judging himself by the standards of religious life and the vows of poverty, chastity and obedience, which had regulated his life in detail in the Wittenberg priory. Without that regime, he realised that he had become undisciplined and subject to the ordinary temptations of the flesh, as well as finding it difficult to cope with the physical hardships of his confinement.

The conditions under which he lived in the Wartburg, isolated in an upper cold and damp chamber with little opportunity for exercise, were challenging to his health. The sedentary lifestyle and perhaps the tensions with which he had lived for months brought on constipation and was the subject of correspondence with Spalatin, who after some time was able to send him remedies. In later years he spoke much about this aspect of health and accepted the general theory about the importance of the body being relieved of fluids. The understanding of the body in terms of 'humours' resulted in misguided approaches to diet and often made medical intervention more harmful than healing, especially because of the frequent recourse to blood-letting. Given the fraught conditions in which Luther spent many years, it is remarkable how well his constitution coped. He did well to live to be 62. (Calvin, who endured much the same maladies and remedies and an equally prodigious literary output, died at 55.)

Isolated as he was, Luther had little contact and less influence on his supporters in Wittenberg, the students and colleagues who had accompanied him at the burning of the bull *Exsurge* the previous December. But his correspondence with Spalatin and others was extensive and showed that in his enforced leisure he reflected on his now-public life, on where he stood in his relationship with his father and family and his religious community. In a letter to a friend in Strasbourg about his work he said he had written expositions of Ps 67 and 36 and a commentary on the *Magnificat* among various other projects. It is worth noting that the two psalms and the *Magnificat* have a role in the church's daily prayer, which may indicate that even in isolation he reflected, perhaps wistfully, on the liturgy of the hours.

His status at this time in relation to life in a religious order was somewhat complicated. After the Augsburg debate in 1519, Staupitz, in a panic because the head of the order wanted him arrested by

Cajetan, released him from his vows. But Luther continued to live in community and according to its rule until sometime in 1520, when through pressure of work he freed himself from the daily round of prayer. As an excommunicate since early 1521, but still living in the Wittenberg Priory, he was in fact excluded from the church's liturgy, but this does not seem to have been implemented in the form of an interdict on his community. On the Wartburg he had opportunity to mull over these things.

He received a draft of a publication by Melanchthon, the young married layman who taught Greek at Wittenberg and who aspired to producing a systematic account of the new theology originating with Luther. Entitled *Loci communes,* it included a section on monastic vows. In response, Luther pointed out flaws in Melanchthon's argument that vows were impossible to keep. The real question was not whether vows could be kept but whether they were enjoined by God. He went on to consider the nature of monastic vows as suited to keeping boys in check rather than men. He concluded that his own vows, taken as a result of the storm, may have been sacrilegious, or at least that his vocation may have had nothing miraculous about it, so that he could ask: 'Am I myself already free and no longer a monk?'[32]

Apart from responding to Melanchthon's draft, a situation which developed in Wittenberg led him to consider the question of celibacy. In his address to the German nobility, he had already called for the freedom of priests to marry. As a result of the marriage of three diocesan priests, there was a lively debate about clerical celibacy and Karlstadt as a diocesan priest contributed a number of theses and a book in which he proposed that all priests should be married. In letters to Melanchthon regarding this situation, Luther expressed the opinion that priestly celibacy was of human, not divine, institution and was not binding upon Christians. On the basis of 1 Tim 4:3 he said that he would allow priests to exercise their freedom.[33] But he continued to distinguish between the case of diocesan priests and monks.

In October, twelve of the Wittenberg Augustinians left the friary and in November three more did so. Luther did not object to their action, but he was concerned that those who left should act with the certainty of a good conscience, which he greatly feared was not the case.[34] (When he returned there in the spring of 1522, the prior was the only friar who had remained.) Because of his concern for such men he decided to deal with the problem in a book, which he wrote in three weeks. This led him to inform Spalatin, in a letter dated 11th November 1521, of a forthcoming work on monastic vows. The preface to the work is a letter to his father, who had been very opposed to his entering religious life. In this preface Luther confesses that by taking vows he had sinned against God's commandment to honour his parents, but that now, sixteen years later, he realizes that his monastic vows were 'not worth a fig'.[35] In a further letter to Spalatin, accompanying the manuscript of the preface, Luther explained the more immediate circumstances which motivated him to write the book. The word had come to him that Karlstadt had proposed a debate on the celibacy of the clergy. Priestly celibacy could be dissolved by anyone, but now he wanted to reflect on the celibacy of monks and nuns about which he had no clear word of God.[36]

Early in his *De votis monasticis,* he approved of St Francis and the dedicated life such as Francis appeared to him to have proposed:

> St Francis, a most admirable man of fervent spirit, wisely said that his rule was the gospel of Jesus Christ. But the gospel holds chastity to be a matter of free choice.... He wanted those little brothers to have the choice of living as celibates or as non-celibates on the strength of their vow and rule, and of remaining in monasteries and under their own regulations as long as they wanted. Those who vowed the gospel vowed nothing other than this and could vow nothing else.

But he believed Francis was in the end deceived: 'he made the universal gospel intended for all the faithful into a special rule for the few. What Christ wanted to be universal and catholic, Francis made schismatic'.[37]

His arguments in *De votis monasticis* are as follows.

1. The vows are contrary to the word of God, having no scriptural support: '[Christ's teachings] clearly show that one is not at liberty to take monastic vows.... St Anthony, the very father of monks and the founder of the monastic life, most wisely and in a Christian manner believed and taught that absolutely nothing should be observed which did not have the authority of scripture. He knew absolutely nothing about monastic vows'. On the other hand, the saintly man Francis was deceived.

2. They are contrary to faith, since they are held to be sources of sanctification.

3. They are contrary to evangelical liberty: 'If celibacy is an evangelical counsel, what is the sense of your making a vow that goes beyond the gospel and makes a rigid commandment out of a counsel? For now you live not according to the gospel but beyond it'.[38]

These are arguments which critique religious life in principle and can be directed to both monastic life, strictly speaking, and to the life of his own Augustinian order, which, as noted earlier, combined a monastic rule with the form of life which emerged at the time of St Francis. When he makes reference to St Francis as 'deceived', he is echoing the common criticism of the mendicant orders of the day and their practice of begging. The monastic communities as such (Benedictines and Cistercians) did not abrogate the right to own property, though the individual monk possessed nothing. In the document he made mention also of St Bernard (as Calvin would in his day), quoting a genuine saying of his: 'I have lost my time, because I have wasted my life. But one thing gives me solace. A broken and contrite heart you will not despise'.[39] 'These were the words of a great Christian soul', Luther says, recognising, he believes, Bernard's acceptance of the principle of justification by faith rather than works.[40] When at other times (especially in his *Table Talk* of later years) he spoke of religious life he focused mainly on the begging practice of the mendicant orders.

In December he wrote to Cardinal Albrecht of Mainz, having heard that indulgences were still being promoted in his diocese, warning him that he, Luther, was not dead as he might suppose and that since indulgences had been shown to be rubbish and lies he should show himself to be a bishop and eliminate them. 'You know that the indulgence is sheer knavery, and that Christ alone ought to be preached to the people. Therefore I openly declare that unless the indulgence is done away with, I must publicly attack Your Grace, as well as the Pope.'[41] It is an indication that Luther was still held to be a threat to good order that the cardinal replied saying that 'the abuses' had been suppressed, though not saying that indulgences had been discontinued, as of course they had not.[42]

In a letter he wrote to a friend, he informed him of various writing projects, including a volume of sermons on the lessons from the epistles and gospels. His main project during these months was, however, the translation of the New Testament into German. This occupied all his energies when other writings were disposed of, as it was a translation not from the Latin Vulgate but from the original Greek. He was apparently helped – from a distance – by Melanchthon, the Greek scholar, and used the second edition of Erasmus' Greek text. It is considered a work of genius as it reshaped the German language itself, because his German became dominant, unifying what had been a wide range of dialects.[43] He had translated various biblical texts already in his writings but, according to Bornkamm, here he rose above his earlier performances and created a new and unified style for the entire New Testament. 'His earlier attempts had retained the colouring of earlier – especially Latin – linguistic usage, his work on the New Testament resulted in a language thoroughly German in all respects.'[44] The poetic richness of his translation resulted in a Bible to be heard and not simply read, a quality which was later to be put to superb use in Lutheran worship. This was because Luther had internalised the message of the scriptures; 'the story had permeated his own life'. As Bornkamm puts it: 'His achievement sprang not simply from poetic intuition; it was the human word being born from the word of God'.[45]

This way of expressing Luther's achievement fits very well with what Roper said about the meaning of *conscientia* in Luther, that is, about a presence of the word in him in the form of a 'with-knowing'. As indicated earlier, he seemed to have an Augustinian sense of internal illumination by Christ which gave him absolute certainty about the meaning and import of the text. That and the fact that he used high German which had been gaining ground – 'I speak the language of the Saxon chancery, which all the German princes are now using' – made his text especially authoritative and shaped the Lutheran religious culture for the future.[46]

It shaped its theology also; Luther's translation embodied his own perspective on what would become controverted issues, such as justification by faith. He expanded slightly the verse of Rom 1:17 which had been so central to his understanding of the righteousness of God. In the translation of another critical text, Rom 3:28, which modern translations simply render as: 'A person is justified by faith apart from works prescribed by the law', he famously added 'alone' to 'by faith'.[47] This insertion was challenged by Roman opponents, especially Hieronymus Emser,[48] and led to Luther's response in *An Open Letter on Translation* (*Sendbrief von Dolmetschen*) of 1530: '[I]f your Papist wishes to make a great fuss about the word "alone" (*sola*), say this to him: "Dr Martin Luther will have it so"'. He also claimed: 'The nature of the German tongue teaches us to say it in the same way ... Furthermore, I am not the only one, nor the first, to say that faith alone makes one righteous. There was Ambrose, Augustine and many others who said it before me'.[49] To his hermeneutical principle of 'scripture alone' Luther had added the *logion* 'faith alone'; 'grace alone' was implied by that. Because of his prioritising justification by faith as the key to understanding the New Testament, he ranked its books in a way differing from the traditional order which accords first place to the gospels. In his Preface to the New Testament he wrote:

John writes very little about the works of Christ, but very

much about his preaching, while the other Evangelists write much of his works and little of his preaching; therefore John's Gospel is the one, tender, true chief gospel, far, far to be preferred to the other three and placed high above them. So, too, the epistles of St Paul and St Peter far surpass the other three gospels, – Matthew, Mark and Luke.[50]

The gospel message was more clearly set out in these epistles:

In them you find not many works and miracles of Christ described, but you do find it depicted, in masterly fashion, how faith in Christ overcomes sin, death, and hell, and gives life, righteousness, and salvation. This is the real nature of the gospel, as you have heard.[51]

He feared that reliance on works would result from concentrating on the narratives of Christ's life, as there would be a temptation to imitate him and try to gain merit by doing so.[52] It was in this Preface that he made his notorious comment that the Epistle of James was 'an epistle of straw'.[53]

CHAPTER EIGHT

Developments in Wittenberg 1521-1522

Meanwhile, in Wittenberg a reshaping of church life was gaining pace without Luther's control or involvement. A pamphlet appeared, using a series of parallel drawings to contrast the pomp and grandeur of the pope with Christ's simplicity, thus initiating a pattern that was to become standard for Lutheran art of antithetical treatment of the Lutheran and the Catholic churches. The obvious changes of lifestyle were, as mentioned, the marriage of some priests and the abandoning of community by religious of both sexes. '[D]uring his absence in 1521 and 1522 one innovation followed another with disconcerting rapidity. Priests married, monks married, nuns married. Nuns and monks even married each other.'[1]

The liturgy was also being altered. The message directly relevant to the liturgy that his sympathisers had gathered from his various publications, especially the *Babylonian Captivity*, was that the mass was not a sacrifice, that the eucharist should be administered to the laity by both bread and cup and that there was no difference between the theological status of ordained clergy and that of the laity – all were priests – though he had maintained there was need for delegated ministers in the community. Changes reflecting these theses began to appear in the rite of mass while Luther was in the Wartburg. In his own situation, he would not offer mass while alone.[2] Having denied it was a sacrifice, he saw no point in its being repeated when there was no community present to receive the sacrament and he therefore decided to produce a document on 'private masses', *De abroganda missa privata* of November that year, addressed to his own community in Wittenberg. He probably had in mind the multiplication of individual masses for the dead in the elector's church which had been such a feature of life in Wittenberg but now, with the departure of many religious, including his own confrères, was becoming a thing of the past and unacceptable to the reforming party in the town. He concluded his tract with an appeal to Friedrich to ensure the practice was eliminated. It was a work which would influence the contents of the *Confession of Augsburg*, nine years later.[3]

In Wittenberg, the lead in altering the mass was taken by Karlstadt, his university colleague. Karlstadt's relationship with the absent Luther, with Friedrich and with the inchoate reform was somewhat complicated. From being Luther's academic senior he became his friend and colleague, but began to be overshadowed by Luther, as had been evident at the Leipzig debate in 1519. He was archdeacon of All Saints Church, the church attached to the elector's palace and also the church of the university, but his relationship with the elector had been under strain for some years because of financial issues. These figured anew when he promoted the marriage of clergy, who would now need added support. He was opposed, like Luther, to individual, or 'private' masses, which provided the income for the All Saints Foundation from which he was paid, and as a result he lobbied Friedrich for some other way of providing clerical income. Despite the elector's opposition, he began to introduce German into parts of the mass and to give both elements of the eucharist to the laity. He eliminated the climactic moment of the celebration, the elevation of host and chalice, a practice that had been of the greatest significance and focus of devotion since the early thirteenth century and so important that when Luther, after his return, began to reform the rite in 1523 he retained the elevation, though he did so also to distance himself from Karlstadt.

Luther's own confrère, Gabriel Zwilling, had only joined the community in 1517 (possibly from another community as he was then thirty). He used his charismatic preaching style to call for more reforms and urged his confrères not to celebrate mass in the community unless it was reformed. As a result, mass ceased to be celebrated in the cloister on October 23rd. All of this was popular with some but greatly offensive to more conservative townspeople and an outbreak of violence was inevitable. The elector was concerned for public safety as well as for what might be the best way forward with religious practice, so he set up a commission, but found that the parties involved, the university, the Augustinian community and the chapter of the Castle Church could not agree.

In that situation, Spalatin felt it was prudent not to have the documents coming from Luther in the Wartburg printed and that prompted a disaffected Luther to make a secret visit to Wittenberg to find out why. Dressed as a knight, he arrived on December 4th 1521, threatening Spalatin that if they were not published more radical ones would replace them. Spalatin relented but never had the letter Luther had sent to Cardinal Albrecht printed. The day before his arrival, there had been a disturbance in which students and some townsfolk invaded the parish church, took away the missals from the altars and drove out the priests. On the day of his arrival, the Franciscans in Wittenberg were intimidated.[4] Zwilling and Karlstadt wished to take drastic action against the devotional environment of the traditional church architecture and Zwilling had led the way in an iconoclastic riot, overturning altars and smashing images of the saints. Luther sensed the revolutionary, anarchic, environment and on his return to the Wartburg issued a letter to the people of Wittenberg, approving the idea of change but warning against violent means of achieving it:

> These innovations have been accompanied by attacks on the mass, pictures, and the sacrament, and other lawless proceedings, which destroy faith and love, thereby wounding the tender feelings of many pious people, which is surely the devil's work. Doubtless it would be a very good thing were such changes made, were it generally desired, and no one objected. But this will never be the case. We cannot all be so learned as Karlstadt, therefore we must give in to the weak, else those who are strong will run into all excesses, and the weak who cannot keep up with you will perish. God has been very gracious to you in Wittenberg, giving you the pure word, so you should have patience with those who

never heard it, or where is your love?[5]

This letter pays a left-handed compliment to Karlstadt, in effect an expression of disapproval, if not contempt. He did not correspond with him while on the Wartburg and this is the only time he is mentioned. It proved a sign of things to come.

Friedrich intervened on December 19th, ruling that there must be no changes in the mass until unanimity had been reached. Karlstadt defied the elector's order and continued his campaign. On Christmas day, 1521, in the elector's own Castle Church, filled with townspeople, he officiated without vestments and in a sermon told the congregation that in preparation for the sacrament they had no need to fast or be absolved. He recited the text in Latin but at the institution narrative, the consecration, changed to German and subsequently distributed the eucharist under both kinds. The town council accepted his lead and issued an ordinance that the mass was to be celebrated as Karlstadt had done and images should be removed from the churches. Prostitution, hitherto vaguely disapproved of, was now forbidden. They further stipulated that begging should cease and the poor be supported from a special fund, picking up on an idea proposed by Luther in his *Address to the Christian Nobility* in the context of his criticism of the mendicant orders. It applied also, however, to students, who customarily supported themselves by begging. The decree was to have unfortunate effects on the university in the years that followed as student numbers dwindled because of the ban.

The temperature of this social and religious upheaval was raised by the arrival in Wittenberg on December 27th from Zwickau of three men claiming to be prophets of the Lord, two weavers, Thomas Drechsel and Nicholas Storch, and a student, Marcus Stübner. As Mullett explains,

> Zwickau was an industrial textile centre close to the rich mining country of the Erzgebirge mountains and the town's sharp economic contrasts of proto-capitalist wealth and working class debt and poverty gave the religious radicalism

that was already flourishing there a militant social tinge.[6]

The reason for their choosing to come from Zwickau two hundred kilometres to the south was that there they were disciples of Thomas Müntzer (1489-1525), who had been recommended for the post of town preacher of Zwickau by Luther. Müntzer had become disenchanted by what he considered Luther's elitist and academic approach to religious reform, one too dependent on and restrained by political patronage, and Luther for his part had come to see Müntzer in a very different light. His judgment is summed up by Lohse:

> Luther saw Müntzer as personally incorporating enthusiasm's distortion of the gospel, its blurring of the Reformation's distinction between law and gospel, its proclamation of a new spiritualised legalism, its revolt against and rejection of the authority of government.[7]

Müntzer was driven out of Zwickau by the city authorities and his radicalism was to lead within a few years to his death in the Peasants' War of 1525. His disciples came to Wittenberg to challenge the slow progress, as they saw it, of the reform party there. Like the movement which was to become known as the Radical Reformation in Zwingli's Zürich at just the same time, the Zwickau prophets were opposed to infant baptism, which Luther (and Zwingli) supported despite emphasising the need for faith in the reception of a sacrament. Luther would return to the question of infant baptism in his *Concerning Rebaptism* of 1528, appealing to the fact that 'baptising has been thus from the beginning of Christianity ... and no one can prove with good reason that (infants) do not have faith'.[8]

While Karlstadt and Zwilling were finding encouragement from the arrival of the 'Zwickau Prophets', the more cautious Melanchthon was quite concerned and consulted Friedrich: 'I can scarcely tell you how deeply I am moved. But who shall judge them other than Martin. Since the gospel is at stake, arrangements should be made for them to meet him.'[9] Luther was kept informed but seems not to have taken these men too seriously. In January 1522, he wrote to Spalatin about his plan to leave the Wartburg: 'It is not because of the Zwickau prophets, nor will they influence me in the least. But I do not wish our people to put them in prison ... See that our prince does not soil his hands with the blood of the Zwickau prophets.'[10] His return to Wittenberg was now very much on his mind; while his original plan was to return after Easter with the translation of the New Testament complete, in fact he would arrive at the beginning of Lent. To come out of hiding while under the ban of the empire would put his life at risk as well as putting Friedrich in an awkward position, so he wrote to him in February, expressing the hope that Friedrich 'would take in good part' his rather strange way of describing his return – it would be as a relic in the form of a cross, 'fully equipped with nails, spears and scourges' which God was now granting him who was always trying to procure sacred relics from all lands. He exhorted Friedrich to accept it cheerfully, even to give thanks. At the end he did admit that he had let the pen run away with him![11] Friedrich, however, had an additional cross to bear. His cousin, Duke Georg of Saxony, whose territory included Leipzig where he had hosted the debate with Eck, raised the question of the Wittenberg reform programme at the spring diet held at Nuremberg. He was a theologically educated Catholic and persuaded the diet to send a complaint in January 1522 to Friedrich and to the Bishop of Meissen, whose diocese included Wittenberg, about the changes which were taking place there. This led the bishop to ask Friedrich's permission to conduct a visitation and caused Friedrich himself to instruct the university and the chapter of the Castle Church to restore the liturgy to its former state. He ruled that Karlstadt (who was under his direct jurisdiction) must cease from preaching.

When Luther was on his way back to Wittenberg in March 1522, he wrote from Borna to justify his move and acknowledge Friedrich's concern for him. This was a reply to a letter from the elector he received just before his departure. He knew too of Duke Georg's recent intervention.

'I write all this to let Your Grace see that I come to Wittenberg under higher protection than that of the elector, and I have not the slightest intention of asking Your Electoral Highness's help. For I consider I am more able to protect Your Grace than you are to protect me.' Friedrich's faith was weak, he said, so rather than seeking to deal with the situation, in which 'he had already done too much', he should simply do nothing and let God alone manage without human intervention. It was enough that he should abide by the safe-conduct he had given. '[S]eeing I decline to follow Your Grace, then you are innocent in God's sight if I am taken prisoner or killed.' Luther had no fear for himself; when he had appeared at Worms he knew that there were as many devils there to combat him as there were 'tiles on the rooftops'. Duke Georg was of less consequence than one devil. 'But I confess I have often wept and prayed for Herzog Georg that God would enlighten him'.[12]

As Luther intended to appear publicly in Wittenberg, he was showing considerable courage, but also putting Friedrich in a difficult position as a ruler who should be implementing the imperial ban. But he had the encouragement of an invitation to return sent in the name of the council and entire city of Wittenberg. With the departure of Karlstadt and Zwilling, the council evidently felt that Luther was the leader who would act in a conciliatory way while promoting the reform the council favoured. The difficulty for Friedrich was resolved to some extent by Luther writing a letter, with help in the drafting from Spalatin, to the effect that he was returning against the elector's will. This was sent to Friedrich's brother with the request that he make copies and circulate them at the diet, ensuring that one came into the possession of Duke Georg.

Luther's reform programme in Wittenberg

He returned on March 6th 1522 and there is an oft-told story of an incident on the way. Dressed as Junker Georg, he stopped for the night at the Black Bear Inn near Jena. While he sat at a table reading, two students arrived. He offered them a drink and entered into conversation. They were from St Gall in Switzerland and on their way to Wittenberg to study. He told them they would find fellow countrymen there, so they asked if he knew whether Dr Luther was there. He replied he was certain that he was not, but it should not be long before they would see him there. The innkeeper had guessed the knight was Luther, but could not persuade the students of this. They were then joined by two merchants and the whole group dined together. One of the merchants proudly displayed a book he had just bought, the *Commentary of Martin Luther on the Epistles and Gospels* and asked the knight if he knew of it, to which he replied that he would get a copy soon. In the morning, Luther was already departing when the merchants approached him, having been told that he was Luther, but he quickly rode away, leaving them and the innkeeper conscious of their obligation to report a sighting of a refugee from justice, but because of how they still felt the 'searing wound of his word' they kept their peace.[13]

Mullett[14] has an incisive comment on the story, which first appeared in 1540 in the memoirs of one of the former students. As told by him, it uses certain familiar conventions to boost its credibility, such as actors identified by what they wear. It has 'genre parallels' with the story of the two disciples on the road to Emmaus (Lk. 24) and with a rich range of European folk tales concerning popular or legendary rulers and involving 'the king in disguise'. Dating from 1540 when Luther's books continued to appear, though he himself was no longer a prominent public figure, it contributed to the creation of a legendary figure to whom much mystery was attached.

The significance of clothing entered the real situation, as the town council presented him with cloth for a new cowl, which was ready for his appearance in the pulpit a few days later, the first Sunday of Lent. In the town church rather than the cloister, he preached the first of eight sermons on successive days (afterwards known as the 'Invocavit Sermons' after the opening word of the Introit of that Sunday). It seems clear that this – including the monastic cowl – was part of a carefully devised plan to get control of the reform in the town;

his Lenten sermons made clear the contrast between his programme and the carnival period that preceded his arrival. The Lenten season, like the religious life symbolised by the cowl, was one of repentance and restraint. The purpose of the sermons was then to further the reform, but in accordance with principles he laid down, 'distinguishing between changes it was necessary to make immediately and changes which were optional but which should become permanent when people were ready'.[15] To accord with what he had already published, changes in the mass could not be postponed, so the words of the institution narrative should be spoken aloud and in German – a rule which Luther in fact did not implement when he issued the reformed rite of the mass, the *Formula Missae*, a year later. But a certain liberty as to how people took part should be allowed, for example in receiving the eucharist. While he had approved of the changes taking place in Wittenberg while he was at the Wartburg, he now moderated his position, implicitly correcting Karlstadt's imposition of rules. Overall, the theme of the series of sermons echoed *The Freedom of the Christian Man*. He named five traditional practices that should remain optional: clerical celibacy, monastic vows, a place for sacred statues and pictures, fasting and private confession. His wearing of the cowl – a traditional symbol of renunciation – expressed both the seriousness of his message and the fact that he was freely choosing to do so.

> If the pope or anyone tried to force me to wear only the cowl, I would defy that person and refuse. But now, of my own free will I choose to wear it as long as I want, and when I no longer feel like wearing it, I will lay it aside.[16]

The sermons were preached in the town church, but Luther was lodged in the Augustinian cloister, where the only other occupant was the prior (fifteen others had left in the months October and November the previous year). Community life had ceased but the elector allowed the two to live there and this large building became Luther's permanent home when it was given to him by the elector on his marriage to Katherina von Bora in 1525.

To refashion the reform according to his own ideas, he had to find ways of dealing with Karlstadt and Zwilling. The latter proved the more amenable. When he apologised and promised to accept the new regime Luther recommended him to the elector for appointment as pastor at Altenburg. The case of Karlstadt, now married and still a member of the university staff, was more complicated. He had been recognised by the staff of the university as the leader of the reform, but now with both Luther and the elector at odds with him he gradually withdrew from university and town life, while still dean of the theology faculty, and even bought a farm as a sign of a new gesture of solidarity with ordinary people. In 1523 he got the consent of the elector to be temporary pastor of Orlamunde, 160 kilometres from Wittenberg, while still officially in the university. By 1524 he wished, with the support of the parishioners, to become permanent but the elector refused his request, whereupon he resigned from the university and became effectively the pastor, with the programme of reform he had not been allowed to develop in Wittenberg. He therefore ceased to be a problem for Luther, but that situation would change.

In his approach to the situation in Wittenberg, Luther was adopting a clever strategy of taking the side of the 'Catholic party' – those not aligned with the reform – against the extreme reforms of Karlstadt and Zwilling, which had undermined civic order, while asserting his own leadership. This meant that he could be seen as aligning himself with the civil authorities, who for their part could be exonerated from any blame for introducing the reform. As Mullett observes:

> Until 1521 Luther had had to define his religious and doctrinal stance only with reference to the catholic system he was inexorably abandoning. Now he was setting a left-of-centre reform course, steering carefully between old tradition and radical innovation. In doing so, he was die-stamping the hallmarks of what historians have come to know as the 'magisterial' (rather than the 'radical') Reformation. Its essence consisted in partnership with the state – the 'magistrate' and hence 'magisterial'.[17]

His credentials, he claimed, came from his combat with the devil, as those whom the devil constantly attacks are those with the strongest faith. In contrast, Karlstadt he described as an 'angel of light', the standard way of describing the devil. To maintain his strategy for resuming his leadership, it was necessary to side-line, even demonise, his former colleague.

A different atmosphere obtained now that he was in charge. Before his arrival, the programme of reform had the support of large numbers of people as well a cohort of students prone to take violent action – sometimes led by Zwilling – while the town council could be said to connive at some of the drastic action such as the removal of images. Now the reformation in Wittenberg was no longer a popular movement even though it was in some other towns such as Zwickau and Nuremberg, while in Switzerland the Zurich town council in 1523 took a lead in implementing Zwingli's ideas. In those towns the overlordship was more remote whereas Friedrich's castle overlooked Wittenberg and he was its active sovereign. The town was small and the university, where diverse views obtained, could not risk alienating its founder. The students were now disadvantaged as the ordinance against begging was still in force and not likely to be revoked, as it meant that a poor fund was now operating in favour of needy citizens. Student numbers began to fall and an element of civic disorder was thereby removed. The move of Duke Georg, with imperial support, to empower the Catholic bishops to deal with priests who had married also meant that Friedrich had to be careful not to be seen to support any radical changes. Still, it had been almost a year since the Edict of Worms and Luther was unmolested. As on previous occasions, political factors led to postponement of plans to deal with him.

The election of Charles as emperor did not end the ambitions of Francis, King of France, while Pope Leo remained alarmed at the hold Charles had over the territories north and south of the Papal States, Milan in the north and Naples to the south. He was offended too that the resolution of the religious question was now in Charles' hands. Inevitably, war broke out between the French and imperial forces and this dynastic struggle would continue in one way or another until 1559. One consequence was that after the Diet of Worms Charles did not set foot again in Germany until 1530 and by then both Pope Leo and Elector Friedrich were dead. Leo died in December 1521 and was succeeded by Hadrian VI (r.1522-23), a Dutchman of humble birth who had been a teacher of Erasmus at Louvain and a tutor to the young Charles V. At the Diet of Nuremberg of 1522, which re-convened in 1523, legates of Hadrian called for the implementation of the Edict of Worms. But the reason for convening the diet was the invasion of Hungary by Suleiman the Turk and so the resolution of the religious question had to yield to the need for unity among the sympathisers and opponents of the reform movement. Hans von Plaunitz, a friend of Luther, represented Friedrich and argued in favour of the policy of promoting peace among the conflicting parties. As a result no concrete actions were decided upon to suppress the reformers; in fact the Lutheran sympathisers were emboldened by Hadrian's inability to institute real reform within the Catholic institution. He was unaccustomed to the ways of the curia and they did not take this unassertive outsider seriously. Luther does not seem to have considered him a worthy target for his invective, even though he had been a member of the committee responsible for the condemnation of Luther's writings issued by Louvain University.

Luther could now turn to considering the details of his own reform programme, with the tacit support of Friedrich who was also conscious of his preferences, the limits he would tolerate. Consequently, when Luther devised his rite for the eucharist, the *Formula Missae*, in 1523, it combined some radical theological changes with a traditional outward form, the use of Latin and of the traditional Latin chants. Feasts of the Lord in the liturgical year were to be retained, but feasts of the saints suppressed. His conservatism prevented him from making some changes at this stage which his theological principles would have called for. As he had said in the *Babylonian Captivity*, he considered that all liturgy was in essence a celebration of the word, the mass being in essence the recitation of Christ's last will and testament, contained in the narrative of institution, or consecration ('Take this all of you ... for the remission of sins').

> You see, therefore, that what we call the mass is a promise of the forgiveness of our sins made to us by God, and such a promise has been confirmed by the death of the Son of God ... From the above it will at once be seen what is the right and what is the wrong use of the mass ... If the mass is a promise, as has been said, then access to it is to be gained, not by works, or powers, or merits of one's own, but by faith alone.[18]

Consequently, it seemed there was no point in celebrating mass if there was no congregation present to hear this promise; it was of vital importance that the people should hear these words. In requiring the presence of a congregation, he did not consider the alternative, as he might have done in logic, of there being just one person present apart from the celebrant to hear the promise of forgiveness.

But there were other ideas underlying his approach. Though he placed great emphasis on the congregation's participation, his theology of church was not based on the Pauline concept of the body of Christ, which has both a spiritual and external manifestation – Paul talks of various ministries. Luther's theology was based on the individual act of faith bringing justification and membership of a community. His emphasis was not on visible community: 'a man consists of two natures, namely, body and soul, yet he is not reckoned a member of the church according to his body, but according to his soul, nay, according to his faith'.[19] A more extensive search through Luther's sermons would perhaps be needed, but it does seem from those examined that he passed over opportunities to speak of the Pauline teaching on the body of Christ. In a sermon on Rom 12:1-6, he stopped short of considering verses 4 to 6, a fundamental mystical body text, and treated instead the individual believer's life of sacrificial offering of oneself.[20] It will be seen later, however, that he did see the church as a visible body but one which could be hidden historically.

Luther's understanding of the mass was very different from the tradition which had considered it a sacrifice offered by the church from the earliest times. Presenting the mass as Christ's testimony placed the emphasis on downward movement, the grace of forgiveness and a sacramental rite rather than also a sacrifice or upward movement of offering. Paradoxically, then, while he required the presence of a congregation because of the focus on forgiveness, the corporate sense of the rite as an act of the church was not evident. Luther was of course heir to a tradition in which the corporate nature of worship had not been evident for centuries. This came about because of the concentration on presence – 'the real presence'.

The concentration on presence had led in previous centuries to special significance being attributed to the one who could bring it about, the priest. It was obvious that the minister and the rite – physical elements and formula – formed a unity, because he handled the elements and said the words. It was necessary then that he should be empowered to carry out this function and do so exactly. How could it be certain that he was empowered to carry out a rite such as the eucharist unless there was another rite to give him the power? This led to the development of the teaching found in Peter Lombard (d. 1160) that the conferring of this power, ordination, was also a sacrament. The priest thereby came to be seen as one having power and to show how specialised this power of the sacrament of order was it was distinguished from the 'power of jurisdiction', which in effect divorced sacramental ministry from pastoral responsibility. But that distinction did lead to the practice of priests being ordained not for a particular pastoral function or a particular congregation but 'absolutely', and to masses being celebrated without a congregation. The role of the congregation, if present, became a passive one, with each person free to engage in their own devotions. The mass was not seen as a corporate action, but a sacrifice offered by the priest.

In this connection, the insightful comments in modern times of a Swedish Lutheran bishop, Yngve Brilioth, in 1926, on the Reformation era are worth recording.[21] In *Eucharistic Faith and Practice: Evangelical and Catholic*, Brilioth noted 'four major strands of eucharistic meaning ... more or less constantly present throughout the history of eucharistic celebration: thanksgiving, communion or fellowship, commemoration or memorial, and sacrifice'.[22] He showed that any period in history in which a tendency arose to reduce eucharistic meaning to any one of these or to a logical ordering of them was by this very fact a period of decay. He noted that the medieval period emphasised commemoration and sacrifice to the relative neglect of thanksgiving and communion, while the reformers from Luther onward reacted by emphasising thanksgiving and communion and diminishing the commemorative and sacrificial aspects of the celebration. Luther was immersed in a tradition which went back to early medieval times, but not to the early church, and in his reaction to it was affected by the breakdown of the medieval synthesis which had not in his time been replaced by an alternative theology of the liturgy.

In sum, his theology of the mass as Christ's testimony combined with the tradition of the 'real presence' of Christ's body in the eucharist, led to a lack of emphasis on the reality of the mystical body as an active agent in the celebration, and this became an obstacle against his appreciation of the mass as a sacrifice, an offering made by a community.

Consequently, he suppressed the offertory prayers, which had the language of corporate offering, of sacrifice, along with the accompanying Latin antiphon, though he retained and even added to music in the mass. The Canon of the mass was reduced to the dialogue preceding it, followed by the words of the institution narrative, again to eliminate the language of sacrifice. Then the *Sanctus* was to be sung, followed by the Lord's Prayer. The greeting, *Pax Domini*, was to be considered an absolution from sin and said facing the people and then communion administered in both kinds while the *Agnus Dei* was being sung.

In adopting the stance which he had already done in the *Babylonian Captivity*, his thinking was in accord with his *De abroganda missa privata* and his decision not to offer mass while he was alone on the Wartburg. Before this development of his thought leading to the rejection of the sacrificial character of the mass, he had probably reacted against the pastoral arrangement obtaining in his early years in Wittenberg. There the celebration of 'private masses' was extraordinarily high in number. In 1519, there were about 24 priests on duty and most of the 1,138 sung masses and 7,856 recited masses in the elector's Castle Church were without a congregation.[23] The priests were in many cases poorly educated and in the small town of Wittenberg had only this limited role of saying mass and reciting the liturgical hours. Theologically, the masses were considered licit as they were actions of the church even when a congregation was not present and canon law required that a server represent the congregation. It made sense pastorally, however, that a congregation should be present and it is not without importance that the 'real presence' of Christ was of the utmost importance to Luther. Though Christ's sacrifice was a historical, unrepeatable event, his was not a voice echoing across the centuries but the incarnate word speaking now to the assembly of believers. But Luther's focus was on the word, rather than the mystical body of the risen Christ, head and members.

Luther's sense of the pastoral significance of worship, which in addition to his anti-sacrificial stance led him to repudiate private celebrations of mass, also prompted him to make the mass understood by the congregation and give it an active role, one greatly facilitated by music. He made a gesture towards the communal nature of the celebration by requiring the words to be chanted aloud rather than in a whisper as the rubrics indicated. But in 1523 they remained in Latin, as did the whole of the celebration, apart from the reading of the epistle and gospel. This meant, however, that much of the old Latin music could be retained. So the Introit, *Kyrie, Gloria, Gradual, Alleluia, Sanctus, Benedictus, Agnus Dei* continued to be sung by a small choir, a *schola*. In the introduction to the rite, he said that these chants were once sung by all the people but now there were no composers (*poetae*) in Germany capable of providing suitable chants in the vernacular for the people.[24]

While he said that there were now no composers to provide

hymns in the vernacular, he was himself capable of contributing to a solution. The books which appeared almost immediately demonstrate this clearly. The history of Protestant hymnals begins in fact with the *Achtliederbuch* of the Nuremberg printer Jobst Gutknecht in 1523-4, containing four hymns by Luther himself. In the same year, Wittenberg's own hymnal appeared with both German and Latin compositions for three to five voices by Johann Walther. Some of the songs of this *Wittenberger Geystliche Gesangk Buchleyn* are first attempts at the sort of German chorale so well-known from the works of later composers.[25] Lucas Lossius's hymnal, *Psalmodia, hoc est: cantica sacra veteris ecclesiae selecta*, went through four editions from 1553 to 1579 and as the name indicates contained liturgical chants from the old church for use in the new.[26]

The congregation in Wittenberg consisted of people of the town and peasants from the farms around it and their needs were not being satisfied by a Latin liturgy in words or music. They would not be likely to perceive that the fundamental change of removing reference to sacrifice had been made. By 1526, Luther accepted the need for further revision and produced the text of his *Deutsche Messe*, most of which was in German. In the introduction, he expressed the wish that his previous Latin mass should still be used, but that in the German mass simplicity should prevail in the chants and in the ritual. The traditional *Kyrie* is retained, but the *Sanctus* and *Agnus* are to be in German. There should be a German hymn between the epistle and the gospel, which is followed by the Creed (these three sung in German).

Taken with what he said about the freedom to retain vestments, candles etc., the somewhat mixed message given by Luther in these liturgical innovations had in the long run the effect of creating a Lutheran liturgy into which much of the former liturgical music fitted.

CHAPTER NINE

Erasmus and the debate on free will

In the preface to the *Deutsche Messe* of 1526, Luther insisted that what he was proposing should not be taken as compulsory, asking that all who used it should do so 'agreeably to Christian liberty at their good pleasure as, where, when and so long as circumstances favour and demand it'.[1] Nonetheless, he was endeavouring to introduce order into the life of the community in Wittenberg and in the villages and towns where the reform had taken hold and where, even before his 1526 initiative, the vernacular in worship was becoming widespread as an expression of the church becoming a people's church.

This was also an indication of course that a new conception of parish was emerging and this had implications for property rights, where hitherto bishops and lay rulers with rights to nominate to benefices had exercised control. In electoral Saxony, the elector was still the authority and while Friedrich was alive and holding off from embracing the reform on a personal level, tensions were inevitable. Luther found it necessary in his leadership capacity to attend not only to reforming the liturgy but to all the aspects of community life as well, such as vesting of parish property, appointments of clergy – mainly by way of advising Friedrich – and making provision for religious instruction in the schools. All this was against a background of social unrest among the peasants, which had pre-existed the religious reform but now became inextricably linked with it. Two areas of practical importance were to occupy him until near the end of the decade, ecclesiastical polity and social justice, while his personal life was also to undergo transformation through entering marriage. In addition, theological controversy had not gone away as he was soon to engage in debate with Karlstadt and the rift between them would eventually be permanent, while debate on another front would open up with Erasmus.

Luther and Karlstadt came face to face while Luther was visiting the parish of Jena, as part of a visitation of parishes authorised by the elector to assess their pastoral and administrative conditions in August 1524. Karlstadt had been present in disguise while Luther preached and afterwards wrote a note to him asking for a meeting. Luther replied that he had no objection and within hours Karlstadt and his party arrived at the Black Bear Inn – the inn of his 'Junker Georg' stay – where Luther and the elector's officials were lodged. An acrimonious debate took place between them, Karlstadt alleging that Luther was placing him in the same category as the group of violent social revolutionaries led by the apocalyptic preacher, Thomas Müntzer. Where he and Luther differed, he said, was only on the sacrament. Behind the confrontation between the two was the fact that Karlstadt was banned from publishing and the upshot of their long argument was that Luther gave him a guilder as a token of what Karlstadt understood to be a challenge to him to write against Luther, freeing him from the ban, while Luther apparently considered it simply a declaration of ruptured relations – a coin exchanged being no more than a symbol of an agreement of a contract or, for that matter, the state of a relationship.

The ensuing conflict between them was uneven as Luther had the support of the elector and this became more pronounced when on the death of Friedrich in 1525 he was succeeded by his brother Johann, who had declared himself to be in favour of Luther's reform. Johann, acting in collaboration with Friedrich, had already banished Karlstadt from Saxony in 1524, suspecting him, unfairly, of being in league with the bloodthirsty Thomas Müntzer. Thus began a period of marginalisation for Karlstadt, wandering among the towns in southern Germany until in 1525 his life was in danger because of the Peasants' War. In fear, he wrote to Luther begging for forgiveness and shelter and in what seems a very generous gesture was invited back to Wittenberg, where he and his wife and child arrived on June

27th, the evening of the celebrations marking Luther's wedding, two weeks after his betrothal to Katherina Von Bora. The Karlstadt family was housed secretly by Luther in the large building and during this time Karlstadt wrote a recantation of his views on the sacrament and it was published with an introduction by Luther.

He wished to stay in the area and was permitted by the Elector Johann to remain only if confined to remote villages near Wittenberg, where he would not be likely to meet and influence others. In 1529 he fled from Saxony and went to Zurich where he was received by Zwingli as one sharing the understanding of the sacrament. Through Zwingli's influence, he earned a position as vicar of Alstatt in Zurich, where he would serve as pastor until 1534. Then, three years after Zwingli's death, Karlstadt resumed academic duties for the first time since 1523. He began teaching at Basel as chair of Old Testament studies, while also serving as parish priest of St Peter's in Zurich. He would remain there until his death from the plague in December 24th 1541. Karlstadt had been unfortunate in adopting a peasant way of life and in recognising the hardships of the peasants at a time when the campaign for peasant rights was escalating into the Peasants' War.

Luther's joust with Karlstadt at Jena in August 1524 proved to be the curtain raiser for a more significant contest. Erasmus had remained mostly uninvolved during the years of Luther's struggles with church authorities, apart from his *Axiomata* of 1520, already referred to, and did not relish a debate. He had a preference, he said in the document he finally published for 'sporting in the wider plain of the Muses rather than engaging in hand-to-hand combat'.[2] He had never met Luther, he said in a letter to Albrecht of Mainz in November 1519 and had 'never had time to read his books beyond glancing over a few pages'.[3] However, when the Edict of Worms failed to put an end to Luther's movement and it had become embedded in parish structures in many places, with ministers appointed and liturgical rites in place, 'it became clear to Erasmus that Luther did not intend a gradual reform within the old faith but a fundamental recasting of traditional doctrines and practices'.[4] Duke Georg was of the same view and encouraged Erasmus to write a rebuttal. While trying to avoid a definitive stance on Luther's theology, at a personal level he had become more distant from Luther because of an innate conservatism and what all commentators agree was a fundamental loyalty to the Catholic teaching authority, despite the many criticisms of Catholic life he had published since 1503. It was an age, also, when intellectual debate was conducted in the form of open letters, which publishers seized upon and sometimes purloined for their own purposes. Erasmus was pulled into the conflict through having some of his letters unofficially published and through having to respond to various public challenges. He had a request from Henry VIII, still defending the old faith, and even from his friend of old, Pope Hadrian VI, to declare himself, after Hadrian's legates had called for the implementation of the Edict of Worms at the Diet of Nuremberg in 1523. His reluctance to engage can be shown by the fact that he moved to Basel in 1524 from Louvain where he had been under pressure from the Dominicans.

The document he issued in September of that year, *De Libero Arbitrio* (*On the Freedom of the Will, a Diatribe or Discourse*), has come to be seen as getting to the heart of the dispute between Luther's theology and what was considered the orthodox teaching up to then, even though free will had not been at the centre of the controversies with the inquisitor at Worms or with Eck at Leipzig (though it was the subject of the Eck–Karlstadt debate). It could be that Erasmus spoke from a platform of late medieval and practical moralistic piety derived from the spiritual doctrine of the *devotio moderna* in which he was educated and so considered the question of free will a tiresome academic one, instead of a matter of common sense. The tone of his famous *Enchiridion Militis Christiani,* on the subject of imitating Christ in simplicity, patience and purity of heart[5] would suggest that this might be his attitude. But Erasmus had noticed the emergence of Luther's career (as witnessed by the letter Luther sent to him through Spalatin) and merely by 'glancing over a few pages' was probably aware that in the Heidelberg Disputation held within his own Augustinian province in 1518 Luther had asserted in Thesis 13: 'Free will, after the fall, exists in name only, and as long as it does what it is able to do, it commits a mortal sin'.[6] In *The Freedom of the Christian Man* (1520) he had declared:

> If works are sought after as a means of righteousness ... and are done under the false impression that through them one is justified, they are made necessary, and freedom and faith are destroyed; and this addition to them makes them no longer good but truly damnable works. They are not free, and they blaspheme the face of God.[7]

From early in his career, therefore, Luther had questioned the existence of free will. In fact, at the Heidelberg Disputation, he had quoted St Augustine in *De Spiritu et Littera* to that effect: 'Free will without grace has the power to do nothing but sin'. From Augustine's *Contra Julianum* 2, he quoted: 'You call the will free, but in fact it is an enslaved will'. This lack of freedom of the will was a consequence Luther drew from his basic conviction about humanity's endemic state of sinfulness, the human inability to please God, to meet the demands of the covenant. The 'enslaved will' expresses this perfectly.

As was clear from the Heidelberg Disputation, Luther (as Calvin subsequently) followed the later Augustine by his acceptance of the theology of predestination understood as involving intellectual foreknowledge of the destiny of the human person to the exclusion of free will. Predestination might be expected to figure prominently in Erasmus' *Diatribe*, especially as he was aware that in 1522 Luther had written disparagingly of his views on the subject in a widely circulated letter which reached Erasmus, as Luther knew it would.

Erasmus argued from a standpoint of common sense, of historical witness and the fact that there were, he claimed, 'some secret places in the holy scriptures into which God has not wished us to penetrate more deeply'.[8] Nonetheless, he goes on to adduce scripture texts to support his position and continues on a theological level, introducing the concept of grace: 'The law of faith commands more arduous things than the law of works, yet because grace is plentifully added to it, not only does it make things easy which of themselves are impossible, but it makes them agreeable also. Faith, therefore, cures reason, which has been wounded by sin, and charity bears onward the weak will'.[9] This is his formula for the practice of true religion and will be the background for all he says about free will.

In the Library of Christian Classics edition, *De Libero Arbitrio* (where *arbitrium* means choosing, rather than just willing) consists of just sixty-five pages, whereas Luther's reply, *De Servo Arbitrio* has two hundred and thirty-three. It was not a debate in the sense of a repeated exchange of views, though Erasmus was in fact responding to what he knew about Luther's position. It was rather a setting out of two visions of human nature and salvation and whether, because of the nature of the human person, one can make any choice in relation to salvation. Erasmus was very much concerned with the *nature* of humanity – 'our disputation was about man, whom God made in his image and likeness'.[10] In accordance with tradition he ascribed to humanity some sort of freedom of choice even in relation to how a person is saved. Luther's very long riposte to Erasmus was concerned with the destiny of humanity and took the form of answering him point by point at such length that he never reached some of the later sections. The ultimate foundation for this stance of Erasmus (whether he knew it or not) was that, according to Aquinas, the will by the necessity of its nature is inclined toward universal goodness.[11] The inclination is a necessary one but according to Aquinas within that inclination humans are free to choose particular things.[12] On the other hand, the context in which Luther's response to Erasmus must be seen is Augustine's theology. (See Appendix 2.)

The approach of Erasmus was to marshal arguments from scripture which appear to support 'free choice' and in so doing he refines the idea of freedom by referring to the fall of man and the subsequent importance of grace in restoring freedom to choose or reject God's offer of forgiveness through Christ. From a consideration of Old Testament passages he concludes:

It is impossible to avoid the conclusion that there is a will in us that can turn one way or the other. If of necessity it is bent toward evil, why is sin imputed? If of necessity it is turned towards the good, why should God from being angry become propitious when there is no further grace due to us?[13]

He concludes his section on the New Testament passages by quoting Luther's statement that everything happens by necessity and adds: 'These many texts have induced learned and holy men not to take free choice entirely away'.[14]

Dealing with the scripture passages which appear to oppose free will, he acknowledges: 'For God to will and foreknow are the same thing', but he then introduces a distinction between God's primary causality and secondary causes to avoid absolute necessity and speaks of God's ordained will, which through secondary causality 'men often do resist'.[15] He discusses the text of Is 45:9, about the potter and the clay, making the point that the human clay is endowed with reason and when admonished can conform to the Lord's will.

Besides if a man is simply to God as clay in the hands of a potter, whatever shape the vase takes must be attributed to no one but the potter ... Yet here a vessel which has been guilty of nothing because it is not its own master is thrown into eternal fire.'[16]

Further on he says that his mind 'encounters many a stumbling block' when he hears that the will does nothing more than clay in the hand of a potter.[17] Towards the end he speaks of good works and adopts a similar view to the earlier Augustine:

Here we can placate those who cannot bear that man can achieve any good work which he does not owe to God, when we say that it is nevertheless true that the whole work is due to God without whom we can do nothing; that the contribution of free choice is extremely small and that this in itself is part of the divine gift, that we can turn our souls to those things pertaining to salvation, or work together (*synergein*) with grace'.[18]

Luther's reply, *De Servo Arbitrio,* a year later had been delayed by the upheaval caused by the Peasants' War and also by his marriage in the summer of that year, 1525. He had dealt already with the issue at the Heidelberg Disputation in 1518 and to have so famous a person as Erasmus return to it, as if it were not already closed, is likely to have stung him into his very long and condescending response. He said he was reluctant to reply because he felt Erasmus was much more eloquent and in any case both he and Melanchthon had dealt with the question already. He then abandons the respectful tone: the book 'is so cheap and paltry that I felt profoundly sorry for you'.[19] Erasmus did leave himself open to attack by showing a lack of enthusiasm for dealing with the issue, for appealing to the fact that 'there are some secret places in the holy scriptures into which God has not wished us to penetrate more deeply',[20] thus introducing a note of uncertainty into discussion of a vital issue. He also said that he had as yet no fixed conviction 'except that I think there to be a certain power of free choice'.[21] Catholic authors later criticised him for this and Paul IV banned his writings in 1559, while the Council of Trent made a clear statement about free will in Canon 5 of the First Decree on Justification in 1547:

> If any one saith, that, since Adam's sin, the free will of man is lost and extinguished; or, that it is a thing with only a name, yea a name without a reality, a figment, in fine, introduced into the church by Satan; let him be anathema.

Luther felt he gained from this approach of Erasmus and wrote to him:

> I owe you no small thanks, for you have made me far more sure of my own position by letting me see the case for free choice put forward with all the energy of so distinguished and powerful a mind, but with no other effect than to make things worse than before.[22]

At the end of his tract he will repeat this sentiment, but with the important addition that he makes clear what the core issue is in his Reformation theology – where the priority lies:

> Moreover, I praise and commend you highly for this also, that unlike all the rest you alone have attacked the real issue, the essence of the matter in dispute, and have not wearied me with irrelevancies about the papacy, purgatory, indulgences, and such like trifles (for trifles they are rather than basic issues), with which almost everyone hitherto has gone hunting for me without success. [23]

There is evidence that Erasmus considered the freedom of the will the core issue to be dealt with, as he sent a copy of his text to the Catholic Duke Georg, saying in an unusually candid comment that it was something to be dealt with because otherwise 'the deceitfulness of these raving maniacs ... if not restrained, will topple both the gospel and good scholarship'.[24] As Luther also felt that it was the core issue, the question arises as to how 'irrelevant' the other named issues were, in particular the authority of the papacy. The issues of Luther's motivation will be discussed at the end of this study.

Erasmus was then not as indifferent as the beginning of his tract may have made him appear. He had read Luther and was not convinced by him, he said, and proceeded to marshal his arguments from both the Old and the New Testaments and in the course of doing so gave a more exact definition of free choice: 'By free choice ... we mean a power of the human will by which a man can apply himself to the things which lead to eternal salvation, or turn away from them'.[25] This in fact accords with Augustine's early view, especially as Erasmus says later: 'it is not wrong to say that man does something and yet attributes the sum of all that he does to God as its author, from whom it has come about that he was able to ally his own effort with the grace of God'.[26] (See Appendix 2.) It is quite significant that Erasmus speaks of grace quite extensively, including reference to Augustine's theology of prevenient grace, showing his alignment with the earlier scholastic tradition of Aquinas and others. Surprisingly, Luther, who owed so much to Augustine, the great proponent of grace, speaks of grace only incidentally. He does speak frequently of the Spirit, however, implying that without the Spirit there can be no grace and charges Erasmus with what he considers the absence of reference to the Spirit and to Christ in Erasmus' discussion of the Christian life, in effect, his reliance on arguments from reason: 'these words of yours, devoid of Christ, devoid of the Spirit, are colder than ice so that they even tarnish the beauty of your eloquence'.[27]

This was a rather telling accusation, given the reputation of Erasmus as a writer who called for a simple and warm-hearted devotion to Christ. Erasmus, for his part, had identified a lack in Luther's spirituality: 'Luther attributes very little importance to scholarship'.[28] Perhaps a better way to characterise the debate between the two is to note that Erasmus was concerned with vindicating the practice of what he called 'true religion' (*pietas*)[29] and used his scholarly gifts to do so, while Luther endeavoured to answer him point by point, but failed to address the issue of what true religious practice amounted to in daily life. He would probably not have accepted what a modern scholar says of St Augustine: 'In pastoral practice Augustine treated men and women as having freedom of choice, whatever his deeper speculation might be'.[30] In the end the difference between the two in the debate was the straightforward one of affirming or denying free choice. Luther was committed to the latter because of what the Synod of Dort (1618-19) would later describe as Lutheran doctrine: the total depravity of human nature. 'Satan now reigns in us with full force', he told Erasmus.[31] The challenge of Erasmus had forced him to accept the logical conclusion of his stance on the enslaved will. As Oberman puts it, for Luther 'the condition of man does not depend on the breadth of his education but on his existential condition as a "mule" ridden either by God or the devil, but with no choice in the matter, no freedom of decision, no opportunity for self-determination'.[32] He had come to this conclusion because of what he took to be Augustine's understanding of human nature and of predestination.

Luther's marriage

As mentioned above, Luther's reply to Erasmus at the end of 1525 had been delayed by two other factors, the Peasants' War and his marriage. His tract against the peasants came in May, his betrothal in June and the wedding celebrations at the end of the month. There was also the demanding issue of the reform of the mass, which had not gone well and required him to address it once more by producing the new text in German, the *Deutsche Messe* at the end of the year, to appear early in 1526. It was clearly an eventful year. Against this background, the circumstances of his marriage take on an almost accidental character. The context was the reform programme in Wittenberg and in the wider Saxony, which had led to the forsaking of the cloister by religious of both sexes as well as the marriage of the secular clergy. The widespread perception – and to a significant extent the truth – was that many young women entered convents as part of a parental policy rather than from free choice. From 1523, groups of women religious began to look for ways of escaping this 'captivity', a project beset with many difficulties because of their own history of submission to authority making such a move psychologically difficult, possible parental opposition and the destitute state in which they might find themselves. On the reformers' side, a desire to help encountered the difficulty that in Duke Georg's territory the abduction of a nun was a capital offence. The Elector Friedrich might not be so severe, but his instinct at all times was to uphold the law.

The incident which was to change Luther's life may or may not have been sparked off by himself. A respected merchant of Torgau, Leonhard Koppe, who was a relative of Luther's friend, Amsdorf, smuggled a group of nuns out of the Nimbschen convent in Duke Georg's territory into Wittenberg. In the agreed account from various sources, Kopfe from time to time delivered barrels of herring to the convent. On Holy Saturday 1523 he bundled twelve nuns into his covered wagon, as if they were empty barrels – or, in some accounts, in empty barrels. Three returned to their own homes. 'The remaining nine arrived in Wittenberg. A student reported to his friend, "A wagon load of vestal virgins has just come to town, all more eager for marriage than for life. God grant them husbands lest worse befall".[33] Among them was Katherina von Bora, who had been placed in the convent at the age of five by her widowed father when he decided to remarry.[34] It is not clear whether Luther organised the flight from the cloister, but in an open letter to Koppe he did reveal that had known all about the plan and regarded it as a snub to his opponent, the Catholic Duke Georg. The women were from the upper nobility of his lands and their families were afraid to welcome them back for that reason.[35]

Luther was now responsible for the nine women – in practice for arranging respectable marriages for them as soon as possible. Six were settled quickly, but Luther was left with three about whom he joked in a letter to Spalatin that he had three wives but had now lost two to other husbands. (This was in a rather salacious letter encouraging Spalatin to marry, as he was hesitating because of his prominence in Friedrich's court.) The one remaining was Katherina von Bora, who two years later was still in domestic service in the house of Lucas Cranach, the painter and friend of Luther. This was unsuited to her social background and it was intended that she marry a young nobleman from Nuremberg then studying at Wittenberg, but when he went home to consult his parents they apparently disapproved, leaving her in an ambiguous position as one virtually betrothed and needing to have her honour upheld. Luther then arranged for her to marry a Dr Glatz but she would not accept him. This put her in a delicate position; she was proving a problem for Luther at a time when he was preoccupied by the Peasants' War. Looking for a solution, Katherina used Amsdorf as a liaison. 'Would he please tell Luther that she could not abide Glatz, but was not unreasonable.'[36] She even said she would accept Amsdorf himself or Luther, thinking that the latter outcome was out of the question.

Luther had more than once declared his intention to remain celibate; for example, when he heard while on the Wartburg that Karlstadt had attacked monastic celibacy, he was shocked and declared in a letter to Spalatin in August 1521: 'they will not foist (*obtrudent*) a wife on me'.[37] As already mentioned, when Melanchthon consulted him on monastic celibacy, he at first defended it but then began to study the question of monastic vows and produced the tract *De Votis Monasticis,* to justify the decision of his confrères to leave the cloister. But when he returned to Wittenberg in 1522 he donned the monastic habit provided by the council as a sign that he had not decided to go down that route. Still, as early as November 1521 he praised marriage in a letter he sent to Nicholas Gerbel from the Wartburg: 'I am daily gaining more insight into the godless lives of the unmarried of both sexes, so that nothing sounds worse to me than the words monk, nun, priest, for I regard a married life of deep poverty as paradise in comparison'.[38] At the time of the arrival of Katherina and the others, he was clearly in favour of freeing at least those religious who wished to do so to leave and be married, though himself hesitant about what he should do.

The decision to marry came when he went home to visit his parents and told them of Katherina's virtual proposal to him. At first it had seemed amusing, but as his father took the idea seriously he began to consider whether it was right for him, as a condemned heretic who might be burned at the stake in a year, to enter upon marriage. It would be counterintuitive to do so, however, as it would leave Katherina in a respected status as a widow, while he would be testifying both by his life and death to the evangelical faith. He acted quickly; the betrothal took place in mid-June and the public marriage ceremony on the 27th in front of the parish church, with his parents and many Wittenberg guests present. A banquet followed in the Augustinian cloister, which the elector gave them as a wedding present.

Like many marriages of the time, it was entered into as a practical arrangement rather than from romantic motives, but it proved a stable and happy marriage. Katherina, who thereafter referred to him as her 'Lord', proved a good manager of their domestic affairs and they had six children, three boys and three girls. One of the girls, Elizabeth (who was named after St Elizabeth of Hungary) died as an infant while Luther was at Coburg Castle and a second died as a teenager. From the Coburg he wrote a letter to Elizabeth's older sibling, three-year old Hans, about the delights of heaven. The Luthers were not well-off, even though the elector increased his salary on his marriage. For this reason, particularly, but also because Luther loved company and the house was very large, Katherina's aunt lived with them for many years, they looked after orphaned nieces and nephews, they took in passing visiting lecturers at the university and student lodgers. These latter were mainly responsible for compiling the collection of Luther's conversations at table, known as *Luther's Table Talk*. They had a garden – and subsequently a small farm – and grew much of their own food. Luther sang and played the lute and composed the well known Christmas hymn 'From Heaven Above to Earth I Come' for the children. He also wrote the pioneering *Small Catechism* for them and the children of the local school.

The Peasants' War

Luther was not unaffected by the social unrest and outbreak of violence of the time. His pastoral programme, carried out in collaboration with the elector's officials, was one which aligned itself clearly with secular authority and began as a reaction to the upheavals, even violence, which had taken place in Wittenberg in his absence. Nonetheless, since in his theology he advocated *The Freedom of the Christian Man*, this policy could not sit comfortably with the manifest lack of freedom endured by the peasants as evolving economic conditions brought them more and more hardship. Nor could the principle he stated in the same document – that the Christian, like Christ, must make himself servant of all – vindicate unjust social conditions.

He came to be associated with the peasants' movement indirectly in that attempts to impose the Edict of Worms led in some places to the arrest of Lutheran pastors and attempts on the part of peasants to release them. The sympathy between the two groups led to the peasants looking to Luther himself as an upholder of their cause and on one occasion to their suggestion that he might act as a mediator between them and the princes. He did react to the growing crisis by responding to the manifesto of the peasants, the *Twelve Articles of the Swabian Peasants*[39] drafted in a few days at the end of February 1525 by a journeyman furrier and lay preacher, Sebastian Lotzer, in Memmingen, from more than three hundred articles.

The title notwithstanding, the articles arose from the grievances not only of the peasant farmers but also workers in the towns and mines who were all affected by increasing overpopulation, encroachment of the nobles on hitherto common land and in general their authoritarian approach to all economic activity. The articles were presented as 'relating to those matters in which they feel themselves aggrieved'[40] and countered the claim that the peasants were using the gospel as an excuse for rebellion. On the contrary they believed in the gospel and lived according to it. The first article is then an appeal to be allowed to live by the gospel through having the right to appoint their own pastors, while the second follows up with an appeal that tithes, which were in accordance with both Old and New Testaments, should be used for the support of the pastors and of the poor. The third article appeals to the freedom Christ has brought as a reason for their request to 'elected and regular authorities', to whom obedience is owed, to grant them freedom from serfdom, 'unless it should be shown us from the gospel that we are serfs'. The fourth to the eleventh articles are concerned with detailed grievances in respect to hunting and fishing rights, wood cutting, commonage, rents, new restrictive laws and death duties, while the final article declares a willingness to renounce any claims not in accordance with the word of God.

The last article shows that peasant demands for justice which had in the past been argued on the basis of ancient customs and laws are now becoming matters concerning divine justice.[41] This will become the background to Luther's response as he points out that 'this matter, then, is great and perilous, concerning, as it does, both the kingdom of God and the kingdom of the world' and he will make much of the distinction. His other principle will be the rejection of violence and will echo the injunctions of the pamphlet he had issued from the Wartburg when he returned there after his visit to Wittenberg in December 1521, where he had become aware of the disturbances which preceded his visit. This was *A Sincere Admonition to All Citizens to Guard Against Insurrection and Rebellion.* There he had made his basic stand quite clear: 'There is no reason for insurrection and generally it does more harm to the innocent than to the guilty'.[42] His reply to the *Articles* was entitled *An Admonition to Peace.* Quite early in the text he lays the blame for the unrest on the authorities:

> We have no one on earth to thank for this mischievous rebellion, except you princes and lords; and especially you blind bishops and mad priests and monks, whose hearts are hardened, even to the present day ... in your temporal government; you do nothing but flay and rob your subjects, in order that you may lead a life of splendour and pride, until the poor common people can bear it no longer.[43]

However, he warns that the peasants must pursue their cause justly and with a good conscience and proceeds to differentiate in his treatment of the two parties. While the abuse of rights by the nobles is a straightforward concept, he feels it necessary to uphold the importance of law, both divine and human, spelling out the consequences of failing to do so. So the content and tone become critical of the peasants and their 'alleged' Christianity. He takes his stance from scripture quotations:

> 'He who takes the sword shall perish by the sword.' That means nothing else than that no one, by his own violence, shall arrogate authority to himself; but as Paul says, 'Let every soul be subject to the higher powers with fear and reverence.'

They will be subject to Paul's judgment in Rom 13: 'He that withstands the ordinance of God shall receive condemnation'. 'In this case you should rid yourselves of the name of Christians and cease to boast of Christian law. For no matter how right you are, it is not for a Christian to appeal to law, or to fight, but rather to suffer wrong and endure evil; and there is no other way.' He also quotes Mt 6 concerning turning the other cheek. It becomes clear that he has Thomas Müntzer in mind when he says he fears that 'prophets of murder' had come among them leading them to violence.

Turning to the individual articles he judges that the peasants' claim on the tithes is 'nothing but theft and highway robbery' and the demand to be free from serfdom 'would make all men equal, and turn the spiritual kingdom of Christ into a worldly, external kingdom'. His argument seems to be that in Christ all are free but in this world inequality must exist, otherwise the earthly kingdom could not function. In support of the status quo, he is determined to maintain the distinction between the two kingdoms which was at the heart of his document on the freedom of the Christian and allows him in the end to distance himself from the peasants' demand for justice in the sphere of human rights. In relation to the more material issues such as hunting, fishing, collecting wood and the amount of tithes and the *Todfall* or death duty, he exempts himself saying that these are matters for lawyers.

Of the two principles on which his intervention is based – violence against legitimate authority cannot be justified and the principle of the two kingdoms – the latter makes him deny that the peasants are acting in accordance with the requirements of the spiritual kingdom, the kingdom of Christ. Because they would defend themselves and suffer neither violence nor wrong, they should rid themselves of the name of Christian and not make it a cloak for 'impatient, disorderly, unchristian undertaking'. While the distinction he makes between the two kingdoms, or two governments as some commentators call it, is not a facile one. It has its foundation in what he said about the two aspects of the Christian's life – being supremely free and yet the servant of all – and it could do little for the peasants in their plight. As Ozment, who supports the legitimacy of the principle, remarks: 'While the distinction between human and Christian rights was simple and clear to Luther, the consequences of his argument proved very painful for the peasants'.[44] He was showing partiality in his approach as he did not use that distinction in addressing the nobles. There was nothing about them being called to be long-suffering.

In a separate intervention, it appears that he advised the two parties to choose some counts and lords from the nobility and some councilmen from the cities to arbitrate and settle the dispute amicably.[45] There was one success in that a treaty was signed on April 17th between the commander of the Swabian League forces and the peasants of the Lake Constance and Allgäu area for pragmatic reasons, both sides being uncertain of victory in battle.[46] The course of events made this strategy redundant very quickly, as violence flared in Swabia, Franconia and Thuringia. Thomas Müntzer took over the government of a Saxon village and organised a peasant force to face the troops of Duke Georg and Landgrave Philip. In the ensuing conflict, six hundred of the peasants were taken prisoner and five thousand killed, while Müntzer escaped only to be caught, tried and executed with fifty others,[47] who were tortured and beheaded, as Bainton graphically puts it.[48]

It was this emergence of Müntzer as a leader of the revolt within the Elector Friedrich's own territory, when he was on his death bed, that caused Luther to issue a call to the nobles to put down the insurrection. *Against the Robbing and Murderous Hordes of the Peasants* came out on the day that Friedrich died, May 5th.[49] Early in the text he refers to Müntzer without naming him: 'It is the devil's work that they are at, and in particular it is the work of the archdevil who rules at Mühlhausen, and does nothing else than stir up robbery, murder and bloodshed'. It was issued as a supplement to the original *Admonition*, as defenders of Luther point out and so as a consequence of the peasants not heeding his warning against violence in that document. It does emphasise that this has been the case:

> Since the peasants, then, have brought both God and man down upon them and are already so many times guilty of death in body and soul, since they submit to no court and wait for no verdict, but only rage on, I must instruct the

worldly governors how they are to act in the matter with a clear conscience.

He then considers the duties and the dangers the rulers will face and concludes:

> Therefore, dear lords, here is a place where you can release, rescue, help.... Stab, smite, slay, whoever can. If you die in doing it, well for you! A more blessed death can never be yours, for you die obeying the divine word and commandment in Rom 13, and in loving service of your neighbour.

Unfortunately, his document appeared just as the peasants were being slaughtered in large numbers and he tried to counteract the effect by issuing another document in which he spoke of mercy to captives, but the effect of the first was that the peasants reproached him as a traitor to their cause, while the Catholic princes, knowing that Lutheran ministers had sided in large numbers with the peasants, considered him responsible for the whole conflagration.

CHAPTER TEN

The Diet of Speyer 1526-1529

If the year 1525 saw Luther somewhat unhappily caught up in politics through his attitude towards the parties involved in the Peasants' War, 1526 brought the unwelcome attention of imperial politics to his reform with the calling of the Diet of Speyer. The successive diets of 1521 and 1522-3 had shown that the fortunes of Luther's movement would be affected as much by secular events as by peaceful preaching and conversions. The calling of this diet showed how much his reform could not be separated from politics; Charles had turned his attention to German affairs when he had defeated Francis I and concluded the Treaty of Madrid in January 1526. This brought a temporary end to a conflict in which Pope Clement VII (r.1523-1534), pope since the death of Hadrian in 1523, was involved. A member of the Medici family and cousin of Leo X, he had joined with Francis and Venice against the emperor in an attempt to protect the Medici hold on Florence and to continue the policy, which had obtained from the time of the imperial election of 1519, of trying to restrict the power of the Hapsburg dynasty represented by Charles. Charles wished to consolidate his position as ruler by endeavouring to bring about German unity but he was aware of the threat posed by the increasing number of estates favouring the reform.

A notable development was the conversion to the reform movement of Philip of Hesse, son-in-law of the Catholic Duke Georg and a man who had been proactive in suppressing the peasants' rebellion. To display his robust new religious convictions, he came to the diet with supporting troops and Lutheran preachers. These latter were refused permission to preach by Archduke Ferdinand, who presided in the absence of his brother Charles, who was now embroiled with the pope in the new conflict. But they took to the balconies of the inns instead and preached to crowds amounting to four thousand. On the cloaks and in the lodgings of the Saxons and Hessians the slogan *Verbum Dei manet in aeternum*.[1] In a rather carnival atmosphere Philip made evident his faith by serving an ox on a Friday. A representative from Strassburg wished he had chosen a more significant testimony than staging a barbecue on a fast day.[2]

The ineffectiveness of the Edict of Worms, Jedin comments[3], became evident to everyone. Philip and a number of secular and ecclesiastical princes formed a committee which recommended liturgical arrangements of a *via media* kind and allowing the marriage of priests. But these were rejected by Ferdinand and the decree concluding the diet in August was that no innovations were to be undertaken in matters of faith or religion. But a council was called for, universal or at least in Germany, to deal with the religious question. The emperor was just then in correspondence with the pope, who had joined a new league against him, claiming in a letter that he was motivated 'by solicitude for peace in Christendom, the freedom of Italy and the security of the Holy See, while Charles V was disturbing the peace'.[4] This led to Charles calling for a general council, something to which Clement could never agree because of fears of a revival of conciliarism, the strengthening of the emperor's central authority and the threat it might bring to his own position as an illegitimate Medici offspring; this might cause a reform council to question his legitimacy as pope. As throughout the decade so far, political considerations had put dealings with Luther's movement and the reform of the church on hold.

This state of affairs dragged on for more than three years, the only progress being that the emperor and the pope settled their differences (after the sack of Rome in 1527 by wages-starved Spanish mercenaries) and Charles was crowned Holy Roman Emperor at Bologna by Clement on February 24th 1530, his birthday (though he had been crowned already by Cardinal Albrecht at Aachen). He and Clement were at that time 'neighbours' there. This seemed to presage a return to a pre-Reformation era, but it was not to be; Clement vacillated in his loyalty to the emperor, in England Henry VIII forced through the Act of Supremacy in 1534 and Clement died in 1534, having taken no decisive step towards the renewal of the church.

In 1529, Charles, while still in Italy, had called yet another diet for Speyer, famous since then for giving rise to the term 'Protestant'. This was a diet which marked a parting of the ways in fact as well as in name. Aid in the combat against the Turks was prominent on the agenda but the religious question was not neglected. Both parties were divided amongst themselves. As so often, there was misinformation in circulation beforehand and in the reformers' camp this was that the Catholics were planning an attack. This led Philip to negotiate an alliance with France and Bohemia, the traditional enemies of the house of Hapsburg, to the horror of the Saxon princes, who had no desire to dismember the empire. On the Catholic side, 'the emperor was for the gloved hand, his brother Ferdinand for the mailed fist', as Bainton puts it.[5] In the absence of the emperor, Ferdinand's view was dominant. Accounts of the motive for the emergence of a 'protesting' lobby vary somewhat. The Protestant view tends to be that in the recess document; Lutheran areas were to respect the rights of Catholics, while in the Catholic areas the same tolerance was not extended to the others. (In neither area were the Zwinglians and the Anabaptists to be tolerated because of their refusal to concede anything more than a commemorative status to the eucharist.) Some of the difficulty arose from the fact that the Edict of Worms was to be applied in the Catholic areas, as had been decided at previous diets, and this of course simply called for the repression of 'heresy'.

Now the diet was calling for the tolerance of the Catholic rites in the Protestant areas: mass was to be allowed 'everywhere'. The Lutheran Bainton conceded that neither side was really tolerant,[5] while the Catholic Jedin (or his Catholic co-editors, Iserloh and Glazik) reproduced a text from the imperial archives (*Reichstagakten*):

We, electors, princes, prelates, counts and estates have

unanimously agreed and loyally promised one another that no one of a spiritual or secular estate is to offer violence to another or compel or attack him because of faith or deprive him of rents, taxes, tithes, or goods.[6]

Jedin adds that no notice was taken officially of the protest of the evangelical states. It would be good to know how divisive the attitudes actually were, given that such a polarised heritage arose from that event. Religious attitudes were certainly overlaid with political ambitions; there were mixed motives for the moves which followed on the Protestant side. On the day of the recess, Philip of Hesse set up a defensive alliance against attacks between Saxony, Hesse, Nuremberg, Strassburg and Ulm. How real the danger was from the Catholic princes (especially Ferdinand of the 'mailed fist') is not clear, but Philip had already shown a lack of regard for the integrity of the empire and was willing to include the Swiss despite their theological stance and their anti-imperial politics. He also brought forward a plan he apparently had for some years to bring the two sides together for a theological colloquy.[7]

Zwingli and the Colloquy of Marburg

Philip's plans were of course made known to Luther by Spalatin, who after Friedrich's death in 1525 was no longer the elector's secretary but remained close to Elector Johann and accompanied him to the diets. Luther was steadfast in his opposition to Zwingli's theology and so did not see the theological consensus now sought by Philip as possible, nor therefore as a basis for a political confederation. In July 1529 Philip sent out invitations to the Wittenberg party and to the Swiss and to their allies. Luther was not inclined to accept, but was under pressure from Elector Johann, Philip's father-in-law to do so. Melanchthon worried about what the consequences of a confederation might be for his own aspirations to reach some accord with the Catholics. The invitation was to Luther, Melanchthon, Zwingli (Zurich), Oecolampadious (Basel), Andreas Osiander and Jakob Sturm

(Strassburg) to convene at his castle overlooking Marburg. Sturm was asked to bring Bucer and in the end there were ten present. The task was to try to establish a common confession of faith concerning the eucharist.

As the parties were for long loudly entrenched in their positions, the colloquy was destined for the most part to fail and so the details of the discussions are less informative or interesting than the circumstances and the environment in which it took place. To gather at the Marburg castle in Hesse involved a long journey for all the participants. For Luther, under the ban of the empire, it was not too hazardous as Saxony and Hesse adjoined each other – though his party was held up at the border as they waited to be assured of a safe pass. However, on the two-week trek he passed through much familiar territory, was greeted in Altenburg by Spalatin and given an escort through Eisenach by the captain of the Wartburg. For the Swiss, there was both a land journey and a thirteen hour passage along the Rhine to Strassburg, before setting off once more for Marburg. They arrived on September 29th, a day before Luther's party. While the official party of disputants amounted to ten (a sheet with ten signatures survives) the entire gathering comprised about sixty people, including various dignitaries, and it has been remarked that for such a high-profile gathering to include Luther eight years after the Edict of Worms was quite significant.

To avoid possibility of rancorous discussion, unsuccessfully as it happened, there were preliminary discussions between Luther, Oecolampadius, Melanchthon and Zwingli. Luther had never met Zwingli, the leader of the Swiss reform, and had made no secret of his disagreement with him. For him, Zwingli was in the same camp as Karlstadt theologically and as people like the Zwickau prophets politically, that of social revolutionaries. This was in part because Zwingli was a republican not averse to military action, while Luther could be said to be a monarchist in the sense that he instinctively sided with the Saxon rulers in the interest of law and order. Zwingli, an almost exact contemporary of Luther (just three months younger), was an early admirer of Luther, whom he described as Hercules, and when they met at Marburg was said to have tears of joy in his eyes. In advance, the two sides had prepared a set of articles and at six in the morning of October 1ˢᵗ began discussions in a room next to Philip's bedroom and in the presence of fifty to sixty people. Always prone to dramatic gestures, Luther's opening gambit has become part of history: he moved aside a velvet cover, drew a circle with chalk on the table and inscribed within it the words 'This is my body' as given in the Latin text of the mass, then replaced the cloth. It was to be some sort of hidden witness and judge of the proceedings. At one point, Zwingli demanded proof of Luther's position and he removed the cloth and pointed to the words.

The arguments of the two sides can be summed up. Luther, basing himself on the words of scripture and his understanding of the person of Christ as having a divine and a human nature intimately united, stated that Christ could maintain a ubiquitous presence, not only in heaven but also in bodily form wherever the eucharist was celebrated. Somewhat surprisingly, the Lutheran party drew on earlier medieval theology, echoing Aquinas (possibly unconsciously), to deal with the question of how Christ's body could be present in the bread. Christ was present substantially, essentially, though not quantitatively, qualitatively, or locally.[8] Zwingli, for whom the important principle was that 'the flesh profits nothing' (Jn 6:63) did not focus on the words of the institution narrative in the gospels; for him Christ's flesh profited enormously, but as put to death, not as eaten. Christ's flesh was now with the Father in heaven. While he believed in the unity of Christ, divine and human, he held that after the resurrection only the divinity of Christ was everywhere. For him, the eucharist was a commemorative meal recalling the Last Supper. In his liturgical arrangements in Zürich this was illustrated by having the participants sit at a long table and pass the elements to one another.

Underlying the dispute, the difference between the two personalities, of Luther and of Zwingli, was important. Both stressed the sufficiency of scripture but Zwingli's humanist training rendered his approach to scripture an objective, somewhat rationalist one, without the subjective religious experience that was so important in Luther's case. Various reasons can be given for Zwingli's iconoclastic attitude to all of liturgical ceremonial and even to music, though he played several musical instruments. The most fundamental one is perhaps indicated by his preference for Jn 6:63. This text he saw as support for direct unmediated conferring of grace by the Holy Spirit and for his disparagement of all mediation by external rites. His was a dualistic approach that involved a distrust of material things where the relationship with God was concerned. Images in churches were idols, organs a distraction, singing made it more difficult to attend to the word of God itself. '[B]y the "flesh" he means the "fleshiness" of the actual physical body, so narrowing the sense in which St Paul uses the word.... The body-soul dualism in Zwingli's thought is not simply a moral but an ontological antithesis'.[9] Yet he was an active, even dominant, citizen of Zürich, with a place on the town council because of his position as *Leutpriester*; he married – secretly – his concubine in 1522 and was a signatory to a letter to the Bishop of Constance seeking a dispensation from celibacy, which was refused.

Luther, on the other hand, retained statues and images in church, loved music and wrote enthusiastic introductions to hymnbooks. He enjoyed the good things of life and, though schooled in the rigorous asceticism of the Observant Augustinians, emerged nonetheless a proponent of family life, which he was now enjoying himself. His references to bodily functions, especially in connection with his own maladies, were frequent and at the colloquy some examples underlined the difference between him and Zwingli. There are seven records of the three-day event, including the *Relatio Rodolphi Collini*, by a Zürich theologian who accompanied Zwingli. He recorded a crude example: Luther, in referring to the Lord's instruction to take and eat, insisted that the Lord was to be obeyed even if he commanded something gross. *Si juberet fimum comedere, facerem, satis sciens hoc esse mihi salutiferum.*[10] The meeting was conducted mostly in Latin and it is not clear whether Luther reverted to German when speaking about his willingness to eat excrement. On another occasion he used the example of eating rotten apples.

The colloquy came to an end not only because of theological stalemate but also because a plague which originated in England was moving quickly through northern Europe, making travel hazardous. At the urging of Philip, Luther assembled fifteen articles which the ten principals were asked to sign. These were based on a previous Lutheran set of articles, the *Articles of Schwabach*, which had been a formulated by the Wittenberg theologians after Speyer and covered the principle articles of the Christian Creed[11] – it had been a fear on Luther's part that the Swiss lacked conviction on fundamental doctrines. All agreed, however, to fourteen, those of an anti-Catholic nature concerning the mass, but the final, also on the eucharist, remaining a sticking point. These became known then as the Articles of Marburg and concluded with a declaration that despite failure to agree each side should show charity to the other in so far as conscience could permit. The political agenda continued, however, and by November Philip had made an alliance with Zürich, Basel and Strassburg. The religious division actually hardened in the months after Marburg – the Lutherans agreed on the Schwabach Articles while the Swiss grouped around the Tetrapolitan Confession. Thus formed the two major streams (Lutheran and Reformed), which divided European Protestantism and remain recognisable all over the world.

Back in Wittenberg and to his lecturing duties, Luther in a letter to Elector Johann in November 1529 commented:

> We cannot in conscience approve such a league inasmuch as bloodshed or other disaster may be the outcome, and we may find ourselves so involved that we cannot withdraw even though we would. Better ten times dead (*wir lieber möchten zehenmal tot sein*) than that our consciences should be burdened with the insufferable weight of such disaster and that our gospel should be the cause of bloodshed, when we should be a sheep for the slaughter and not avenge or defend ourselves.[12]

CHAPTER ELEVEN

The Diet of Augsburg 1530

The political situation took on a new complexion when the emperor, having made peace with France and Pope Clement, turned his attention to Germany with new determination and ordered that a diet should convene at Augsburg in April 1530. He had been crowned by Clement in Bologna in February, but even before that he had sent out the proclamation, hoping that this recognition of his dignity and his plan to preside, would make this a more successful diet in relation to the unity of the empire by a solution to the religious question. From a position of strength, he could then muster forces against the Turks. This would be the first diet he attended since as a twenty-one year-old he encountered Luther at the Diet of Worms in 1521. Now thirty years old, hardened by wars and conscious of his guardianship of the faith after his coronation, he was determined to deal with what he saw as religious rebellion. He had already demanded of Pope Clement the calling of a general council of the church to deal with the underlying causes of religious dissent.

The Elector Johann had his residence at Torgau (though he would be buried in Wittenberg like his brother Friedrich) and from there he sent orders to the Wittenberg theologians to prepare for the diet. Luther, Melanchthon and Justus Jonas were to join the elector's party at Torgau, be joined by Spalatin in Thuringia, before going on to Coburg. From there the elector's party would travel the final one hundred and fifty miles to Augsburg. Coburg was the last town before the Saxon border and there Luther would have to remain. The party arrived there on April 24th and Coburg Castle became his residence from then until October 4th. It had been conjectured that he might be able to travel to Nuremberg, a free city, but the authorities there preferred to keep good relations with the emperor rather than risk his anger by harbouring a man under the ban. Luther would have dearly loved to be at the diet but the circumstances were different now; he could no longer make a stand before the emperor. The elector's party had to receive safe conducts to pass through Catholic Bavaria. Before the emperor reached Augsburg, the elector had made efforts to reach agreement with him on the religious question by sending embassies to him at Innsbruck, without involving the more politically active Philip. But his efforts were rebuffed, with the added disapproval that he had allowed Lutheran pastors to preach at Augsburg.

The emperor's arrival at Augsburg on June 15th brought tensions out into the open. The dignitaries went out to greet him. As they knelt to receive the blessing of the papal legate, Campeggio, the elector of Saxony stood upright. According to Bainton:

> On the following day came one of the most colourful processions in the history of medieval pageantry. In silk and damask, with gold brocade, in robes of crimson and the colours appropriate to each house, came the electors of the Empire followed by the most exalted of their number, Johann of Saxony, carrying in accord with ancient usage the gleaming naked sword of the emperor. Behind him marched Albrecht, the Archbishop of Mainz, the bishop of Constance, King Ferdinand of Austria and then his brother, the emperor.[1]

They processed to the cathedral and there the emperor and his entourage knelt in prayer – all except Johann and his son-in-law, Philip. A further embarrassment arose when the emperor required all the nobles to take part in the Corpus Christi procession of the following day, but the Lutherans stayed away. This division highlighted the fact that the diet had as its proximate purpose the resolution of the religious question, but ultimately had to do with the political one of the empire's cohesion. Its conclusion several months later would be to clarify the political situation, while leaving the religious one as before. At the start things went well; on both sides there was readiness to reach understanding. The papal legate, for his part, spoke of issues which would have to be referred to a council and believed the Lutherans would yield on some issues.

Luther meanwhile lodged in spacious quarters in Coburg Castle, most comfortable and suitable to study, as he wrote to Melanchthon, adding that his absence left him sad. He also got news of the death of his infant daughter while there. Those who were with him told how he retired to his room to grieve in private. He had realised that he could not appear at the diet, so he had prepared a document in Wittenberg, which he completed in the Coburg, expanding it in scope and vehemence, as he wrote to Melanchthon. It went to the printers in Wittenberg on May 12th. In early June five hundred copies were delivered to Augsburg and quickly sold out.

It has been described as Luther's 'alternative Augsburg Confession' and was entitled *Exhortation to All Clergy Assembled at Augsburg*. The title is significant in not being addressed to the emperor and the princes at a diet which was principally concerned with the politics of the empire, a fact which influenced Melanchthon's irenic approach – his hope that the princes might let an ecumenical approach to the religious issue influence their political relationships. Luther was concerned simply with a theology to be vindicated and he began by referring to the previous Diets of Speyer where the religious issue had been put to one side. He wanted to remind all that at Worms the German nobility brought a list of 'about four hundred grievances against the clergy'. He listed among the worst abuses 'butter-letters', the dispensations from the Lenten fast which could be bought. (These related to the ban on *lacticinia*, foods derived from animals, but in the fifteenth century dispensations could be got by paying a fee. By the end of the century these were being bought on a sufficient scale to pay for the 'Butter Tower' of Rouen Cathedral. That fact greatly offended Luther.)[2] There was a double abuse here, in that these things had been given by God freely to all people, but the clergy bound them and then required payment to make them free. The rite of confession brought the abuse that while God in Christ has forgiven mankind, the church required people to make satisfaction and go to heaven by their own efforts. From this misunderstanding of repentance flowed all the other abuses, endowments of cloisters and masses, pilgrimages, venerating the saints. He concluded with an offer – it is difficult to know whether he was being naïve, serious or engaged in wishful thinking – to the clergy, by which he meant bishops, especially the prince bishops: let them not give up their temporal possessions but their spiritual office and allow the Lutherans to fulfil these duties in their stead. 'Do not persecute and resist that which you cannot do and are nevertheless obligated to do and which others want to do for you.'[3] Much of what he wrote would appear in summary form in the second part of Melanchthon's text of the *Confessio*, that dealing with abuses.

In all of his text, Luther uses significant labels to make a distinction: 'the true Christian church' and 'the pretended church'. He reminds his readers that at the Nuremberg Diet of 1523 Pope Hadrian VI had acknowledged the need to correct long-standing abuses. Among his readers, as it turned out, was the Papal Legate, Campeggio, who ordered one of his staff to make a Latin translation of the pamphlet – whether as a salutary warning to the prelates or as further ammunition against Luther is not known.

The Confession of Augsburg 1530

Before the diet opened on June 20th, the irenic Melanchthon met with the emperor's secretary and assured him that the Lutheran affair was not as divisive as the emperor had been led to believe; it had to do merely with communion under both kinds, the marriage of priests and private masses. The first two were disciplinary issues, but Melanchthon seems to have underplayed the significance of the prohibition of private masses. The theological implication of the latter issue was more than pastoral; it was also a denial of the sacrificial nature of the mass. He was in communication with Luther through what must have been a rapid courier service. On June 23rd twenty-three Lutheran theologians and princes gathered for a reading and signing of a document by Melanchthon. On June 25th Melanchthon wrote to Luther to say that his text of the Lutheran *Confession* would be presented to the emperor that day. On the following day he asked in a letter what concessions should he make, particularly in relation to private masses, as his text had given the reasons for their prohibition. Two days later he wrote to say he was expecting much conflict over the private mass issue. On June 29th Luther wrote saying he should concede nothing and next day wrote again saying: 'In private disputes, I am less firm than you, but in public ones, you are like me in private ones, and I like you in private ones' (The Latin is more elegant!).[4] On June 30th the text was read out publicly in German in the presence of the emperor, who understood German only poorly, and the next day Melanchthon sent Luther a copy and described the hostility it had aroused. Luther, however, was dissatisfied that the *Confession* did not reject the papacy and its authority completely; 'too much has been granted'.[5] The text of Article VIII had however given a strong hint when it stated:

> Although the church properly is the congregation of saints and true believers, nevertheless, since in this life many hypocrites and evil persons are mingled therewith, it is lawful to use sacraments administered by evil men, according to the saying of Christ: the scribes and the pharisees sit in Moses' seat, etc. Mt 23:2.

Further than that Melanchthon could not have gone if there was going to be any chance that the emperor would accept Lutheranism as an acceptable form of church.

The Catholic response, *Confutatio Pontificia,* was prepared by twenty theologians and read to the diet on August 3rd. According to it, ecclesiastical and monastic properties were to be restored to their previous owners and the Lutheran presses in the Evangelical cities and states were to be silenced. The Imperial Court of Justice was to be empowered to enforce these prescriptions.[6] During that month there were meetings between theologians from the two sides and, while some progress was reported, the sticking point proved to be the section at the end of the *Confession* which spoke of the 'abuses corrected'. These were the practical aspects of Christian living which the *Confession* claimed had been corrupted. The last article contains the only explicit criticism of the papacy:

> The pontiffs, emboldened by the power of the keys, not only have instituted new services and burdened consciences with reservation of cases and ruthless excommunications, but have also undertaken to transfer the kingdoms of this world, and to take the empire from the emperor.[7]

Some of the criticisms were couched in subtle terms; for example, about the mass it says: 'Public ceremonies for the most part like those hitherto in use, are retained; only the number of masses differs.' This is the vindication of the suppression of private masses, which Lutheran theology in fact held were clearly based on the theology of the mass as sacrifice. The other practices criticised were also based on a theology which was being repudiated, though not always explicitly.

Melanchthon got to work on a response to the *Confutatio* and claimed on September 19th to have rebutted it satisfactorily, but on September 22nd the emperor gave his verdict that the Catholic *Confutatio* had refuted the *Augsburg Confession;* its prescriptions were to come into effect and he gave all the evangelical rulers until April 15th of the following year to inform him whether or not they would return to Rome. One practical result of the diet was that Lutheranism now had a confession of faith which would be the basis for later articulation of its standards of belief. The other was that the Elector Johann formed the League of Schmalkalden by the beginning of the following year to pre-empt any plans to impose the recess of the Diet of Augsburg and to oppose Charles' plans to strengthen his empire by giving greater authority to his brother Archduke Ferdinand by having him styled King of the Romans. Charles' struggle to unite his empire was to involve various bloody conflicts before and after Luther's death in 1546, until Charles' own resignation and retirement to a monastery in 1556.

The year 1530, which saw the statement of Lutheran belief in the *Confession of Augsburg* and Luther's own 'Confession' in his *Exhortation*, marks a turning point in his career. He was satisfied by the outcome of the diet: 'If Christ would allow himself to appear a bit weak, that does not mean he has been ousted from his seat'.[8] The gospel, in his view, was no longer negotiable and, following the 'Confession', would never become so again. Before the diet ended he had added to his *Exhortation* the 'Letter to the Cardinal Archbishop of Mainz' urging him to be a voice of moderation at the diet; let others believe as they wished, while permitting the Lutherans to believe the truth of their confession. He pointed out that no one could or should force anyone to believe. In the aftermath of the diet the severity of the prescriptions of the *Confutatio* was a stimulus to the participants to activate the Schmalkaldic League by preparing plans to defend themselves by force.

In anticipation of an outbreak of violence and before the Recess of the diet, Luther began writing his *Warning to His Dear German People* on October 1st. It had a somewhat modified approach to the current situation compared with what he had said a year before in his letter to the Elector Johann after the Marburg colloquy: better be ten-times dead than that the gospel should be the cause of bloodshed. Now he gave approval to defensive action against the 'murderers and bloodthirsty papists'. He had to reconcile this with his deep seated respect for secular authority and took refuge in the idea of evil counsellors being behind oppressive imperial policy. As a subsequent document, *Comment on the Alleged Imperial Edict* showed, the real enemies were Pope Clement VII and the papal legate Cardinal Campeggio. In effect he was introducing a distinction into his teaching on the two kingdoms, by raising the question of who actually might hold the real power in a secular state.

What he would write in his remaining years would be going over old ground and become increasingly vituperative. Some biographies lay little stress on his development from then until his death in 1546 and it is true that declining health brought a decline in creativity but a hardening in attitudes and in consequence several years before his death he was excluded from the attempt at rapprochement at Regensburg in 1541, convened in anticipation of the coming general council at Trent. As will be seen later, his reaction was to produce the most polemical of his writings in his last year, 'the virulent, rambling'[9] *Against the Papacy at Rome Founded by the Devil*, in which he railed against the pope of the time, Paul III (r.1534-1549), describing him as a sodomite and a transvestite.

But there was also an output of academic activity and important literary work as part of the legacy of those years. Despite his frequent headaches, on his return to Wittenberg he continued his lectures on the Song of Songs which had been interrupted by the stay at the Coburg. He worked also on introductions to each psalm and on revising the translation of the Psalter, which had first appeared in 1524. The translation of the whole Bible into German became a team effort with a team assembling in his house fifteen times between mid-January and mid-March 1531. Luther explained[10] that the team refrained from literal translation of the Hebrew and at times differed from the interpretations of the Jewish rabbis. Once they understood the meaning of the text, they looked for ways a German might say the same thing, a technique which is known today as seeking the dynamic equivalent. For Luther the Hebrew Bible was not exclusive to the Jewish religion but was the Old Testament part of the Christian Bible and it was this integrated whole which appeared in 1534 and incorporated a revised version of the New Testament he had translated in 1522. In this way, the religion of the Reformation became a religion of the book in a way that the Hebrew Bible had made Judaism a people of the book in earlier times. The Lutheran scholar, Scott Hendrix, has noted, however that Luther did not anticipate

> how many Protestants would ignore his claim that the ultimate importance to reading the Bible was to encounter the gospel.... Luther had no way of foreseeing that once people could read the Bible, going to church to hear the gospel in its various forms might seem superfluous. Or that people reading

the Bible on their own would use parts they liked to support bizarre beliefs and practices.... Instead of finding freedom through the good news contained in the Bible some readers would end up enslaving themselves verse by verse to a paper pope.[11]

Luther was clear about the importance of the Old Testament – he may have known the dictum of Augustine that the New lies hidden in the Old and the Old is unveiled in the New (*Quaest. in Hept.* 2,73). But in that case his attitude to the people of the Hebrew Bible was oddly negative.[12] His attitude towards the Jews, which changed over the years, has always attracted severely critical comment.

CHAPTER TWELVE

Luther and the Turks

In Luther's day, there were two forces perceived as hostile to the fabric of Christian society, Islam (an external force) and Judaism (an internal one). Over the course of the years he had varying degrees of awareness of them both, according to the degree to which their existence impinged upon his career, and attitudes that varied from indifference to outright hostility. He made a casual reference to the Turks, praising their way of governing according to the Koran, in his *Address to Christian Nobility* of 1520.[1] While eight years later he said the Turk's *Koran*, or creed, teaches him to destroy not only the Christian faith, but also the whole of government. This was in a document of 1528, *War Against the Turks*.[2] In the intervening years, the call of successive popes for Christian crusades to retake Constantinople had taken the form of lobbying by papal legates at the diets for the necessary taxes to be imposed on the estates. But the focus changed because of the concern of the Emperor Charles to mobilise military forces against the advance of the Turks, who under Suleiman the Magnificent took large parts of Hungary in 1526 and in 1529 failed, because of the winter conditions, to take Vienna. As noted earlier, the concern for the safety of the empire in face of military threats from outside caused treatment of the perceived internal religious threat from Luther's movement to be put on hold, even though it was recognised that internal divisions in the empire weakened its capacity to deal with the Turks. During that decade, Luther was himself concerned with internal religious divisions but maintained a hard-line stance against the Swiss even though this frustrated Philip of Hesse's plans for a political alliance that would strengthen Protestantism – but not the empire at a time of external threat. Luther was also alarmed by the social disturbances that culminated in the Peasants' War, but, as noted earlier, only reluctantly became a supporter of physical force. The *War Against the Turks* expressed his new attitude and is of interest because of his acceptance of the need for the use of arms in defence. His earlier avoidance of support for war had been based on his concept of the two kingdoms, which separated the religious and secular realms in such a way that he counselled the Christian to be long-suffering in face of hostility while recognising the right of the secular authority to resort to physical force when necessary.

In his 1528 document, he begins by quoting one of his theses condemned in *Exsurge Domine*: 'to fight against the Turk is the same thing as resisting God, who visits our sin upon us with this rod'. He agrees he said this but things are different now:

> This was the state of things at that time – no one had taught, no one had heard, and no one knew anything about temporal government, whence it came, what its office and work was, or how it ought to serve God ... princes and lords who wanted to be pious men held their rank and office as of no value and did not consider it a service of God.

He goes on to reiterate his teaching on the two kingdoms:

> What I would do is keep the callings and offices distinct and apart, so that everyone can see to what he is called, and fulfill the duties of his office faithfully and with the heart, in the service of God. Of this I have written more than enough elsewhere, especially in the books *On Soldiers* and *On Temporal Government*.

The losses in the battles with the Turks up to now he blames on failure to maintain this distinction; the involvement of the church in battle has led to disaster. His solution:

> If I were emperor, king, or prince in a campaign against the Turk, I would exhort my bishops and priests to stay at home and mind the duties of their office, praying, fasting, saying mass, preaching, and caring for the poor.

He then describes the appropriate way of life for the Christian calling in this distinction of roles; it is that of prayer and penance because the attack of the Turk is in the end God's punishment for sin, though he sees it also as the work of the devil: '[he] justly gives us into the hands of the devil and the Turk'. To encourage people to practise prayer and penance he gives an account of the true nature of the religion of the Turks, as he had acquired a copy of the Koran. The sum of its teaching, according to Luther, is:

> Since Christ's office of prophet is now complete, it has been commanded to (Mohammed) to bring the world to his faith and if the world is not willing, to compel it or punish it with the sword; and there is much glorification of the sword in it.

His summing up of the threat: 'Thus the Turk is, in truth, nothing but a murderer or highwayman, as his deeds show before men's eyes'. But he also recognised what he would describe as natural virtues in them as a people.

> It is said, indeed, that the Turks are, among themselves, faithful and friendly and careful to tell the truth. I believe that, and I think that they probably have more fine virtues in them than that.

Towards the end, however, he accuses the Turks:

> I hear one horrible thing after another about what an open and glorious Sodom Turkey is, and everybody who has looked around a little in Rome and Italy knows very well how God there revenges and punishes the prohibition of marriage, so that Sodom and Gomorrah, which God overwhelmed in days of old with fire and brimstone, must seem a mere jest compared with these abominations.

Linking the Turks and Italians in his various condemnations is especially strong in relation to that of homosexual practices. Luther believed that what he described as Sodom and Gomorrah type of activity was widespread in Rome and that the Fifth Lateran Council

(1512-17) had allowed each cardinal to have five 'Ganymedes' (the youth described in Homer's *Iliad* as Zeus's beautiful young cup-bearer, in Latin 'Catamitus') in his entourage.[3] In fact this reforming council, though considered by historians as ineffective in its outcome, laid down strict rules concerning such things as ankle length clothing for attendants on cardinals and called for canonical or even civil punishment of those 'found guilty of a charge on account of which the wrath of God comes upon the sons of disobedience'. Reference to the wrath of God was a veiled way of referring to the consequences of sodomy and the fact that such a decree was included presumably attests to the practice being a problem at the time. As he showed in his tract *On the Estate of Marriage*, Luther was well aware of such misdemeanours as adultery among his own people, but he viewed Italians as particularly prone to sexually deviant practices and held that this was due in the end to the church's deviance from divine law – especially by the exaltation of virginity.

The long tract, after various comparisons of the pope with Turks, eventually come to the point:

> What the emperor can do for his subjects against the Turk, that he should do, so that even though he cannot entirely prevent the abomination, he may yet try to protect and rescue his subjects by checking the Turk and holding him off.

Luther and the Jews

The attitude towards the Turks needs to be borne in mind when Luther turns his attention to a perceived internal threat to the German people, the Jewish community. In both cases his judgment was influenced by eschatological passages in the scriptures concerning the final elimination of all evil and his apocalyptic belief that this was at hand. At the same time, the threat from the Turks was obviously more imminent, while the Jewish community had been part of German society for centuries. But perceptions were changing and in 1538 Philip of Hesse restricted the rights of Jews because of protests from the Protestant clergy against his renewal of a policy of protection and his fears of a threat from their presence to the newly established Protestant cities. The tone of Luther's writing against the Turks was more measured, while that of his writings on the Jews became more vindictive with time.

His attitude towards the Jews can be traced through successive publications, most of them precipitated by events. For example, *That Jesus Christ Was Born a Jew* (1523) arose from a controversy in which the humanist scholar, Johannes Reuchlin opposed the call of a convert from Judaism, Johann, for Hebrew books to be confiscated and burned. In 1513 Reuchlin was charged with heresy but eventually vindicated. At the time Luther came out in favour of Reuchlin in a letter to Spalatin, on the basis of the usefulness of Hebrew literature for philological and grammatical studies of the Old Testament. Like Reuchlin, he believed that knowledge of Jewish literature would help towards the conversion of Jews. His book *Jesus Christ was Born a Jew* was written as a result of a rumour spread at the Diet of Worms after Luther's departure and disappearance that he held that Joseph was in fact Jesus' physical parent. In the book he professes loyalty to traditional teaching and in a well-known passage says of the Jews: 'so long as we treat them like dogs how can we expect to work any good among them?' Against Lull's view that in this book Luther 'urged a new beginning guided by love' but later 'became more hostile' to the Jews, Whitford argues that Luther's attitude did not undergo a fundamental change, but that what changed was his attitude to those who refused to convert. 'At no time in his life did he regard Jews as worthy members of the community in their own right.'[4]

His sermon for the twenty-fifth Sunday after Trinity in 1525 was entitled *Ein Sermon von den judischen Reichs und der Welt Ende.*[5] The text was Mt 24:15-28, Christ's description of the signs of the end of the age. Luther says that the text refers not only to the Jews and the end of their world but also to the Pope's kingdom, the the pope being 'the greatest arch-abomination of all abominations, to whom Christ and Daniel refer; and the true antichrist, of whom it is written that he sits in the temple of God'. It is another example of the pope and the Jews, as in the case of the pope and the Turks, being considered equivalent agents of the devil.

Of the publications of his last years, the *Commentary on the Book of Genesis, Against the Papacy at Rome Founded by the Devil, On the Jews and their Lies* (1543), the third is the most violent in tone and the most vulgar in its language. Roland Bainton, a Lutheran and naturally sympathetic biographer, stated: 'One could wish that Luther had died before ever this tract was written'[6] and other biographers have been equally embarrassed by it, especially because it can appear proto-Nazi and did apparently 'fall into the lap of the Nazi propaganda machine'.[7] Lohse admits that 'leading National Socialists at the time of Hitler felt they were entitled to claim Luther as a patron of their persecution of the Jews'.[8] In fact, at his trial in Nuremberg in 1946 the Nazi propagandist, Julius Streicher, said that anti-Semitic publications had existed in Germany for centuries, giving the example of this book and quoting Luther's call for the synagogues to be burned down.[9] But Lutheran biographers point to the fact that Luther's opposition to the Jews, as was true of the anti-Semitism of medieval Europe, was based on religion, on their anti-Christian stance and supposed practices, while the National Socialist belief was racist; it predicated the supremacy of the Aryan. Luther's perspective had always been the need to convert Jews to the Christian faith.

On the Jews and their Lies[10] was an indirect reply to another book, *Messiahs of the Christians and the Jews*, in which a Hebrew professor, Sebastian Münster, had expressed the hope that learning Hebrew and reading Hebrew books would lead to the mutual toleration of Christians and Jews.[11] Luther did not share either the conclusion or the aspiration. At the beginning of his book, he makes it clear that by now he has despaired of being able to convert the Jews by debating with them:

> From their youth they have been so nurtured with venom and rancour against our Lord that there is no hope until they reach the point where their misery finally makes them pliable

and they are forced to confess that the Messiah has come and that he is our Jesus.

He wrote the book partly to support the restrictions being imposed by such people as Philip of Hesse and to help vindicate the policy of his own elector, Johann Friedrich, who had already expelled the Jews from Saxony. While Philip forbade the building of new synagogues, Luther now went further and advised that existing ones should be burnt down.[12] He called his advice 'sharp mercy' that might 'save at least a few'.[13] But he did not advocate violence against their persons. Preachers should advise parishioners to be on guard against Jews and avoid them, but not 'curse them or harm their persons'.[14] He advocated their return to Jerusalem, leaving to Germans their government, their way of life, their property and their faith.

In the introduction to *Vom Schem Hamphoras und vom Geschlect Christi* (1543), which came out soon afterwards, he explains that he deliberately gave the title *On the Jews and their Lies* to that work

> so that we Germans know historically what a Jew is and to warn our Christians about them, as of the devil himself, and to strengthen and honour our faith; not to convert the Jews who are as possible to convert as the devil.[15]

He does not advocate action against them but his language is even more vulgar than in the preceding work. In *Vom Schem Hamphoras* he attacks both the papacy and the Jews:

> We also reject the pope together with all his church, which has filled all the world with the same jugglery, sorcery, idolatry, for he also has to be particularly a 'Schem Hamphoras'; as he goes enchanting the water with loose, bare, single letters, pretends it is holy water that washes away the sin, chases away the devil, and has many other virtues.[16]

Vom Schem Hamphoras gets its title from a Kabbalistic term containing a secret name of God and Luther's book is devoted to discrediting the myth about the power derived from its use. The anti-Semitic image, the *Judensau* (Jewish sow), carved on the façade of the town church in Wittenberg (as on many other German churches since the thirteenth century) provides him with a way of linking the mythical term with an insulting reference to the rabbis' reading of the Talmud, comparing it to the sow's anus:

> Carved here in Wittenberg on our parish church is a sow in stone, also young piglets with Jews among them who suckle; behind the sow stands a rabbi who raises the right leg of the sow up, and with his left hand he pulls the tail over himself, stooping forward and looking with great diligence under the tail inside the sow to the Talmud, as he wants to read and see something incisive and peculiar; here they certainly have their Schem Hamphoras'.[17]

Luther dies at the place of his birth

Despite increasing ill-health, Luther continued to teach in the last decade of his life and in 1545 published his *Commentary on Genesis*, from the material of his lectures in the decade up to then. His last publication came at the end of March 1545, *Against the Papacy at Rome Founded by the Devil*. It therefore appeared almost nine months before the first session of the Council of Trent which was originally meant to open on March 13th that year, but because of the small number of bishops who had arrived was postponed to December. The purpose of the treatise was to discredit the council so its timing was successful, though the members of the Schmalkaldic League had already boycotted the event. Its chief result was to strengthen their resolve on the eve of the outbreak of the war against them by Emperor Charles, ostensibly because of the takeover of the Duchy of Braunschweig by the forces of the league (to be described in the next chapter), but also as part of his campaign for the restoration of the Catholic religion.[18] In the ongoing struggle between him and the league, he had made substantial concessions at the Diet of Speyer in 1544 in return for their support in the imperial war against the Turks and France. These included an acceptance of the Protestant demand that a 'general Christian free council' be held in Germany territory – against the express decision of Pope Paul III in 1539 that a reforming council would take place in Italy. In addition, Charles renewed the decision of previous diets that no action would be taken against the Protestant territories. His action caused the pope to send him an admonitory letter charging him with having grossly overstepped the mark by presuming to consider a council without reference to him. Charles was to 'desist from infringing on the ecclesiastical sphere, from discussing religious questions at the diet and from disposing of ecclesiastical property'.[19] Luther was encouraged by the Elector Johann to engage in a counterblast against the papal claims in order to discredit the Council of Trent and inform Protestants, wherever that was still needed, of the true nature of the papal antichrist. During his career, Luther had written tracts which were primarily theological and some which were as much polemical as instructive, as in this case.

In his later years, his decline in health and a feeling that his own end was near brought an apocalyptic mentality to the fore and led to a lack of restraint in language. What he now produced was at the end of the polemical range; he no longer felt the need to consider the papacy as anything more than the work of the devil. As noted earlier, in various writings from 1520 onwards, he had associated or identified the papacy with the antichrist; in this latest tract, the identification is complete. In a work devoted to Luther's last years, *Luther's Last Battles,* Edwards says: 'This treatise is the most violent and vulgar to issue from Luther's pen'.[20] It was a document written to order and Johann and his associate Philip of Hesse may have received more than they bargained for, though they were said to be pleased with the result. The main body of the treatise goes over old ground, Luther's argument from history against papal supremacy, but now with a new claim – there was evidence he believed that the seventh-century Pope Boniface III was the first pope to be acknowledged as head of all the churches. That was as 'clear as the sun' from all the ancient decrees of councils and from the writings of the Fathers, Jerome, Augustine, Cyprian and all of Christianity.[21] He then argued theologically that since the two powers in society, the secular and the spiritual (the councils and bishops) had not established the papacy, it must have been founded by the devil. The identity then is threefold – papacy, devil, antichrist, as had been suggested particularly in his treatises on the Turks and on the Jews.

When some of the Protestant party at the Diet of Worms in 1545 were taken aback by the harshness of Luther's language, Philip of Hesse came to his defence, saying that he had a special spirit (*sonderlicher geist*) that did not allow him to be moderate in this matter, particularly in relation to the papacy.[22] The way Luther actually showed this special spirit was not only in his text but also in the notorious woodcuts which he commissioned from Lucas Cranach to illustrate his text. They are filled with violent and scatological images, reflecting what he says in his text, for example, that the tongues of the pope and his cohorts should be torn out and nailed with them to the gallows. They could hold a council there or in hell among the devils.[23] This scene is presented in detail in one of the eight cartoons.

Text and image were designed to create a sense of identity amongst the evangelical audience, united through hatred of the enemy. But it was also intended to provoke laughter, as Luther used coarse humour to destroy the papal aura of holiness.[24]

His old friend, Amsdorf, whom he had consecrated as a bishop in 1541, wrote to congratulate him on the book and he replied on April 14th 1545 thanking him and saying that not everyone was pleased with it but that it was not his way to write to please people. In any case, the Elector Johann had spent twenty florins purchasing copies to put into circulation.[25]

During the year he became aware of a publication by the theology faculty of the University of Louvain containing a list of articles confirmed and issued by the emperor. By September he had issued a response, *Against the Thirty-Two Articles of the Louvain Theologians*, consisting of seventy-five counter-theses. As in his response to Erasmus twenty years previously, he denies what the others affirm, dealing with one after another of the articles on the sacraments. When the Louvain party says in Article 21 that there is one true and visible church established by Christ and handed on by the chair of Peter, Luther denies the claim, saying that the laity who form the greater part of the church have not believed this theory. There is one church but these heretics and their 'abominable idol' do not belong to it. It was a document lacking his customary rhetorical skills, rarely mentioning the devil and indicating perhaps declining physical energy.[26]

He was in poor health when he journeyed to Mansfeld, his home town, in October, to arbitrate between the five Counts of Mansfeld and the lease holders of the mines in the area (of whom his father was one), which the counts had now revoked, making the smelters their employees' instead. His father was one of the people affected. The town, incidentally, was divided by the allegiance of three of them to the old faith and the two younger to the reform, with the result that the St Andreas Church had two entrances; the pastor was a Catholic, whom Luther bitterly opposed, and the preacher one of Luther's early associates. Luther was unsuccessful in defending the rights of the leaseholders but undertook another journey for this same purpose. In severe weather in January 1546 he travelled to the town of his birth, Eisleben, accompanied by his three sons, ranging in age from nineteen to thirteen.

He wrote a number of letters during the three-week journey and from Eisleben during his last days. On January 19th 1546 he wrote to Amsdorf saying he was praying for the day of redemption and the destruction of the world with all its pomps and malice. 'Let it come quickly'.[27] On February 1st he wrote to Melanchthon saying he felt unwell on the journey, suffering from palpitations, and also wrote to Katherina. He wrote again to Melanchthon on February 6th from Eisleben asking him to arrange that the elector would send him a letter recalling him to Wittenberg, in the hope that this might lead the disputants to reach an agreement, a tactic which turned out to be the successful. In a letter to Katherina at the same time, he complained of breathing problems and said that in Eisleben he did not have a way of dealing with the ulcer on his leg, which she had at home. The doctors in Eisleben kept the wound open to release, as it was thought, the 'harmful humours' and in fact were hastening his death.

He preached four times while in Eisleben and in one of the services ordained two ministers. He preached his last sermon three days before his death, which came on February 18th. The sermon was on Mt 11:25-30, Jesus' praise of the Father 'for hiding these things from the learned and the clever and revealing them to mere children'. The text seems to have been specially chosen for the occasion, as preaching on a Monday would normally have been on the Catechism. It allowed him to underscore a point which had been central to his entire career as a reformer: God's word bypasses the paths of human wisdom laid out by philosophers and the theology of the scholastics and by its own power guides and rules the church. The pope was then an obvious target; he has subverted the order of things established by God. The tone of the sermon is milder, however, than that of the notorious treatise of the preceding year. He turns to a theme of suffering; it will be the lot of those who, like him, hold on to the word and let everything else go. He calls on his hearers to turn away with eyes shut from all great personages and cling only to Christ's word 'and come to him as he so lovingly invites us to do, and say: Thou alone are my beloved Lord and Master, I am your disciple'. Luther finished on this note, saying that he was too weak to continue.[28]

Three days later, on the evening of February 17th, he was suddenly taken ill when he went with his sons to his room to pray. He recovered later and in periods of relief prayed: 'Into your hands I commend my spirit'. He had a number of relapses and was attended by his sons and a small group of his friends. His confessor, Bugenhagen, was in Wittenberg so he did not receive the rite of penance to which he was accustomed during his life. When the clergy present asked him if he were ready to die trusting in the Lord Jesus Christ, he answered with a distinct 'yes' and died a short time later.[29] His body was returned to Wittenberg on February 22nd, where a great procession was formed to meet it, led by officials of the elector, two of the Mansfeld Counts and forty-five horsemen. The body reposed overnight in the Castle Church, where the next day Bugenhagen preached and Melanchthon gave an oration in Latin, in which he gave Luther the title of 'Charioteer of Israel' – a reference to Elijah's ascent to heaven. He was buried in a grave opened near the pulpit.

There was an element of triumph in the celebrations of Luther's death and intimations of lasting fame, shown by the printing of a memorial booklet and pamphlets and the plaster casts of his hands and face – still displayed in the Marketkirche of Halle. This is one of the ironies that marked the whole period of Luther's struggle with the church of his day; it is the church in which Albrecht had his display of relics, with attendant indulgences. When Charles V visited the Castle Church a year after Luther's death, he ordered his troops to leave the grave undisturbed, even though imperial law required that heretics' bodies be exhumed and burned. But his policy towards the Protestants was now becoming more detailed and aggressive and on their side some of the princes of the Schmalkaldic League took up arms against Charles. At the battle of Mühlberg in 1547, they were defeated and both the Elector Johann and Philip of Hesse were captured and imprisoned. Victory there led to the Augsburg Interim of 1548, which sought reconciliation of the two religious parties.

Charles oversaw the subsequent peace treaty at Westphalia in 1555, which gave the rulers of Western Europe the *ius reformandi* – the right of reforming their territories and making them Lutheran, or remaining Catholic. It was not the outcome of his reform movement that Luther had expected when the die was cast at the Diet of Worms in 1521, but the coining of the term Protestant at the diet there in 1529 was a sign of the reality which would exist through subsequent centuries. He would have repudiated the name Lutheranism, but the church bearing his name is today one of the principal denominations that arose out of his original protest against Rome.

The widowed Katherina and the four living children had the protection of Elector Johann and because of Luther's estate and financial support from friends their situation was comfortable initially. They could remain in the large house, but the situation soon changed. After the defeat of Mühlberg they fled to the fortified city of Magdeburg, which belonged to the Schmalkaldic League, where they were joined by Melanchthon and his family. That was soon overcrowded with refugees and as the King of Denmark had offered financial support, Katherina proposed to move there. With Melanchthon as escort they got as far as Lüneborg but then the moving areas of conflict made it possible to return to Wittenberg, where she opened a hostel for students. A plague broke out in 1552, endangering the boarders and making it likely that the university would move away from Wittenberg, so Katherina and her two youngest fled once more. Before reaching Torgau, the horses shied and Katherina fell or jumped from the wagon; she was injured in the fall and never recovered. She died at Torgau on December 20th 1552 and was buried there.[30]

CHAPTER THIRTEEN

Luther's challenge to the church and society of his day

In the interests of simplicity, the narrative up to now has avoided as far as possible issues of motivation and other factors arising from Luther's personality, but has thereby left aside aspects of the story which call for deeper reflection. To consider the issue of his challenge to the church of his day now requires attending to what were his stated intentions and as far as possible his underlying motives, how these influenced his teaching, how important was his preoccupation with the devil or the antichrist and, objectively, what the results of his activities were – at least within his lifetime. Biographers and theological commentators ask corresponding questions. The answers can be expected to be diverse and there is surprising variety too in relation to the first and basic question of what his intentions were. That he was trying to reform the church of his day is a common view; Lull[1] says that at one point Luther 'thought that he so spoke for the hopes of Christendom that the reforms he proposed might sweep through the Roman church, especially if assisted by a General Council' – a reference to Luther's *Address to the German Nobility*. However, the authoritative Oberman thought: 'He never set himself up as a healer of the church and never regarded the renewal of the church as his task'.[2] In a recent biography, Peter Stanford comments: 'He did not set out with a vision to change the church and had no interest in refashioning society'.[3] In a study of Luther's place in modern (as opposed to ancient) church history, James Kittelson's thesis is that Luther 'did not set out to solve a particular problem or to correct errors within the church as a distinct area for thought and action. He was indeed driven by other concerns that were related to the church, but tangentially and even contingently so.... Luther was seized with the problem of the *cura animarum*, the care of souls'.[4] The judgment of his contemporary, Erasmus, was that he was not trying to create reform within the old faith but seeking to recast doctrine in a new form. Somewhere between all these views, the truth lies.

Yet it is abundantly clear from Luther's writings that he called for the elimination of abuses such as the impoverishment of the faithful for the enrichment of church dignitaries, that he saw all the baptised as having equal dignity in the church, thus relativising the status of the ordained, and above all that he wished to give scripture its supreme normative role in the life of the church. He could reasonably be called a would-be reformer of the Catholic Church, before he became a declared foe of that institution, as Mullett[5] puts it. There is the further question of if and when, according to himself, he ceased to be a member of the visible institution, the Catholic Church, and belonged thereafter to a new body, which would in time be called the Lutheran Church.

Eight popes reigned during Luther's lifetime, five of them during his active years. In order to assess his relationship with the church of his day it is necessary to take account of a distinction between his attitude to the pope and his attitude to the papacy. Julius II was pope when Luther visited Rome in 1510. According to anecdotes recorded at different times in his *Table Talk* of later years, and not easy to reconcile, he arrived full of devotion and, on seeing Rome, prostrated himself, saying, 'Hail, holy Rome'.[6] But he was soon scandalised. He stayed with Carthusians, according to one entry in the *Table Talk*, and as a young and devout monk was taken aback by things said at the table. For example, they joked about the way some of them interpolated the words 'Bread you are and bread you will remain' into the mass. (An odd thing about this is that the Carthusians have the reputation of never having had need of reform.) In that same entry he talks of celebrating mass and being told by a neighbouring celebrant to hurry.[7] In a commentary on Mt 21 in later years, he said that he had arrived in Rome 'with onions and left with garlic', which appears to mean that he arrived with some doubts and left with greater ones.[8]

What he thought about the rebuilding of St Peter's Basilica begun by Julius, or of Julius himself, is not known. Leo X, Julius' successor, issued the Bull *Exsurge* and also excommunicated him. His attitude towards Pope Leo was respectful at the time of the indulgences controversy and exaggeratedly so when he sent an open letter to him with the tract *To the Christian Nobility of the German Nation*. But when Leo died the following year, Luther had already ceased to take account of who was pope, as the idea of the pope as antichrist had by now begun to monopolise his thoughts.

His attitude had changed fundamentally in the course of 1520. In February of that year, he had written to Spalatin about the tract by Lorenzo Valla (1407-57) which showed that the *Donation of Constantine* (attesting the donation by Constantine I of the Roman Empire to the church) was a forgery. Valla's tract was published only in 1517 and Luther had just received a copy of it from the Knight Hutten. This was the final proof for him that the papacy's claim to authority over the secular realm was bogus and he was distressed but could no longer doubt that the papacy was the antichrist.[9] June was a month of feverish literary activity for Luther.[10] Early in that month, he wrote to Spalatin about Prierias' attack on him in his *Epitome* (*Epitome responsionis ad Lutherum,* a follow-up to his original *Dialogue*),[11] saying that 'the mysteries of the antichrist must be brought out into the open, since they push themselves forward and no longer wish to remain hidden'.[12] He responded to Prierias by publishing the *Epitome* himself, with an introduction in which he said that if this is what is taught in Rome, with the knowledge of the pope and cardinals ('I hope not'), then the true antichrist has his seat and reigns in 'empurpled' Rome, while the curia is the synagogue of the devil.[13] He added a note, saying that whatever Christians were not under the Roman antichrist were happy compared with 'us unhappy Christians'.[14]

But his judgment appears to have been not quite final at that stage, from the evidence of his tract *On the Papacy at Rome*[15] of June that year – a response to a Franciscan, Alfeld, who had written a treatise defending the papacy as of divine origin. In it he asks,

> Why is the occupant of the papal throne so furious to possess the whole world, and has not only stolen lands and cities, principalities and kingdoms, but has arrogated to himself the power to make kings and princes, seat and unseat and change them according to his pleasure, as if he were antichrist?

This he asks against the background of a proverb he attributes to the 'Romanists': 'Squeeze the gold from German fools, in any way you can'. However, he would 'let the pope remain' if two conditions were satisfied: no new articles of faith established and if the pope were to deny that 'the fellowship is a bodily thing', that is, if he agreed that the church was not simply a visible institution, but 'by its very nature, is of the things which no one sees or feels, as St Paul says in Heb 11:1'.

However, the distinction he had made between the visible institution and the church 'which no one sees or feels' was becoming fundamental and his challenge now amounted to dissociating himself from the rule exerted in Rome. He no longer had any hesitation in this regard when in response to the Bull, *Exsurge Domine,* he issued the tract, *Against the Execrable Bull of the Antichrist,* in November 1520 and his attitude did not change as the years passed.[16] In 1545, in the autobiographical preface to the edition of his Latin works, he asked for yet more preaching against the devil, 'because he is powerful and evil, more furious and dangerous than ever, because he knows his pope's reign (*regnum sui papae*) is endangered and only a short time remains'.[17]

From the foregoing it is clear that his attitude to the papacy had both practical and theoretical foundations. There was the German resentment at the gold 'leaping over the hills' to Rome, but, more importantly, his view was based on his theological convictions, ultimately on his theology of justification, as will be seen below. However, there seems to have been a parallel process: his view of the church was influenced by his experience even as his theological conviction about its nature was maturing as a result of his insight into justification. He was one of many – Erasmus being the most famous – who were disenchanted, to put it mildly, by the church's reputation at institutional level. After his debate with Eck at Leipzig in 1519, he began to speculate more deeply on the nature of the church and several of the publications of 1520 were the result.

The tract of June 1520, *On the Papacy at Rome: An Answer to the Celebrated Romanist at Leipzig*, includes the first radical statement of the alternative to the received theology of the church: '[the] church is a spiritual community, which can be classed with a temporal community as little as spirits with bodies, or faith with temporal possessions'.[18] This statement has led many critics to attribute to Luther an understanding of the church as wholly invisible and a further statement in the same tract seems to reinforce that view: 'though a man consists of two natures, namely, body and soul, yet he is not reckoned a member of the church according to his body, but according to his soul, nay, according to his faith'. However, there is a subtlety in this statement; Luther can be regarded as reacting against the commonly accepted theology of the time, according to which membership of the church came about through three bonds: participation in the sacraments, acceptance of the authority of the church and faith. Society was so ordered, however, that baptism into the church had marked civic connotation and consequences. Conversely, being a citizen presumed church affiliation with the result that simple outward conformity was considered to be adequate, with little regard to how active or real faith was at the internal level.

Luther saw the inadequacy of this practical theology and in due course would elaborate a theology which attempted to rectify it. At this initial stage, his emphasis is on faith as the criterion for membership and he will subsequently (in the *Babylonian Captivity* of the same year) turn his attention to the importance of the sacraments. The third criterion, acceptance of authority, gets short shrift at this point:

This, indeed, is true, that just as the body is a figure or image of the soul, so also the bodily community is a figure of this Christian, spiritual community, and as the bodily community has a bodily head, so the spiritual community has a spiritual head. But who would be so bereft of sense as to maintain that the soul must have a bodily head?

He amended his view on external authority in the 1520s when his idea of reform began to be implemented in Wittenberg without him and when he undertook visits to parishes in 1524. But at the beginning of the decade the nature of faith and justification governed his thinking about membership of the church and its external manifestation. As Torrance saw it, for Luther justification was an act of Christ, 'the eschatological act of pure grace which anticipated Christ's ultimate vindication of the sinner at the final judgment'.[19] Torrance pointed out that 'in the *Commentary on Galatians,* Luther is also concerned to emphasise the fact that we can only understand justification in terms of a duality which reaches out to the advent of Christ, when our perfect righteousness in Christ will be revealed'.[20] This establishes the justified sinner in a state that transcends the purely historical. Luther uses the term 'the bosom of mercy' to describe this transcendent existence:

> In the meantime, as long as we live here, we are carried and nourished in the bosom of the mercy and the longsuffering of God until the body of sin is abolished and we are raised up as new creatures in that great day. Then there shall be new heavens and a new earth in which righteousness shall dwell.[21]

There is the obvious question as to what justification of this 'eschatological' kind can mean in the life of the believer in time and critics of Luther's theology have often presented it as '*merely* forensic', some kind of legal fiction that does not affect the believer's ontological status. In his article, 'Luther's contemporary theological significance', Robert Jenson draws attention to a 1525 sermon on Eph 3:14-21.[22] In it Luther states:

everything [Christ] is and does is present in us and there works with power, so that we are utterly deified, so that we do not have some part or act of God, but his entire fullness. [23]

Jenson rightly points out that apart from differences of diction this could be from any of the Greek Fathers. It should also be noted, of course, that the Greek Fathers introduced the concept of divine energies to create a necessary distinction between God and the creature in this deification or *theosis,* while Luther lacks this device. But as again Jenson notes, Luther in *The Freedom of the Christian Man* had articulated this union of the believer with God in terms of an ethical union: 'the soul of the one who clings to the word in true faith is so united with it that all the virtues of the word become virtues of the soul also'.[24] This divinisation would appear to be instantaneous – on hearing the word – but Luther continues in his sermon:

> In this passage is designated the truest way to attain godlikeness. It is to become filled to the utmost with God, lacking in no particular; to be completely permeated with him until every word, thought and deed, the whole life in fact, be utterly godly. But let none imagine such fullness can be attained in this life. We may indeed desire it and pray for it, like Paul here, but we will not find a man thus perfect. We stand, however, upon the fact that we desire such perfection and groan after it. So long as we live in the flesh, we are filled with the sinfullness of Adam.[25]

The important detail here is that 'none should imagine that such fullness can be attained in this life'. Luther is presenting a view of the church derived from an eschatologically dimensioned concept of justification according to which the justified, deified believer is also a sinner dealing with the ethical challenges of the Christian life. This goes some way to explain the advice Luther gave to Melanchthon, which took the enigmatic form: 'Be a sinner and sin boldly, but believe and rejoice in Christ even more boldly'. It was his way of emphasising that the grace of Christ was 'true and not fictitious' and that the same applied to sin in the Christian life. 'This life is not the dwelling place of righteousness but, as Peter says, we look for a new heavens and a new earth in which righteousness dwells.'[26] Despite the somewhat unedifying advice to Melanchthon, Luther does seem to present an authentically scriptural and catholic understanding of the church and this has to be taken seriously as a way of avoiding the temptation to identify too readily the church in history with the 'church without a spot or wrinkle or anything of the kind' of Eph 5:27.

While the insight concerning the eschatological status of the Christian life was also prominent in the early Christian tradition, it has to be said that it was not obviously characteristic of the church of Luther's day; instead the interests of this world were pursued with considerable dedication. The lifestyle of prelates had much in common with that of secular princes and even the religious orders, which in theory expressed in a special way the eschatological dimension of the Christian life, were in many places characterised by a worldly way of life. The situation that prevailed helps to explain how Luther came to the conclusion that, from the nature of the gracious act of Christ, the bodily or historical state of the Christian existence not only has no need, but excludes, a leadership role corresponding to Christ's headship. In effect, his view of the church's eschatological nature, that it anticipates Christ's final victory, more than hints at a belief on his part that the time in which he was living was the end time, the climax of the period in which the devil held sway and ruled the church through the antichrist, the papacy. But defeat for the devil and his representative was imminent.

Luther's eschatological perspective has then an apocalyptic dimension to the extent that it seems reasonable to speak of his 'apocalyptic eschatology'.[27] The apocalyptic colouring of his thought has been mentioned above in relation to his treatises on the Jews and the Turks and it was dominant in his tract on the papacy the year before his death. For Bayer the sixteenth century was in a certain sense an apocalyptic time because of the Turkish threat, the Peasants' War and the splits between the confessional groups: 'apocalyptic is not so much about a chronology as it is of the quality of the era ... Luther could not conceive that settled and less apocalyptic times would follow once again'.[28] It is significant that in his last years, he wanted to know when the world would end, as indicated by the title of his *Supputatio Annorum Mundi* of 1541.[29]

In *Luther's Last Battles,* Mark Edwards says:

> Heightening Luther's sense of cosmic struggle was his conviction that the End Time was nearly at hand; that with the exposure of the papal antichrist seated within the church, Satan had unleashed all his minions for one final climactic battle. Luther's own ill-health and expectation of death, combined with his disappointment about the reception of the gospel within Germany, fed his sense of the imminence of the Apocalypse and his desire to do final battle with the devil.[30]

The difference between eschatology and apocalyptic eschatology needs elaboration. The standard explanation of eschatology (not taking account of different kinds of it) is that the Christian lives in a tension between the present life and its consummation with the return of Christ, and has the belief that Christ has already achieved victory over death and evil, but that this has yet to be fully realised in time, in the ongoing history of the age. An additional apocalyptic perspective has an effect on the perception of historical time. For people who have an apocalyptic outlook, that is, have entered 'apocalyptic time', time itself is altered:

> everything quickens, everything enlivens, everything coheres. In apocalyptic time, believers become semiotically aroused – everything has meaning, patterns. The smallest incident can have immense importance and open the way to an entirely new vision of the world, one in which forces unseen by other mortals operate.[31]

The question is how apocalyptic Luther's attitude may be said to be. Reference in the definition above to forces unseen by other mortals evokes Luther's frequent reference to the presence of the devil in events affecting him – there is the legend of his having thrown an inkpot at the devil when he was on the Wartburg – but also his reference to the true church as hidden. The principal evidence of such a mentality, however, is his identification of the papacy with the antichrist; in his appeal to the German nobility he had said: 'we wrestle not against flesh and blood, but against the rulers of the darkness of this world'.

This judgment of his involves more than a dismissal of the authority of the papacy; he proposes instead a congregation of true believers whose reality can at times be hidden because it belongs to the 'already and not yet' reign of Christ. In the interest of this sometimes secret eschatological community, he identifies an institution, the Roman church, existing in historical time, with the reign of the antichrist, which rules in apocalyptic time, but the climax of the conflict with the reign of Christ was now entering historical time.

Luther's use of the term antichrist had precedence in church history (apart from the New Testament references in 1 Jn and 2 Jn). From about the tenth century it was used both by and against popes and prelates, one of the more notorious examples being the accusation by Eberhard II, Prince-Archbishop of Salzburg, in 1241 at the Council of Regensburg, that Pope Gregory IX was the antichrist. In history, however, the term had been used against individuals, not institutions. This awareness of the antichrist was still common in Luther's day; he included Bernard's twelfth-century sermon in his lecture and may have known about an elegantly printed book with coloured illustrations published in Nuremberg in 1493, *Liber Chronicarum*, by Hartmann Schedel. It was a history of the world, concluding with the seventh age, the end of the world, and had an illustration of the antichrist. Luther, however, brought the term to a new level of usage and identified it clearly with the papacy, thus beginning a tradition that continued in the Reformation era and beyond. His particular theology of the church arose not only from genuine eschatological insight but also from an apocalyptic assessment of the papal church.

It can be asked, of course, if highlighting his apocalypticism can form part of a balanced assessment of a man who married, had children and a happy family life, sang and played the lute, wrote hymns, shared his large residence with needy students, cultivated a garden and made great efforts to ensure that children received a good schooling. He devoted much energy to providing pastoral care for the communities of his reform, which emerged as a result of his preaching and publications, and ensured also the continuation of these communities by ordaining men to the ministry. But the preoccupation with the reign of the antichrist and its identification with the papacy cannot be ignored; it is a constantly recurring theme from about 1520 and goes well beyond the commonly polemical character of debate at that time.

It is almost as if one were dealing with two Luthers, especially as even in later years he makes uncharacteristically positive comments about the papal church. Health considerations come into it. Many biographers have dealt with the issue of Luther's health, physical and mental, with special attention to his later years. The physical symptoms which he himself reported at various times do allow a hypothesis to be formulated, if not a confident diagnosis.[32] He was not reluctant to describe his condition and the picture which emerges is of a man with the many ailments, which the primitive medicine of the time could not cure and tended in fact to aggravate. It has been suggested that a basic problem may have been an unusually high level of uric acid in his system, which would account for acute and very painful attacks of kidney stones. When isolated in Coburg Castle he wrote to Melanchthon, describing his suffering from piles and headaches and dizziness – the latter possibly caused by Meniere's syndrome.[33] Like many contemporaries, he suffered from toothache. All of these conditions were more acute in his later years and could reasonably explain increasing irritation and polemical tendencies in his writing.

But the state of his mental health and his type of personality are clearly also of fundamental importance in assessing his theological development and his career as a dominant figure on the ecclesiastical scene, especially in relation to his apocalyptic cast of thought as it developed over the years. Speculation about a father fixation and about depression and mood swings has already been mentioned. In *Table Talk* entries from January and March 1532, he said that he had no better resource than anger; it helped him to write, to pray and to preach and drove away temptations.[34] Avarice was not a problem for him, or lust because of age and infirmity, but he acknowledged that anger remained.[35]

A clinical psychologist in conversation with this writer has suggested that the root of his anger may in fact have been fear, that his positive assessment of his anger may have been his way of taking the focus off other emotions, especially fear, in a process which externalised sources of pain and threat going back perhaps to his relationship with his father. As Taylor says of the whole Reformation period: '[it] is, as Delameau argues, an age of anxiety. An age of great fears. Fear of magic, of outsiders, of disorders, and of course sin, death and judgment'.[36] By focusing on what appeared to be external threats – his various opponents or the papacy – it may be that Luther avoided dealing with a state of inner resentment and even self-disgust. It is noticeable that he never accepted he could be wrong – this was always seen by him as a temptation. By a process which psychologists call inverse inference he may have boosted his own internal authority by disputing external authority. This would be in addition to his 'conscience being captive to the word', as already discussed.

As he advanced in years, a failure to achieve a healthy psychological state could be expected to be externalised in somatic symptoms and to alter behaviour. There was the incident, for example, in 1545 when he became suspicious that Melanchthon was not holding fast to the doctrine of real presence of Christ in the eucharist. He became enraged and appeared to have Melanchthon in mind when he preached against the 'sacramentarians'. That summer he set out to visit his friend Amsdorf in Zeitz and while there wrote to Katherina telling her to sell all and leave Wittenberg, as he had heard bad things about it during his visit. In the end calm was restored.

In the winter of 1542-3, he had expressed the wish publicly that he and all his children were dead. Though it came at a time when his daughter Magdalena had died and plague was raging in Wittenberg, it points to an unhealthy psychological state as much as to an apocalyptic desire for the world to end. To speculate along these lines may of course lead to the mistake that early psychoanalytical studies, such as those of Reiter and Erikson, made. They failed to give sufficient weight to profound theological insights. However, there lurks in the background the possibility that his personal psychology predisposed him to accept and even carry to an extreme Augustine's pessimistic assessment of human nature by the denial of free will, especially.

Despite this disturbing picture, there is also Luther's impressive pastoral care which says as much about his aims in life as does the campaign against Rome. As his vision of what he saw as the true church began to form while he was on the Wartburg in 1522, the pastoral Luther was clear on what he wanted to see happen; he did not want it to centre on himself and he wanted a peaceful transition from the old way. In late 1521 rioting students attacked the Franciscan community in Wittenberg and this was one of the excesses that led him to write to the people of Wittenberg:

> In the first place, I ask that men make no reference to my name; let them call themselves Christians not Lutherans. What is Luther? After all, the teaching is not mine (Jn 7:16). Neither was I crucified for anyone (1 Cor 1:13). St Paul, in 1 Cor 3, would not allow the Christians to call themselves Pauline or Petrine, but Christian. How then should I – poor stinking maggot-fodder that I am – come to have men call the children of Christ by my wretched name? Not so, my dear friends, let us abolish all party names and call ourselves Christians after him whose teachings we hold. The papists deservedly have a party name.[37]

He had come to realise that establishing a contrast with the 'papists' was not sufficient; it was leading simply to actions against them. His difficulties were more often with extremists than with traditionalists, as is evident from his tract *Concerning Rebaptism* of 1528, where his complaint against the Anabaptist groups is that in rejecting the pope they reject also the church, and he makes a distinction:

> If now this pope is (and I cannot think otherwise) the veri-
> table antichrist he will not sit in the devil's stall, but in the
> temple of God ... For he is an antichrist and must be among
> Christians. And since he is to sit and reign there it is neces-
> sary that there be Christians under him.... The Christendom
> that is now under the papacy is truly the body of Christ and a
> member of it... We do not rave as do the rebellious spirits, so
> as to reject everything that is found in the papal church. For
> then we would cast out even Christendom from the temple of
> God, and all that it contained of Christ.

He came to the surprising conclusion that:

> If the pope will suffer and accept this dissembling of mine,
> then I am and will be, to be sure, an obedient son and devoted
> papist with a truly joyful heart, and take back everything I
> have done to harm him.[38]

As noted earlier, the year 1530 marked a turning point in Luther's
career. The Diet of Augsburg followed quickly on that of Worms in
1529, where a party had emerged with a Protestant identity and determination to exert pressure on the emperor and the Catholics. Luther was excluded from participation and was confined to the Coburg
fortress, from which he issued his *Exhortation to all the Clerics Gathered at Augsburg 1530*. In it he declares: 'Living, I am your nemesis;
dead, I will be your death, O pope'.[39] In his *Address to his Beloved Germans* the following year, he uttered similar sentiments. He had lived
too long; after his death they would begin to talk honestly about him,
that he had taken a whole house of bishops, popes and monks with
him in the procession to the grave and was greater than them all.[40] In
light of this, his offer two years earlier to be an 'obedient son' seems
to have been made tongue in cheek.

The situation became complicated in the 1530s when the religious
division affected also in a significant way the relations between secular authorities. Elector Friedrich's successor, his brother Johann, was

on Luther's side but Duke Georg remained Catholic even though his son-in-law, Philip of Hesse, was a leader of the Schmalkaldic League of Protestant princes. Cardinal Albrecht lived on until 1545, a powerful prince as well as prelate. Territorial disputes religious in origin flared up and Luther and the Wittenberg theologians were called in to advise. A dispute arose in 1539, for example, between the Catholic Duke Heinrich of Braunschweig-Wolfenbüttel and the Protestant Philip of Hesse over two cities in Heinrich's territory which had gone over to the reform. To protect themselves from the former they joined the Schmalkaldic League, so Heinrich found himself in dispute with Philip and Elector Johann, principal proponents of the league. Heinrich therefore joined in a Catholic league with the emperor, Cardinal Albrecht and several others. The ensuing conflict remained – mostly – at the level of pamphlets in large numbers and with extraordinarily long titles – the Diet of Regensburg in 1541 was flooded with them. Luther became unwittingly involved when Heinrich made an insulting reference to Philip and attributed it to Luther. Luther was provoked into attacking Heinrich in a pamphlet and the relevance of this to the present study is that it caused him to undertake a Protestant against Catholic polemic, going beyond the anti-papal rhetoric to claim that the Protestants remained faithful to the 'true ancient church', while the Catholics, including Duke Heinrich, had apostatised from it.[41]

The conclusion must be, therefore, that Luther's attitude to the papacy allowed him little choice in the end other than to go his own way, ignoring or in places combatting the parishes maintaining Roman allegiance. On one occasion he appealed to the common saying, found also in Augustine: 'No one can or ought to be forced to believe'.[42] In his last sermon he was less sanguine about the future of his own movement when he acknowledged that people soon grow weary of all the preaching and ask what do they get out of it. He challenged his hearers, knowing that in this fundamental respect his reform had not yet won out. If people did not want God to speak to them every day, they could:

be wise and look for something else: in Trier is the Lord God's coat, in Aachen are Joseph's pants and Our Lady's chemise; go there and squander your money, buy indulgences and the pope's second-hand junk; these are valuable things.[43]

To the end, Luther was challenging the deep-rooted traditions and devotional practices of medieval Christianity and proposing instead a religion of the word. Elector Johann described him as a man 'through whom God's word has again been brought to light'.[44] His conscience was captive to the scriptures and he had no doubts about the authenticity of his message. But the old church tradition continued as before and pope succeeded pope.

CHAPTER FOURTEEN

Luther's challenge to the church and society of today

Luther's challenge to the church of his time was marked above all by a prodigious output in quill and ink, but also by salvoes from a tower (even two towers), journeys in disguise and dramatic confrontations. There was the excitement of missives-turned-missiles, though the notorious hand to hand combats were few. Luther challenged the church in its structures and its theology, the heart of his theology being his doctrine of justification. The question is whether as regards both structures and theology he can now issue a challenge across the centuries, diachronically. It is a real question not only for the Catholic Church but also for today's secularism and especially for Lutheran theologians in their attempt to formulate a Lutheran theology for a secular culture. According to Mark Mattes in *The Role of Justification in Contemporary Theology*,[1] some Lutheran theologians accommodate the doctrine of justification to goals aligned with secular modernity – endeavour to make it 'relevant' today – while others challenge secularity. (He devotes chapters to five prominent theologians.) For them the challenge has to do with how justification relates to their Lutheran theologies; the Catholic Church has its own theology of justification (since Trent) and the theological challenge is basically to assess how that may be refined, deepened, by understanding Luther's doctrine more fully, especially in light of the *Joint Statement on Justification* of the Lutheran World Federation and the Catholic Church of 1999. As to structures, the possibility of challenge will be considered below.

The Catholic Church has changed in important ways since the sixteenth century. It has outgrown the perspective of a European institution, becoming more authentically 'catholic' as it has spread throughout the world. Hundreds of years of missionary work, inaugurated to a large extent by the programme of renewal mandated by Trent (the so-called Counter Reformation), have made a great difference to what it means to be a Catholic as an acculturation process occurs through the meeting of traditional Catholic culture with the cultures of far-flung indigenous societies. This has been more the case since Vatican II – the initial Catholic missionary movement sought to spread a European Catholicism worldwide.

At the same time, the world of the sixteenth century has given way to a new and greatly enlarged one, with many cultures, political systems and religions. The civic culture which was once 'European' has now grown to be that of the 'Western world' and is one to which the rest of the world seems drawn, perhaps fatalistically, given that culture's secular orientation, addiction to consumerism and, in various areas, indifference to ecological warnings. Like the Lutherans, the Catholic Church has to establish how it addresses the secular world.

The church today

At the simplest level of analysis, Luther's challenge to the 'papal' church has been dealt with. He called for a general council in 1520; there have been three such councils since then. While the revolutionary character of Vatican II is rightly lauded, it may be forgotten that the difference between the perspective of that council and that of its predecessor of little less than a century depended in a major way on the demise of the Papal States. Blessed Pius IX, who built a cigarette factory in Rome to give employment, was a temporal ruler as well as being Peter's successor. The remains of the sixteenth-century Customs Post at the boundary of the Papal States can still be seen on the Via Aurelia at Capalbio in the Province of Grosseto. The days of papal alliances with other European powers are long gone. The quaintly armed and accoutred Swiss Guard is a conveniently romantic reminder of a body which in the days of Julius II was of lethal purpose. These are the externals, as is the diminutive Vatican state; the transformation of the papacy for those who have not known anything but its present mode of being can be very difficult to envisage. It is safe to say that Luther could never have envisaged it, especially the role of papal ministry as it is filled by Pope Francis. The filling of the role is of course to an extent a matter of personal discernment but it is a role defined also by the theology of Vatican II, and has for its setting a theology of the church and its life which meets the challenge Luther posed in his day to a remarkably identifiable extent. The council went a long way to satisfying his call for a council as a representative body; there were lay and also Protestant 'observers' there and it turned out that the latter had significant influence. Today, instead of offering more and more indulgences to mitigate the punishment due to sin, Pope Francis speaks of God's mercy, echoing, it has to be said, Pope John XXIII's discourse at the opening of Vatican II.

Luther would still of course have great difficulty with the concept of papal infallibility, but that decree of Vatican I, in its unanticipated closing session, was subtly fenced about by the later council taking up the issue of the local church and its leadership. Luther's anti-Roman stance was to an extent a provincially German one – and important for his hope of a fair trial – but there was a prophetic element also in his seeking what might be called devolution of power. Even if up to now in the church centralisation has been something of a problem, the importance of the local church is acknowledged to an increasing degree, especially by Pope Francis. And Vatican II went a long way towards reforming another aspect of the hierarchical nature of the church in recognising the importance of the common priesthood of the baptised.

The baptismal priesthood had assumed a dominant role when Luther's theology of the church excluded visible headship, thus eliminating a hierarchy; when Vatican II spoke of the church 'constituted and organised as a society in the present world' (*Lumen Gentium* 8), it still recognised the baptismal priesthood as fundamental to its structure as the people of God. In fact, it gave a fuller account of 'the priesthood of all believers than one can find in *The Book of Concord*', according to Harry McSorley.[2] By seeing all ministries in the context of the church as mystery, rather than simply speaking about a visible, hierarchical institution, the council was able to maintain a distinction between the common and ministerial priesthood in terms of a difference not only of degree but of kind (No. 10). This highlights the difference between Luther's denial of visible headship and the Catholic position; it is not simply a case of repudiation of his belief, there is a deeper principle here arising from the council's reliance on the concept of mystery for its theology of the church.

In the end the Pauline teaching about the body of Christ is fundamental to the theology of the church and of its liturgy. As the constitution on the liturgy says:

> The liturgy is considered as an exercise of the priestly office of Jesus Christ. In the liturgy the sanctification of man is signified by signs perceptible to the senses, and is effected in a way which corresponds with each of these signs; in the liturgy the whole public worship is performed by the mystical body of Jesus Christ, that is, by the head and his members. (*Sacrosanctum Concilium* 7)

A downward movement, 'sanctification', as well as an upward movement, 'worship', is evident in this description of the liturgy. Luther simply saw the mass as an expression of God's promise of forgiveness.

The theologies of the liturgy in the Catholic Church and in Luther are derived from two different theologies of the church, which may be summarised in one case as that of the mystical body doctrine and the other the community of the justified (as detailed in Chapter Eight). Nevertheless, Luther's pastoral reform of the liturgy in his day challenged the liturgical life of the church at that time. There is a sense in which aspects of his challenge, repudiated at the Council of Trent (though he was not named) were accepted as valid at Vatican II (though again he was not mentioned). At Trent, the vernacular in the mass liturgy was already an issue for delegates from some countries, but it was decided at a session in September 1562[3] that it was not expedient that the vernacular should be used 'everywhere' and the proposal that mass should be celebrated in the vernacular *only* was condemned. This allowed Vatican II to be consistent with past decrees in introducing the vernacular as a favoured option.

As many are aware, the liturgical reforms mandated by Vatican II were consonant with much of what Luther had actually introduced in his day – the use of the vernacular, prominence given to the liturgy of the word, greater participation by the faithful, especially through music, communion under both kinds – all of which can leave the more traditionally minded alarmed by an apparent surrender to Protestant theological principles. But the Catholic Church could and did introduce a renewal of the liturgy which made it look very similar to that of Luther's reform without embracing his theology of the church. Luther's challenge at the liturgical level was met in a very discerning way by the council.

But it is true also that Luther has been seen as one whose original challenge now provides inspiration for both Catholic and ecumenically minded Lutheran and other Protestant scholars in their search for an ecumenical theology of the eucharist. Here considerable ecumenical convergence has emerged. This has come about through study of the early liturgy which allows scholars to present the theology of the eucharistic liturgy in terms which avoid the medieval pre-occupation with 'real presence'. It is ironic that Luther should have so energetically defended this doctrine against the reductionist views of Zwingli and others when, following a period of ecumenical consensus in various bilateral dialogues on the real presence, today the scholars of different churches have moved on from discussion of this doctrine and concentrate instead on agreeing a way of describing the eucharist as a celebration of the paschal mystery, a dynamic rather than a static view of the liturgy that takes account of the church's life in Christ, its participation in his mysteries.

The extent to which Luther's challenge has been met in relation to the place of scripture in the life of the church can be assessed at the level of ecumenical agreement by referring to the Fourth World Conference of the Faith and Order Commission of the World Council of Churches at Montreal in 1963 and at a practical level by referring to the growing interest in meditative reading of scripture, *lectio divina*, which has become widespread throughout the church. Luther's *sola scriptura* principle could not in the most literal way be accepted by the Catholic Church, but the members of the Faith and Order Commission (which included representatives of the Catholic Church) meeting at Montreal were able to agree on a way to overcome the polarity which arose from Luther's principle. According to it, no human authority could claim to give an interpretation of scripture which would become a definitive part of the church's teaching, its normative tradition. Montreal made a distinction between the gospel itself (Luther's *sola scriptura*) and how it is transmitted through the ages by the use of the terms 'Tradition' and the 'traditions':

> By the term Tradition is meant the gospel itself, transmitted from generation to generation in and by the church, Christ himself present in the life of the church. By tradition is meant the traditionary process. The term traditions is used in two senses, to indicate both the diversity of the forms of expression and also what we call confessional traditions, for instance the Lutheran tradition.[4]

While the language used is technical and subtle, the reality underpinning it is that Christ himself is the final revelation of all that is contained in the scriptures. The statement from the Vatican Council's *Constitution on Revelation* (2) two years after Montreal, 'Christ ... is the mediator and sum total of Revelation', gave significant confirmation to the agreement.

Luther's challenge to the church today, in the terms of this study, necessarily relates to the same church as five hundred years ago, the papal church. It is true, however, that ecumenical progress over at least half a century has recognised – as Bishop Elchinger said at Vatican II – that where the Spirit is, there too is the church,[5] and a fruitful dialogue over many years made it possible for the Lutheran World Federation to make a joint statement with the Catholic Church in 1999 on the issue of justification which Luther raised five hundred years ago. The churches' perception now seems to be that Luther's challenge still centres today on justification and that this is an issue relevant to all the churches in their programme of evangelisation. In a recently published book jointly authored by Cardinal Walter Kasper and the Lutheran Bishop Ulrich Wilckens, *Weckrufökumene*, Kasper acknowledges that

> in our day many do not understand what is meant by the word 'justification', or are not really interested. However, if we go more deeply into the question we find that there is now more to be concerned about than was the case in the sixteenth century. For the question today for many people is not whether justification is by faith alone or (also) by good works. Today, many ask if we need to be justified by God or if we can resolve the issue ourselves pedagogically, psychologically, sociologically, politically or technologically. In the modern world, awareness of being lost because of sin has to a large extent disappeared and instead the conviction of the possibility of self-justification (*Selbstrechfertigung*) has become predominant.[6]

Kasper is rightly concerned about the contemporary problem of religious indifference and lists the various approaches people adopt for finding fulfilment – from the pedagogical to the technological. He feels that an ecumenical theological approach is needed and cannot be simple; the 'wake-up call' is for new thinking about the salvific meaning of the death and resurrection of Christ in order to set out the ethical consequences for the Christian life in a deeply uncertain world.[7] He holds that the churches should call a spiritually tired and sluggish world to repentance and decisive action against pessimism and should hold up the torch of hope for the coming kingdom of God and his righteousness – in other words that the churches should take an eschatological stance, challenging secularism.[8] His co-author, Wilckens, adopted a similar view, calling for the churches to profess 'publicly' faith in the Resurrection of Christ.[9]

To assess how Luther's theology of justification may be relevant to today's uncertain world, it will be helpful to examine that post-Christian ethos in which, as Kasper says, people have turned to so many ways of finding fulfilment without the resource of religion.

Religion in today's world

As mentioned at the beginning of this work, commentators such as Dilthey, Troeltsch and Weber held that a religious culture arose from Reformation theology and has had a formative influence on the over-all culture of today's Western world. While Dilthey saw the autocracy of the human person, an appreciation of the secular world and the fostering of a new kind of personal religion emerging from the writings of Luther, Troeltsch and Weber speculated about the effects of Protestantism on the economic outlook and ethics in the centuries after the Reformation. In all three writers, secularism implied awareness of the transcendent giving way to focusing only on this world.

There are various identifiable reasons why this occurred, including the heritage of the whole Reformation period. Taylor begins his *A Secular Age* with the deceptively simple question, 'Why was it virtually impossible not to believe in God in, say 1500, while in 2000 many of us find this not only easy, but even inescapable?'[10] Later, he asks: 'what stopped people (that is, almost everybody) from being able to adopt stances of unbelief in 1500?'[11] The answer for him is 'the enchanted world ... a cosmos of spirits and forces, some of them evil and destructive'. He sees the beginning of secularisation in the Reformation as 'an engine of disenchantment' and holds that a consequence of it was the rise of humanism, so that, overall, secularisation was a consequence of anthropocentric versions of religion arising from the Reformation. It is interesting that he traces this path back to Calvin and makes no mention of Luther.[12]

Carlos Eire suggests that 'three essential reconfigurations of reality',[13] going back to the religion of Luther but continuing in the later Reformation, have produced the secularism which he prefers to call desacralisation. These are, first, how matter relates to spirit, second, how the natural relates to the supernatural and third, how the living relate to the dead. If Luther and later Protestantism were the cause of

desacralisation, it needs to be established how his theology of justification can still be relevant, and it would appear to be a difficult task.
For example, Luther's elimination of masses for the dead did create
a hiatus between this world and the next which did violence to the
sensibilities of many of his contemporaries who were devoted to the
saints and prayed for the souls in purgatory. But he never dismissed
the reality of the other world, spoke to his little son about the joys
of heaven and honoured the memory of such saints as Elizabeth of
Hungary, as well as being respectful, even devout, in his regard for
the Virgin Mary. Today, however, the secular world is hardly aware
of those traditions and Catholics, influenced by that culture, are challenged to maintain awareness of them. As regards relations between
the natural and the supernatural, the very terms go back to earlier
scholasticism, to a more positive view of human nature and a linking
of the two which was at ease with irruptions of the sacred into human
life by way of miracles. Luther would have none of that, believing
that these 'signs' were for the 'ignorant, unbelieving crowd', but with
belief in the gospel 'what do we want them for?'[14] That does play into
the reductionist approach to miracles common in today's world of
empirical science.

But Luther's tenacious defence of the 'real presence' in the eucharist shows his belief that the sacred can be found in human life
and he cannot be faulted for the dichotomy between matter and spirit
which today leads some to reduce mind to the physical processes of
the brain. Going back beyond Descartes, it can be seen in Zwingli
and in Karlstadt, Luther's opponents with regard to eucharistic presence, while Luther remained convinced of the importance of the sacraments.

The relation between Luther and secularism is a complex one;
centuries of cultural change lie in between and include the rise of
modern science and the Enlightenment. Luther's religion of the word
always contained an element of resistance against the process of secularisation, to the extent that in the seventeenth century a form of
Lutheranism, Pietism, arose spontaneously to counteract an interpre-

tation of Lutheran orthodoxy influenced by the Enlightenment. At the other end of the spectrum from rationalism, Luther invoked his theology of the word to condemn superstitious practices, yet these are to be found throughout Christianity today. Catholic theology is committed to the view that all that is needed of God's self-revelation is contained in the person of Christ and in the scriptures' record, yet many look for new revelations elsewhere.

In the discussion at Vatican II of the preparatory text, the schema of the *Pastoral Constitution on the Church in the Modern World (Gaudium et Spes)*, tensions emerged among the drafting groups in relation to the theology of the human person as image of God. As summarised by Joseph Ratzinger before he was made a cardinal, some draft versions were committed to an optimistic view of human nature which was opposed by 'theologians from the German-speaking countries', though 'it was not a question of imposing a pessimistic view of man ... because of a certain correspondence with some forms of Lutheran thought'. He denied Lutheran influence but at the same time Lutheran theology of the person was closer to German minds, compared with, as he noted also, the French understanding.[15] In fact, Luther's theology of justification (based on a theology of the person which Catholic theology does not share because of the denial of free will) was regarded in a number of Catholic–Lutheran dialogues as offering ecumenical possibilities more than a decade before the international statement, the *Joint Declaration on Justification* between the Catholic Church and the Lutheran World Federation, was finalised in 1999. In the final stages of its formulation Cardinal Ratzinger had a significant role. The central truth, namely the grace of Christ, on which the two sides declared agreement, was quoted by Pope Francis on October 31st 2016, at Lund in Sweden:

> The spiritual experience of Martin Luther challenges us to remember that apart from God we can do nothing. 'How can I get a propitious God?' This is the question that haunted Luther. In effect, the question of a just relationship with God is the decisive question for our lives. As we know, Luther

encountered that propitious God in the Good News of Jesus, incarnate, dead and risen. With the concept "by grace alone", he reminds us that God always takes the initiative, prior to any human response, even as he seeks to awaken that response. The doctrine of justification thus expresses the essence of human existence before God.[16]

The pope's two final sentences are interesting in that they speak of what actually happens, that grace brings about a just relationship with God. There is no mention of human nature being entirely corrupt or simply defective. These are theological theories on which agreement is lacking, but they are simply theories, though important ones on which ecumenical agreement needs to be found.

The agreement on justification does allow an ecumenical understanding of Luther's application of it to the Christian life in his principle *simul justus et peccator*, that the justified person remains a sinner. As discussed in the previous chapter, Luther's theology of justification depended on seeing the Christian life from an eschatological perspective; while he talked of a deification of the justified sinner, he emphasised that

> In the meantime, as long as we live here, we are carried and nourished in the bosom of the mercy and the longsuffering of God until the body of sin is abolished and we are raised up as new creatures in that great day. Then there shall be new heavens and a new earth in which righteousness shall dwell.[17]

Elsewhere he said: 'none should imagine that such fullness can be attained in this life'.[18]

Catholic theology and practice acknowledge that all members of the church are in this situation of incompletion in their spiritual journey, though the traditional theology of merit tended to highlight the positive element of holiness deriving from prayer and the sacraments – the *justus* aspect of the Christian state. It is true also, however, that the church's official prayer, the liturgy of the hours, allocates Ps 51 (50), 'a Plea for Mercy', to morning prayer on Friday and prayers such as the *Confiteor*, the *Our Father* and the *Hail Mary* all make a similar plea. Likewise, *The Jesus Prayer* is characteristic of the Orthodox Church.

There is another theme more fundamental to the liturgy, its eschatological perspective, and there is common ground here with Luther's vision of the Christian life. The communion rite in the mass puts the immediate preparation for meeting the Lord in the sacrament into the context of greater expectancy of the coming of the kingdom and of final union with the Lord at the banquet of the lamb. It gives a particular tone to this anticipation by introducing the prayer, 'Lord, I am not worthy', thus recognising the need for God's mercy while reaching out to the coming of Christ in glory. The challenge to believers who participate in the celebration is to deepen awareness of this perspective so as develop an appropriate spirituality for coping with life in relationship with the world.

Such a spiritual outlook makes a difference in the way many issues are perceived. There are obvious practical reasons why ecological issues are considered vital today, but the person of profound eschatological outlook sees these issues in light of the end or *telos* of creation, that humanity and all of creation is meant to return to God through Christ: 'When all things are subjected (to him), then the Son himself will also be subjected to him who put all things under him, that God may be everything to everyone' (1 Cor 15:28). The believer thus motivated can be empowered for counter-cultural activity in a way that can hardly be possible for one with a secularist outlook.

The challenge Luther posed to the church of his day in *De votis monasticis*[19] involved a judgment based on what was, not on what could be, and he no doubt failed to recognise examples of genuine vocations. Today, at a time when the number of religious in the Western world is declining rapidly, he could well challenge those who profess to be believers to look more deeply into their lives as people who live with the tension between being *justus et peccator* and, if inspired by a further grace from Christ (through the Spirit), opt as vowed religious for a way of life which brings Christ's kingdom to a special degree of realisation in their personal lives. This would be a choice made while recognising personal unworthiness. Because of his theology of human nature, for Luther this would be a rare grace, but in the Catholic view it should not be so rare among those with a truly eschatological perspective, because of a positive orientation towards the good in human nature, as Aquinas says.[20] Communities with such orientation are emerging and it is not accidental that one of these (Bose in Italy) has a cock at the entrance as a symbol of looking towards the dawn. It could be asked what difference greater eschatological awareness would make to the number and kind of vocations there are in the church today, at least in the West, where it appears that vocations arise sometimes among those who collapse the tension mentioned above and tend to identify the church with the kingdom of God. Inevitably triumphalist tendencies manifest themselves in this situation.

In his reply to Erasmus in 1525, Luther had acknowledged: 'unlike all the rest you alone have attacked the real issue, the essence of the matter in dispute, and have not wearied me with irrelevancies about the papacy, purgatory, indulgences, and such like trifles (for trifles they are rather than basic issues)'. For Catholic theology, the papacy and its place in the theology of the church is far from irrelevant and this study has been unsparingly critical of Luther as someone who succumbed, for complex reasons including health, to the temptation to an apocalyptic dismissal of the papacy. The issue for Luther was the unfree will arising from the corruption of human nature, while the assessment of Erasmus was more positive in accordance with Catholic tradition. It would be difficult, then, to accept the correctness of a challenge from Luther in those stark terms.

At the same time, Erasmus' common-sense approach may have tended to reduce God to an equal partner in dialogue with humankind, while Luther could be charged with making the human person, made in the image of God, something of a mannequin which God may choose, or not choose, to bring to life by an act of irresistible grace. His theology could make the human being a mule ridden by God or the devil, as Oberman put it.[21] Erasmus was educated in the tradition of the 'imitation of Christ' and his spirituality was one of warm devotion to Christ encountered in the gospels; his humanism made him a humane Christian who avoided extremes in views and feelings. Luther's spirituality was equally Christocentric, but his Christ was the *deus crucifixus,* who by his sufferings revealed both the hidden God and the enormity of human sin. Luther's spirituality was passionate, encompassing a whole range of feelings, ranging originally from hatred of a God whose justice he could not satisfy to the joy akin to rebirth on recognising the God of mercy.

It may be that today's widespread dismissal of God on the one hand and religious fundamentalism on the other are traceable to rejection of both of these understandings of the divine-human relationship. There are fundamentalists whose unsophisticated idea of justification causes them to enquire of people if they are 'saved', while, as Kasper noted, the secular world is indifferent in that regard. There is also a not uncommon Catholic view that one need not be concerned over the issues which Erasmus and Luther believed were crucial but could not agree upon and perhaps this indicates a failure to engage at a deep level with issues which are crucial for one's spiritual development. It is easier not to think either of growth in merit or minor sinful reverses. When linked with sporadic religious practice, this may be called de-traditionalisation and indicates, at best, the lack of a theological foundation for spirituality, or, at worst, secularism encroaching on people's lives. There seems to be a need for a theology of the human person adequate to understanding the complexity of human life and accompanying ethical issues, which scientific studies, biological and psychological, have revealed. Such a project could bring about a theology which was beyond the grasp of both Erasmus and Luther, resolve their dispute and provide a basis on which to bring the gospel to today's secular society.

In these circumstances, the approach of this study has been to look, as Pope Francis has done, for fruitful theological content in Luther's theory of justification as an expression of the activity of the gracious Christ, whatever the nature of the one to be justified may be.

This has meant analysing closely what is often simply considered an example of his paradoxical utterances, his *simul justus et peccator*, in the theology of justification. It would be easier follow a different path and dismiss Luther and his theology as irrelevant to today's world or as a divisive and destructive force in the progress of the church towards its end, the kingdom of God. But seeing what is best in another Christian tradition is at the heart of the ecumenical movement. At Lund, Pope Francis pointed to the importance of 'forgiveness, renewal and reconciliation' among Christians in order to proclaim the message of God's mercy in the world and to the world. Otherwise, he said, 'the Christian faith is incomplete'.[22]

Ninety-Five Theses[1]

Out of love for the truth and the desire to bring it to light, the following propositions will be discussed at Wittenberg, under the presidency of the Reverend Father Martin Luther, Master of Arts and of Sacred Theology, and Lecturer in Ordinary on the same at that place. Wherefore he requests that those who are unable to be present and debate orally with us, may do so by letter.

In the name our Lord Jesus Christ. Amen.

1. Our Lord and master Jesus Christ, when he said *Poenitentiam agite*, willed that the whole life of believers should be repentance. 2. This word cannot be understood to mean sacramental penance, i.e. confession and satisfaction, which is administered by the priests. 3. Yet it means not inward repentance only; nay, there is no inward repentance which does not outwardly work divers mortifications of the flesh. 4. The penalty [of sin], therefore, continues so long as hatred of self continues; for this is the true inward repentance, and continues until our entrance into the kingdom of heaven. 5. The pope does not intend to remit, and cannot remit any penalties other than those which he has imposed either by his own authority or by that of the canons. 6. The pope cannot remit any guilt, except by declaring that it has been remitted by God and by assenting to God's remission; though, to be sure, he may grant remission in cases reserved to his judgment. If his right to grant remission in such cases were despised, the guilt would remain entirely unforgiven. 7. God remits guilt to no one whom he does not, at the same time, humble in all things and

bring into subjection to his vicar, the priest. 8. The penitential canons are imposed only on the living, and, according to them, nothing should be imposed on the dying. 9. Therefore the Holy Spirit in the pope is kind to us, because in his decrees he always makes exception of the article of death and of necessity. 10. Ignorant and wicked are the doings of those priests who, in the case of the dying, reserve canonical penances for purgatory. 11. This changing of the canonical penalty to the penalty of purgatory is quite evidently one of the tares that were sown while the bishops slept. 12. In former times the canonical penalties were imposed not after, but before absolution, as tests of true contrition. 13. The dying are freed by death from all penalties; they are already dead to canonical rules, and have a right to be released from them. 14. The imperfect health [of soul], that is to say, the imperfect love, of the dying brings with it, of necessity, great fear; and the smaller the love, the greater is the fear. 15. This fear and horror is sufficient of itself alone (to say nothing of other things) to constitute the penalty of purgatory, since it is very near to the horror of despair. 16. Hell, purgatory, and heaven seem to differ as do despair, almost-despair, and the assurance of safety. 17. With souls in purgatory it seems necessary that horror should grow less and love increase. 18. It seems unproved, either by reason or scripture, that they are outside the state of merit, that is to say, of increasing love. 19. Again, it seems unproved that they, or at least that all of them, are certain or assured of their own blessedness, though we may be quite certain of it. 20. Therefore by 'full remission of all penalties' the pope means not actually 'of all,' but only of those imposed by himself. 21. Therefore those preachers of indulgences are in error, who say that by the pope's indulgences a man is freed from every penalty, and saved. 22. Whereas he remits to souls in purgatory no penalty which, according to the canons, they would have had to pay in this life. 23. If it is at all possible to grant to any one the remission of all penalties whatsoever, it is certain that this remission can be granted only to the most perfect, that is, to the very fewest. 24. It must needs be, therefore, that the greater part of the people are deceived by that indiscriminate and high-sounding promise of release from penalty. 25. The power which the pope has, in a general way, over purgatory, is just like the power which any bishop or curate has, in a special way, within his own diocese or parish. 26. The pope does well when he grants remission to souls [in purgatory], not by the power of the keys (which he does not possess), but by way of intercession. 27. They preach only human doctrines who say that so soon as the penny jingles into the money-box, the soul flies out [of purgatory]. 28. It is certain that when the penny jingles into the money-box, gain and avarice can be increased, but the result of the intercession of the church is in the power of God alone. 29. Who knows whether all the souls in purgatory wish to be bought out of it, as in the legend of St Severinus and Paschal. 30. No one is sure that his own contrition is sincere; much less that he has attained full remission. 31. Rare as is the man that is truly penitent, so rare is also the man who truly buys indulgences, i.e. such men are most rare. 32. They will be condemned eternally, together with their teachers, who believe themselves sure of their salvation because they have letters of pardon. 33. Men must be on their guard against those who say that the pope's pardons are that inestimable gift of God by which man is reconciled to him. 34. For these 'graces of pardon' concern only the penalties of sacramental satisfaction, and these are appointed by man. 35. They preach no Christian doctrine who teach that contrition is not necessary in those who intend to buy souls out of purgatory or to buy confessionalia. 36. Every truly repentant Christian has a right to full remission of penalty and guilt, even without letters of pardon. 37. Every true Christian, whether living or dead, has part in all the blessings of Christ and the church; and this is granted him by God, even without letters of pardon. 38. Nevertheless, the remission and participation [in the blessings of the church] which are granted by the pope are in no way to be despised, for they are, as I have said, the declaration of divine remission. 39. It is most difficult, even for the very keenest theologians, at one and the same time to commend to the people the abundance of pardons and [the need of] true contrition. 40. True contrition seeks and loves penalties, but liberal pardons only relax penalties and cause them to be hated, or at least, furnish an occasion [for hating them]. 41. Apostolic pardons are to be preached with caution, lest the people may falsely think them preferable to other good works of love. 42. Christians are to be taught that the pope does not intend the buying of pardons to be compared in any way to works of mercy. 43. Christians are to be taught that he who gives to the poor or lends to the needy does a better work than buying pardons. 44. Because love grows by works of love, and man becomes better; but by pardons man does not grow better, only more free from penalty. 45. Christians are to be taught that he who sees a man in need, and passes him by, and gives [his money] for pardons, purchases not the indulgences of the pope, but the indignation of God. 46. Christians are to be taught that unless they have more than they need, they are bound to keep back what is necessary for their own families, and by no means to squander it on pardons. 47. Christians are to be taught that the buying of pardons is a matter of free will, and not of commandment. 48. Christians are to be taught that the pope, in granting pardons, needs, and therefore desires, their devout prayer for him more than the money they bring. 49. Christians are to be taught that the pope's pardons are useful, if they do not put their trust in them; but altogether harmful, if through them they lose their fear of God. 50. Christians are to be taught that if the pope knew the exactions of the pardon-preachers, he would rather that St Peter's church should go to ashes, than that it should be built up with the skin, flesh and bones of his sheep. 51. Christians are to be taught that it would be the pope's wish, as it is his duty, to give of his own money to very many of those from whom certain hawkers of pardons cajole money, even though the church of St Peter might have to be sold. 52. The assurance of salvation by letters of pardon is vain, even though the commissary, nay, even though the pope himself, were to stake his soul upon it. 53. They are enemies of Christ and of the pope, who bid the word of God be altogether silent in some churches, in order that pardons may be preached in others. 54. Injury is done the word of God when, in the same sermon, an equal or a longer time is spent on pardons than on this word. 55. It must be the intention of the pope that if pardons, which are a very small thing, are celebrated with one bell, with single processions and ceremonies, then the gospel, which is the very greatest thing, should be preached with a hundred bells, a hundred processions, a hundred ceremonies. 56. The 'treasures of the church,' out of which the pope grants indulgences, are not sufficiently named or known among the people of Christ. 57. That they are not temporal treasures is certainly evident, for many of the vendors do not pour out such treasures so easily, but only gather them. 58. Nor are they the merits of Christ and the saints, for even without the pope, these always work grace for the inner man, and the cross, death, and hell for the outward man. 59. St Lawrence said that the treasures of the church were the church's poor, but he spoke according to the usage of the word in his own time. 60. Without rashness we say that the keys of the church, given by Christ's merit, are that treasure. 61. For it is clear that for the remission of penalties and of reserved cases, the power of the pope is of itself sufficient. 62. The true treasure of the church is the most holy gospel of the glory and the grace of God. 63. But this treasure is naturally most odious, for it makes the first to be last. 64. On the other hand, the treasure of indulgences is naturally most acceptable, for it makes the last to be first. 65. Therefore the treasures of the gospel are nets with which they formerly were wont to fish for men of riches. 66. The treasures of the indulgences are nets with which they now fish for the riches of men. 67. The indulgences which the preachers cry as the 'greatest graces' are known to be truly such, in so far as they promote gain. 68. Yet they are in truth the very smallest graces compared with the grace of God and the piety of the Cross. 69. Bishops and curates are bound to admit the commissaries of apostolic pardons, with all reverence. 70. But still more are they bound to strain all their eyes and attend with all their ears, lest these men preach their own dreams instead of the commission of the pope. 71. He who speaks against the truth of apostolic pardons, let him be anathema and accursed! 72. But he who guards against the lust and license of the pardon-preachers, let him be blessed! 73. The pope justly thunders against those who, by any art, contrive the injury of the traffic in pardons. 74. But much more does he intend to thunder against those who use the pretext of pardons to contrive the injury of holy love and truth. 75. To think the papal pardons so great that they could absolve a man even if he had committed an impossible sin and violated the Mother of God – this is madness. 76. We say, on the contrary, that the papal pardons are not able to remove the very least of venial sins, so far as its guilt is concerned. 77. It is said that even St Peter, if he were now Pope, could not bestow greater graces; this is blasphemy against St Peter and against the pope. 78. We say, on the contrary, that even the present pope, and any pope at all, has greater graces at his disposal; to wit, the gospel, powers, gifts of healing, etc. as it is written in 1 Cor 12. 79. To say that the cross, emblazoned with the papal arms, which is set up [by the preachers of indulgences], is of equal worth with the Cross of Christ, is blasphemy. 80. The bishops, curates and theologians who allow such talk to be spread among the people, will have an account to render. 81. This unbridled preaching of pardons makes it no easy matter, even for learned men, to rescue the reverence due to the pope from slander, or even from the shrewd questionings of the laity. 82. To wit: 'Why does not the pope empty purgatory, for the sake of holy love and of the dire need of the souls that are there, if he redeems an infinite number of souls for the sake of miserable money with which to build a church?' The former reasons would be most just; the latter is most trivial. 83. Again: 'Why are mortuary and anniversary masses for the dead continued, and why does he not return or permit the withdrawal of the endowments founded on their behalf, since it is wrong to pray for the redeemed?' 84. Again: 'What is this new piety of God and the pope, that for money they allow a man who is impious and their enemy to buy out of purgatory the pious soul of a friend of God, and do not rather, because of that pious and beloved soul's own need, free it for pure love's sake?' 85. Again: 'Why are the penitential canons long since in actual fact and through disuse abrogated and dead, now satisfied by the granting of indulgences, as though they were still alive and in force?' 86. Again: 'Why does not the pope, whose wealth is today greater than the riches of the richest, build just this one church of St Peter with his own money, rather than with the money of poor believers?' 87. Again: 'What is it that the pope remits, and what participation does he grant to those who, by perfect contrition, have a right to full remission and participation?' 88. Again: 'What greater blessing could come to the church than if the pope were to do a hundred times a day what he now does once, and bestow on every believer these remissions and participations?' 89. Since the pope, by his pardons, seeks the salvation of souls rather than money, why does he suspend the indulgences and pardons granted heretofore, since these have equal efficacy? 90. To repress these arguments and scruples of the laity by force alone, and not to resolve them by giving reasons, is to expose the church and the pope to the ridicule of their enemies, and to make Christians unhappy. 91. If, therefore, pardons were preached according to the spirit and mind of the pope, all these doubts would be readily resolved; nay, they would not exist. 92. Away, then, with all those prophets who say to the people of Christ, 'Peace, peace,' and there is no peace! 93. Blessed be all those prophets who say to the people of Christ, 'Cross, cross,' and there is no cross! 94. Christians are to be exhorted that they be diligent in following Christ, their head, through penalties, deaths, and hell; 95. And thus be confident of entering into heaven rather through many tribulations, than through the assurance of peace.

Augustine's theory of knowledge

Eugène Portalié, in *A Guide to the Thought of St Augustine,* stresses the idea that for Augustine 'the understanding has need for the light of God, its sun, to attain truth just as the will needs the grace of God, the supreme good, to attain virtue'.[1] This parallel is important because it means that for Augustine, the illumination of the soul in intellectual knowledge has the same effectiveness as that which he attributes to grace in the moral order. For him intellectual ideas are totally different from the inferior knowledge given by the senses. In *Solloquia* I.viii.15, he said that intellectual truths cannot be understood unless they are illuminated by another as by their sun. In *De Trinitate* XIV. xv.21 he describes 'this incorporeal light as a transcription which transports eternal truth from the divine book into our soul, where it is imprinted, just as a seal leaves its mark on wax'. In the *City of God* x.2 he develops the idea that the word is this light of every soul. In *De Magistro* xi.38, he identifies this word as the indwelling Christ: 'Our real teacher is he who is listened to and is said to dwell in the inner man, namely Christ, the unchangeable power and eternal wisdom of God'. 'Illumination' was also an important concept in the theology of the Eastern Fathers, especially in relation to baptism. In his *Commentary on the Second Letter to the Corinthians,* Cyril of Alexandria uses terminology very similar to that of Augustine: 'since the only-begotten shone upon us, we have been transformed into the word, who gives life to all things' (5:5-6). He speaks of the righteousness of Christ gaining possession of the Christian, so he is treating principally of the ontological and moral condition.

The debate on free will

In considering the exchange of views between Erasmus and Luther, it is worth noting how dependent on Augustine Luther was and how problematic, even inconsistent, Augustine's stance was in relation to the theology of predestination and the relationship between predestination and free will. Thomas Allin[2] points to 'two distinct theologies' in Augustine, an earlier and a later in relation to Christian anthropology. While the later one is couched in terms of 'foreknowing' in the Western epistemological sense, the earlier follows the Eastern tradition of deification (which had made its way from Eastern theology to the West). The basic concept here is not that of 'knowing' in the later sense, but that of 'choosing' humanity for participation in God's own life as described in 2 Pet 1:4. The foundation for this process is outlined in Eph 1:4, where Paul uses predestinarian language: 'God chose us in Christ before the foundation of the world to be holy and blameless before him in love'. Here predestination (as in Rom 8:28-30 and 1 Cor 2:7) has to be understood in semitic terms as God looking lovingly on his creation and calling humankind to participate in the divine life by being 'in Christ'. Augustine uses terms of this kind in *Tractate* 81 on John's Gospel: 'He loved us before the foundation of the world that we also should be his children with the Only Begotten'. He also uses the related Pauline term 'mystical body': 'we have been made his members: he is the head, we are his body' (*Sermo* 32).

As the concept of grace will be treated differently by Erasmus and Luther, Augustine's teaching on the subject is of particular interest. The first point to note is the Neoplatonist framework of much of his thinking. He saw human existence as having come from God by creation and tending to return to God as creation's final resting place.[3] Grace, then, is the work of the Spirit implanting the desire for self-transcendence and enabling the act of love which constitutes real freedom. In his treatise *On Grace and Free Will* addressed to Valentinus and the monks of Adrumetum, he made the important point (which will be taken up by Erasmus): 'He, therefore, who wishes to do God's commandment, but is unable, already possesses a good will, but as yet a small and weak one' (33). In this he is not giving assent to the Pelagian heresy, according to which man can contribute to his salvation through natural ability, before receiving God's grace, but rather that man may express a desire for salvation, has the capacity to will it, and grace will cooperate with it. But he introduces a dichotomy (which Luther will rely upon): 'There is, however, always within us a free will – but it is not always good; for it is either free from righteousness when it serves sin – and then it is evil – or else it is free from sin when it serves righteousness – and then it is good' (31). This 'either or' addresses the existential situation of fallen man's condition; 'Augustine was overwhelmed by the dynamics of concupiscence, temptation and sin.... Human existence for Augustine is freedom and this freedom is clearly manifested in the power of free choice. But on another level this this freedom is held in bondage.'[4] He moves more definitely to the position of an enslaved will while still retaining the idea of cooperation, when in the same treatise he refers to Peter's declaration that he is willing to lay down his life for Christ (Jn 13:31) and subsequent betrayal:

> And who was it that had begun to give him his love, however small, but he who prepares the will, and perfects by his co-operation what he initiates by his operation? Forasmuch as in beginning he works in us that we may have the will, and in perfecting works with us when we have the will.... He operates, therefore, without us, in order that we may will; but when we will, and so will that we may act, he co-operates with us. We can, however, ourselves do nothing to effect good works of piety without him either working that we may will, or co-working when we will.

There is then some ambiguity in Augustine's approach to the subject of free will, but on the whole Augustine attests to free choice while still affirming the role of grace.

The situation becomes more complex, however, in his later writings, which reflect the 'maturer working of his mind'. As Haight re-

marks: 'Augustine's cosmic doctrine of double predestination finally undermines his conception of personal freedom'.[5] He sees God's
choice as following on foreknowledge as understood in a Western
intellectual sense: 'This and nothing else is the predestination of the
saints, God's foreknowledge and preparation of his benefits whereby
whoever is liberated is most certainly liberated' (*Gift of Perseverance*,
14, 35). But God's foreknowledge, if it is truly such, extends not only
to the saints, it must include those who will not be saved as well.
Hence there is no room for free will. Such a difference of destiny
obtains because of the fall. Because of the fall, man no longer has free
will and God has foreknown this from eternity and decreed that some
will be saved – only a few – from the *massa peccati.*

In light of this difference between the earlier and the later Augustine, the comment of the Augustinian scholar, Gerald Bonner is
not surprising: 'In pastoral practice Augustine treated men and wom-
en as having freedom of choice, whatever his deeper speculation
might be'.[6] Bonner adds: '[He] never attempted to bring together his
thoughts into a single system, in which every apparent contradiction
was reconciled'[7]

Augustine's thinking about free will underwent an important
change between the writing of *On the Free Choice of the Will* (*De libero arbitrio*) soon after his conversion in 387, while *On Grace and Free
Choice* (*De gratia et libero arbitrio*) and *On Reprimand and Grace* (*De
correptione et gratia*) came forty years later and the emphasis is on
grace rather than innate freedom. In the first book he had argued
that in order to have a good will all that one needed to do was to will
it (I.xii.26) while ten years later in *Ad Simplicianum* he had 'worked
hard in defense of the free choice of the human will, but the grace of
Christ won out' (iv.8).

NOTES

Abbreviations

WA: *D. Martin Luthers Werke, Kritische Gesamtausgabe*, 58 vols, Weimar, 1883-1929

WA BR: *D. Martin Luthers Werke, Briefwechsel*, 15 vols, Weimar, 1930

WA TR: *D. Martin Luthers Werke, Tischreden*, 6 vols, Weimar, 1912-21

LW: *Luther's Works*, J. Pelikan and H. Lehmann, eds, Philadelphia and St Louis, 1955

MPL: *Migne Patrologia Latina*

Preface

1. Scott H. Hendrix, *Martin Luther: Visionary Reformer* (New Haven: Yale UP, 2015)
2. Lyndal Roper, *Martin Luther: Renegade and Prophet* (London: The Bodley Head, 2016)
3. Peter Stanford, *Martin Luther: Catholic Dissident* (London: Hodder & Stoughton, 2017)
4. Owen Chadwick, *The Reformation* (Harmondsworth: Penguin Books, 1972)
5. *Ibid.*, 11
6. WA 6.604, 19-38
7. Martin Luther, 'Concerning the Promise of the Sacraments' in Timothy Lull ed. *Martin Luther's Basic Theological Writings* (Minneapolis: Fortress Press, 1989) 344; LW 40:131-2

Introduction

1. Lyndal Roper, *Martin Luther: Renegade and Prophet* (London: The

Bodley Head, 2016) 2

2. Brad Gregory's *The Unintended Reformation: How a Religious Revolution Secularized Society* (Harvard MA: Belknap Press, 2012) is premised by the idea that Luther did not intend his movement to be revolutionary.

3. C.f. Hubert Jedin, ed., *History of the Church*, Vol. 5 (London: Burns & Oates, 1980) 217

4. Roland Bainton, *Here I Stand* (Oxford: Lion Publishing, 1978) 384

5. WA TR 5, 6250. Luther's *Table Talk*, a record of Luther's *obiter dicta*, at table with the large group of students and others, exists in various collections, mostly recorded by students.

6. Carlos M. N. Eire, *Reformations: the Early Modern World, 1450-1650* (New Haven: Yale UP, 2016) 741-57

7. Karl Rahner, *Theological Investigations*, Vol. 4, trans. Kevin Smyth (London: Darton, Longman & Todd, 1974)

8. John Zizioulas, *Being as Communion* (Crestwood NY: St Vladimir's Seminary, 1993) 22

9. Andrew Pettegree, ed., *The Early Reformation in Europe* (Cambridge: Cambridge UP, 1992) 6

10. B. J. Kidd, ed., *Documents Illustrative of the Continental Reformation* (Oxford: Clarendon Press, 1911) 390

11. *Ibid.*, 391

Chapter One

1. R. W. Southern, *Western Society and the Church in the Middle Ages* (Harmondsworth: Pelican, 1970) 141

2. Patrick Geary, *Furta Sacra: Thefts of Relics in the Middle Ages* (Princeton: Princeton UP, 1992) 35

3. Roland Bainton, *Here I Stand* (Oxford: Lion Publishing, 1978) 25

4. John M. Todd, *Martin Luther: A Biographical Study* (London: Burns & Oates, 1964) 18

5. Timothy George, *Theology of the Reformers* (Nashville: Broadman Press, 1988) 55

6. Steven Ozment, *The Age of Reform 1250-1550: An Intellectual and Religious History of Late Medieval and Reformation Europe* (New Haven: Yale UP, 1980) 232; John M. Todd, *Martin Luther: A Biographical Study* (London: Burns & Oates, 1964) 22

7. Jane E. Strohl, 'Luther's Spiritual Journey' in Donald K. McK-

im, ed., *The Cambridge Companion to Martin Luther* (Cambridge: Cambridge UP, 2003) 150

8. Roland Bainton, *Here I Stand* (Oxford: Lion Publishing, 1978) 361

9. *Ibid.*, 41; WA 43:382; LW 4:340-1; WA TR 2:1558. In another account of the event, he said that at the words 'Eternal and living and true God' he became afraid and wanted to run from the altar but the prior constrained him, saying 'Courage, courage'. WA TR 2 1558; LW 54:156-7

10. Martin Brecht, *Martin Luther: His Road to Reformation 1483-1521*, trans. J. L. Schaaf (Philadelphia: Fortress Press, 1985) 186

11. Frank C. Senn, *Christian Liturgy: Catholic and Evangelical* (Minneapolis: Fortress Press, 1997) 259

12. WA TR 4:4174; LW 54:325

13. John M. Todd, *Martin Luther: A Biographical Study* (London: Burns & Oates, 1964) 41

14. Lyndal Roper, *Martin Luther: Renegade and Prophet* (London: The Bodley Head, 2016) 67

15. Roland Bainton, *The Reformation of the Sixteenth Century* (Boston: Bacon Press, 1985) 33

16. John M. Todd, *Martin Luther: A Biographical Study* (London: Burns & Oates, 1964) 36

17. WA TR 2 2252a, 379

Chapter Two

1. Jordanus, cited in Hastings Rashdall, *The Universities of Europe in the Middle Ages*, Vol. 1 (Oxford: Clarendon Press, 1895) 4

2. This was a more profound concept than the contemporary 'Three States' theory, which was popular in France and referred to the trio of clergy, nobles and commoners, and gave rise in modern times to the idea of the 'Fourth Estate', by which is generally meant the modern media of communication.

3. Carlos M. N. Eire, *Reformations: The Early Modern Word, 1450-1650* (New Haven: Yale UP, 2016) 742

4. Pope Innocent III, 'Sermo 2: In Consecration', MPL 217:657-8; Colin Morris, *The Papal Monarchy: The Western Church from 1050 to 1250* (Oxford: Clarendon Press, 1989) 431

5. Joseph H. Lynch, *The Medieval Church: A Brief History* (London: Longman, 1992) 320

6. Henricus Denzinger and Adolfus Schönmetzer, *Enchiridion Symbolorum Definitionum et declarationum de rebus fide et morum, Editio XXXIV* (Freiburg: Herder, 1927) 870-875

7. Hubert Jedin, ed., *History of the Church*, Vol. 4 (London: Burns & Oates, 1980) 277

8. David Knowles, *The Christian Centuries: The Middle* Ages (London: Darton, Longman & Todd, 1969) 336

9. Steven Ozment, *The Reformation in the Cities* (New Haven: Yale UP, 1975) 36

10. Thomas Madden, *Venice: A New History* (New York: Viking Penguin, 2012) 182-90

11. Cited in Steven Ozment, *The Age of Reform, 1250-1550: An Intellectual and Religious History of Late Medieval and Reformation Europe* (New Haven: Yale UP, 1980) 156

12. George H. Tavard, *Holy Writ or Holy Church: The Crisis of the Protestant Reformation* (London: Burns & Oates, 1959) 49

13. Steven Ozment, *The Age of Reform, 1250-1550: An Intellectual and Religious History of Late Medieval and Reformation Europe* (New Haven: Yale UP, 1980) 67

14. Martin Luther, cited in *ibid.*, 239

15. Peter Matheson, *The Rhetoric of the Reformation* (Edinburgh: T & T Clark, 1998) 34

16. Euan Cameron, *The European Reformation* (Oxford: Clarendon, 1991) 64

17. Desiderius Erasmus, *The Essential Erasmus*, ed. John P. Dolan (New York: Mentor Omega, 1964) 25

18. *Ibid.*, 193

19. Roland Bainton, *Here I Stand* (Oxford: Lion Publishing, 1978) 125

20. Martin Luther, cited in Heinrich Bornkamm, *Luther in Mid-Career, 1521-1530* (Philadelphia: Fortress Press, 1983) 338

21. A. G. Dickens, *The German Nation and Martin Luther* (London: Edward Arnold, 1974) 51

Chapter Three

1. Walther Köhler, cited in Roland Bainton, *Here I Stand* (Oxford: Lion Publishing, 1978) 78

2. *Ibid.*, 77

3. LW 41:232; 'Solche predigt hatte ich auch zuvor gethan hie auff

im Schlosse, wider das Ablas, Und bey Hertzog Friderich damit schlechte gnade verdienet, Denn er sein Stifft auch seer lieb hatte.' (WA 51:539.8-10:)

4. Timothy Wengert, 'Martin Luther's *Preaching an Indulgence* in January 1517', *Lutheran Quarterly,* Spring 2015, 62
5. WA 1 141
6. LW 48:43-49
7. Lyndal Roper, *Martin Luther: Renegade and Prophet* (London: The Bodley Head, 2016) 1
8. *Ibid.,* 109
9. Martin Luther, cited in Daniel Olivier, *The Trial of Luther,* trans. John Hopkins (London: Mowbray, 1978) 27
10. WA 1 529 23-26
11. Martin Luther, *Dr Martin Luthers Sämmtliche Schriften,* ed. Johann Georg Walch (St Louis: 1880-1910); WA 2 *Reformationsschriften* 1, Von Reichstag zu Augsburg 1518 Cap. 3 Col. 470
12. WB 1. 129
13. Lyndal Roper, *Martin Luther: Renegade and Prophet* (London: The Bodley Head, 2016) 113
14. *Idem*
15. Martin Luther, *Dr Martin Luthers Briefe, Sendschreiben und Bedenken,* Vol. 1, ed. Wilhelm Martin Leberecht de Wette (Berlin: 1825) 142-145
16. *Ibid.,* 147-149
17. Martin Luther, cited in Roland Bainton, *Here I Stand* (Oxford: Lion Publishing, 1978) 97
18. Martin Luther, *Dr Martin Luthers Briefe, Sendschreiben und Bedenken,* Vol. 1, ed. Wilhelm Martin Leberecht de Wette (Berlin:1825) 149-158
19. *Ibid.,* 162-163
20. *Ibid.,* 163-165

Chapter Four

1. Roland Bainton, *Here I Stand* (Oxford: Lion Publishing, 1978) 103
2. Daniel Olivier, *The Trial of Luther,* trans. John Hopkins (London: Mowbray, 1978) 83
3. John M. Todd, *Martin Luther: A Biographical Study* (London: Burns & Oates, 1964) 163

4. Ludwig Pastor, *History of the Popes,* Vol. 7 (London: Kegan Paul, 1908) 384; Hubert Jedin, ed., *History of the Church,* Vol. 5 (London: Burns & Oates, 1980) 62
5. Lyndal Roper, *Martin Luther: Renegade and Prophet* (London: The Bodley Head, 2016) 131
6. Klaus Schatz SJ, *Papal Primacy: From its Origins to the Present* (Collegeville: Michael Glazier, 1996) *passim*
7. Lyndal Roper, *Martin Luther: Renegade and Prophet* (London: The Bodley Head, 2016) 134
8. Roland Bainton, *Here I Stand* (Oxford: Lion Publishing, 1978) 117
9. *Idem.*
10. Ibid., 119
11. Daniel Olivier, *The Trial of Luther,* trans. John Hopkins (London: Mowbray, 1978) 90
12. Hubert Jedin, ed., *History of the Church,* Vol. 5 (London: Burns & Oates, 1980) 62

Chapter Five

1. Bernard Hamilton, *Religion in the Medieval West* (London: Edward Arnold, 1986) 129
2. Alister McGrath, *The Intellectual Origins of the European Reformation* (Oxford: Blackwell, 1987) 74-85
3. Lyndal Roper, *Martin Luther: Renegade and Prophet* (London: The Bodley Head, 2016) 100
4. WA 2 714-23; LW 35:9-22
5. Heiko A. Oberman, *Luther: Man Between God and the Devil* (New Haven: Yale, 1989)
6. Paul Reiter, *Martin Luthers Umwelt, Charakter und Psychose,* 2 Vols (Copenhagen: Leven & Munksgaard, 1937-41)
7. Erik Erikson, *Young Man Luther* (New York: W. W. Norton & Co., 1958)
8. Lyndal Roper, *Martin Luther: Renegade and Prophet* (London: The Bodley Head, 2016) 206
9. Roland Bainton, *Here I Stand* (Oxford: Lion Publishing, 1978) 143
10. Scott H. Hendrix, *Martin Luther: Visionary Reformer* (New Haven: Yale, 2015) 84
11. Ludwig Pastor, *History of the Popes,* Vol. 7 (London: Kegan Paul, 1908) 400-2

12. LW 44:123-217
13. WA 3 417
14. Saint Bernard of Clairvaux, *St Bernard's Sermons on the Canticle of Canticles*, Vol. 1, trans. a priest of Mount Melleray (Dublin: Browne and Nolan, 1909) 406-408
15. Saint Bernard of Clairvaux, *The Letters of St Bernard*, trans. B. Scott James (Kalamazoo: Cistercian Publications, 1998) 86

Chapter Six

1. LW 36:11-126
2. *Ibid.*, 11
3. *Ibid.*, 29
4. *Ibid.*, 31
5. Martin Luther, *Luther's Basic Theological Writings*, trans. and ed. Timothy F. Lull (Minneapolis: Fortress Press, 1989) 252
6. LW 36:37
7. LW 36:51
8. LW 36:57
9. LW 36:60
10. LW 36:13
11. Martin Luther, *Luther's Basic Theological Writings*, trans. and ed. Timothy F. Lull (Minneapolis: Fortress Press, 1989) 274. WA 6 501 translates it as 'endeavouring to bring me back by some thongs of rhetoric'.
12. LW 31:333–377
13. Martin Luther, *Luther's Basic Theological Writings*, trans. and ed. Timothy F. Lull (Minneapolis: Fortress Press, 1989) 590
14. Lyndal Roper, *Martin Luther: Renegade and Prophet* (London: The Bodley Head, 2016) 106
15. Martin Luther, *Luther's Basic Theological Writings*, trans. and ed. Timothy F. Lull (Minneapolis: Fortress Press, 1989) 597
16. *Ibid.*, 608
17. *Ibid.*, 610
18. LW 31: 375
19. Lyndal Roper, *Martin Luther: Renegade and Prophet* (London: The Bodley Head, 2016) 168
20. Roland Bainton, *Here I Stand* (Oxford: Lion Publishing, 1978) 166
21. Michael A. Mullett, *Martin Luther* (Abingdon: Routledge, 2015) 155

22. Peter Matheson, *The Rhetoric of the Reformation* (Edinburgh: T & T Clark, 1998) 34

Chapter Seven

1. Roland Bainton, *Here I Stand* (Oxford: Lion Publishing, 1978) 170
2. Daniel Olivier, *The Trial of Luther*, trans. John Hopkins (London: Mowbray, 1978) 141
3. Charles Butler, *Life of Erasmus: With Historical Remarks on the State of Literature Between the Tenth and Sixteenth Centuries* (London: J. Murray, 1825) 188
4. John P. Dolan, ed., *The Essential Erasmus* (New York: Mentor Omega, 1964) 193
5. Roland Bainton, *Here I Stand* (Oxford: Lion Publishing, 1978) 172
6. Martin Luther, cited in *ibid.*, 174
7. *Ibid.*, 176
8. Scott H. Hendrix, *Martin Luther: Visionary Reformer* (New Haven: Yale, 2015) 100
9. Roland Bainton, *Here I Stand* (Oxford: Lion Publishing, 1978) 178
10. WA BR 1 383 No. 1
11. WA BR 1 391
12. Michael A. Mullett, *Martin Luther* (Abingdon: Routledge, 2015) 158
13. Daniel Olivier, *The Trial of Luther*, trans. John Hopkins (London: Mowbray, 1978) 160
14. Lyndal Roper, *Martin Luther: Renegade and Prophet* (London: The Bodley Head, 2016) 177
15. WA 7 808-13; LW 51:65
16. Daniel Olivier, *The Trial of Luther*, trans. John Hopkins (London: Mowbray, 1978) 164
17. WA 7 838; LW 32:112-3
18. Lyndal Roper, *Martin Luther: Renegade and Prophet* (London: The Bodley Head, 2016) 183-4
19. Scott H. Hendrix, *Martin Luther: Visionary Reformer* (New Haven: Yale, 2015) 106
20. WA 7 97
21. Martin Luther, *Luther and Erasmus: Free Will and Salvation*, trans. and ed. E. Gordon Rupp, Philip S. Watson (Philadelphia: Westminster Press, 1969) 112
22. Steven Ozment says of Augustine's theory of knowledge:

'Through the illumination of Christ, indwelling truth, the mind received divine light by which it could know truly.' *The Age of Reform, 1250-1550: An Intellectual and Religious History of Late Medieval and Reformation Europe* (New Haven: Yale UP, 1980) 47

23. Hubert Jedin, ed., *History of the Church*, Vol. 5 (London: Burns & Oates, 1980) 74

24. *Deutsche Reichstagsakten unter Kaiser Karl V*, Vol. 2 (Gotha: Friedrich Andreas Perthes, 1896): *'il est certain que ung seul frère erre en son opinion, laquelle est contre tout(e) la crestiennité, tant de temp passé mille ans et plus que du present.'*

25. Daniel Olivier, *The Trial of Luther*, trans. John Hopkins (London: Mowbray, 1978) 170

26. Johannes Cochlaeus, cited in Lyndal Roper, *Martin Luther: Renegade and Prophet* (London: The Bodley Head, 2016) 189

27. WA BR 2 401

28. WA BR 2 410; LW 48:221

29. Martin Luther, cited in Roland Bainton, *Here I Stand* (Oxford: Lion Publishing, 1978) 194

30. Heiko A. Oberman, *Luther: Man Between God and the Devil* (New Haven: Yale, 1989) 102

31. LW Letters I: 257; WB 2 418

32. LW Letters 1: 296-304

33. C.f. LW 48: 277-279

34. LW 48:337-338

35. LW 48:330-338

36. LW 48:332

37. Scott H. Hendrix, *Martin Luther: Visionary Reformer* (New Haven: Yale, 2015) 113-114

38. LW 44:251-400

39. MPL 183, 867

40. LW 44:290

41. Martin Luther, *The Letters of Martin Luther: Selected and Translated by Margaret Currie*, trans. Margaret Currie (London: Macmillan & Co. 1908) 89-91; WA BR 2, No. 442, 405

42. See WA BR 2, No. 448, 420 for Albrecht's response.

43. Lyndal Roper, *Martin Luther: Renegade and Prophet* (London: The Bodley Head, 2016) 207

44. Heinrich Bornkamm, *Luther in Mid-Career, 1521-1530* (Philadelphia: Fortress Press, 1983) 46-7

45. *Ibid.,* 48
46. Martin Luther, cited in *ibid.,* 50
47. Lyndal Roper, *Martin Luther: Renegade and Prophet* (London: The Bodley Head, 2016) 208
48. Michael A. Mullett, *Martin Luther* (Abingdon: Routledge, 2015) 188
49. Martin Luther, *Dr Martin Luthers Werke,* Band 30, Teil II, trans. Gary Mann, Project Wittenberg (Weimar: Hermann Boehlaus Nachfolger, 1909) 632-646. 'Throughout all the revisions of his lifetime he would never relinquish that word "alone".' Roland Bainton, *Here I Stand* (Oxford: Lion Publishing, 1978) 334
50. LW 31:362
51. LW 31:331
52. Michael A. Mullett, *Martin Luther* (Abingdon: Routledge, 2015) 187
53. LW 31:362

Chapter Eight

1. Roland Bainton, *Here I Stand* (Oxford: Lion Publishing, 1978) 198
2. John M. Todd, *Martin Luther: A Biographical Study* (London: Burns & Oates, 1964) 203
3. WA 8 411-76
4. Roland Bainton, *Here I Stand* (Oxford: Lion Publishing, 1978) 205
5. Letter 71, 'To Wittenbergers', http://www.godrules.net/library/luther/208luther2.htm
6. Michael A. Mullett, *Martin Luther* (Abingdon: Routledge, 2015) 176
7. Bernhard Lohse, *Martin Luther: An Introduction to His Life and Work* (Edinburgh: T & T Clark, 1986) 58
8. Martin Luther, *Luther's Basic Theological Writings,* trans. and ed. Timothy F. Lull (Minneapolis: Fortress Press, 1989) 353
9. Martin Luther, cited in Roland Bainton, *Here I Stand* (Oxford: Lion Publishing, 1978) 208
10. Martin Luther, *Dr Martin Luthers Sämmtliche Schriften* ed. Johann Georg Walch (St Louis: Concordia Publishing House, 1890) 5:11, Appendix 104
11. Letter 75, 'to Elector Friedrich', http://www.godrules.net/library/luther/208luther2.htm
12. Martin Luther, *The Letters of Martin Luther 1483-1546,* ed. and trans. Margaret Currie (London: Macmillan and Co., 1908) 98-100

13. Daniel Olivier, *The Trial of Luther,* trans. John Hopkins (London: Mowbray, 1978) 193
14. Michael A. Mullett, *Martin Luther* (Abingdon: Routledge, 2015) 178-9
15. Scott H. Hendrix, *Martin Luther: Visionary Reformer* (New Haven: Yale, 2015) 128
16. LW 51: 87
17. Michael A. Mullett, *Martin Luther* (Abingdon: Routledge, 2015) 181
18. Martin Luther, *Luther's Basic Theological Writings,* trans. and ed. Timothy F. Lull (Minneapolis: Fortress Press, 1989) 294-5
19. LW 39:68
20. Martin Luther, *Sermons of Martin Luther,* Vol. 7, ed. and trans. J. N. Lenker (Ohio, 1884) 6-16
21. He also contributed to the early ecumenical convergence, at a time when the studies of Catholic scholars, especially Benedictine communities in Belgium and Germany, were laying the groundwork for it by developing the theology of the Paschal Mystery.
22. Yngve Brilioth, cited in Frank C. Senn, *Christian Liturgy: Catholic and Evangelical* (Minneapolis: Fortress Press, 1997) 615
23. Helmar Junghans, 'Luther's Wittenberg' in *The Cambridge Companion to Martin Luther,* ed. Donald McKim (Cambridge: Cambridge UP, 2003) 22
24. Martin Luther, *Documents of the Continental Reformation,* ed. B.J. Kidd (Oxford: Clarendon Press 1911) 128-32
25. Howard Brown, *Music in the Renaissance* (New Jersey: Prentice-Hall 1976) 273
26. Frank C. Senn, *Christian Liturgy: Catholic and Evangelical* (Minneapolis: Fortress Press, 1997) 346-7

Chapter Nine

1. Martin Luther, *Documents of the Continental Reformation,* ed. B. J. Kidd (Oxford: Clarendon Press 1911) 193
2. Desiderius Erasmus, *Luther and Erasmus: Free Will and Salvation,* trans. and ed. E. Gordon Rupp, Philip S. Watson (Philadelphia: Westminster Press, 1969) 36
3. Desiderius Erasmus, cited in *The Reformation in its Own Words*

ed. Hans Hillerbrand (London: S.C.M. Press, 1964) 424

4. Steven Ozment, *The Age of Reform, 1250-1550: An Intellectual and Religious History of Late Medieval and Reformation Europe* (New Haven: Yale UP, 1980) 292

5. Bernard Reardon, *Religious Thought in the Reformation* (London: Longman, 1981) 36

6. LW 31:40

7. Martin Luther, *Luther's Basic Theological Writings*, trans. and ed. Timothy F. Lull (Minneapolis: Fortress Press, 1989) 615

8. Desiderius Erasmus, *Luther and Erasmus: Free Will and Salvation*, trans. and eds E. Gordon Rupp and Philip S. Watson (Philadelphia: Westminster Press, 1969) 38

9. *Ibid.*, 50

10. *Ibid.*, 93

11. Saint Thomas Aquinas, *De Veritate*, Q.22 A.5

12. Saint Thomas Aquinas, *De Veritate*, Q.24 A.1

13. Desiderius Erasmus, *Luther and Erasmus: Free Will and Salvation*, trans. and eds E. Gordon Rupp and Philip S. Watson (Philadelphia: Westminster Press, 1969) 58

14. *Ibid.*, 64

15. *Ibid.*, 68

16. *Ibid.*, 71

17. *Ibid.*, 87

18. *Ibid.*, 89-90

19. Martin Luther, *ibid.*, 102

20. Desiderius Erasmus, *ibid.*, 38

21. *Ibid.*, 37

22. Martin Luther, *ibid.*, 104

23. *Ibid.*, 333. There is a variant of this text as two versions are found in WA, 'You and you alone have seen the question on which everything hinges and aimed the knife at the vital spot, for which I heartily thank you.' LW 33:294; 'Lectures in Galatians' WA 40: 687; LW 26:459

24. Martin Luther, cited in Scott H. Hendrix, *Martin Luther: Visionary Reformer* (New Haven: Yale, 2015) 169

25. Desiderius Erasmus, *Luther and Erasmus: Free Will and Salvation*, trans. and eds E. Gordon Rupp and Philip S. Watson (Philadelphia: Westminster Press, 1969) 47

26. *Ibid.*, 84-85

27. Martin Luther, *ibid.*, 114
28. Desiderius Erasmus, *ibid.*, 37
29. *Ibid.*, 38
30. Gerald Bonner, *Freedom and Necessity: St Augustine's Teaching on Divine Power and Human Freedom* (Washington DC: Catholic UP, 2007) 107
31. Martin Luther, *Luther and Erasmus: Free Will and Salvation,* trans. and ed. E. Gordon Rupp, Philip S. Watson (Philadelphia: Westminster Press, 1969) 187
32. Heiko A. Oberman, *Luther: Man Between God and the Devil* (New Haven: Yale, 1989) 219
33. Roland Bainton, *Here I Stand* (Oxford: Lion Publishing, 1978) 286-7
34. Michael A. Mullett, *Martin Luther* (Abingdon: Routledge, 2015) 235
35. Lyndal Roper, *Martin Luther: Renegade and Prophet* (London: The Bodley Head, 2016) 274
36. Roland Bainton, *Here I Stand* (Oxford: Lion Publishing, 1978) 288
37. WA BR 377
38. Letter 105, 'To the Learned and Saintly Nicholas Gerbel', http://www.martinluthersermons.com/luther-letters-500pl-index.pdf
39. Martin Luther, *Documents of the Continental Reformation,* ed. B. J. Kidd (Oxford: Clarendon Press 1911) 174-9
40. *Ibid.*, 174
41. Steven Ozment, *The Age of Reform, 1250-1550: An Intellectual and Religious History of Late Medieval and Reformation Europe* (New Haven: Yale UP, 1980) 277
42. Martin Luther, cited in Heinrich Bornkamm, *Luther in Mid-Career, 1521-1530* (Philadelphia: Fortress Press, 1983) 39
43. *Ibid.*, 366; Michael A. Mullett, *Martin Luther* (Abingdon: Routledge, 2015) 208
44. Steven Ozment, *The Age of Reform, 1250-1550: An Intellectual and Religious History of Late Medieval and Reformation Europe* (New Haven: Yale UP, 1980) 283
45. Heinrich Bornkamm, *Luther in Mid-Career, 1521-1530* (Philadelphia: Fortress Press, 1983) 368
46. *Ibid.*, 371
47. *Ibid.*, 385
48. Roland Bainton, *Here I Stand* (Oxford: Lion Publishing, 1978) 280
49. LW 49-55

Chapter Ten

1. Hubert Jedin, ed., *History of the Church*, Vol. 5 (London: Burns & Oates, 1980) 212
2. Roland Bainton, *Here I Stand* (Oxford: Lion Publishing, 1978) 317
3. Hubert Jedin, ed., *History of the Church*, Vol. 5 (London: Burns & Oates, 1980) 213
4. *Ibid.*, 239
5. Roland Bainton, *Here I Stand* (Oxford: Lion Publishing, 1978) 318
6. Cited in *History of the Church*, Vol. 5, ed. Hubert Jedin (London: Burns & Oates, 1980) 243
7. Bernhard Lohse, *Martin Luther: An Introduction to His Life and Work* (Edinburgh: T & T Clark, 1986) 75
8. Roland Bainton, *Here I Stand* (Oxford: Lion Publishing, 1978) 320
9. Bernard Reardon, *Religious Thought in the Reformation* (London: Longman, 1981) 100
10. Martin Luther, *Documents of the Continental Reformation*, ed. B. J. Kidd (Oxford: Clarendon Press 1911) 249
11. Heinrich Bornkamm, *Luther in Mid-Career, 1521-1530* (Philadelphia: Fortress Press, 1983) 632
12. Roland Bainton, *Here I Stand* (Oxford: Lion Publishing, 1978) 318-9; WA BR 1496

Chapter Eleven

1. Roland Bainton, *Here I Stand* (Oxford: Lion Publishing, 1978) 323
2. John Bossy, *Christianity in the West 1400-1700* (Oxford: Oxford UP, 1985) 51
3. WA 30:340 23; LW 34:49
4. WA BR 1611; 412
5. WA BR 5 405, 19
6. Michael A. Mullett, *Martin Luther* (Abingdon: Routledge, 2015) 279
7. Martin Luther, 'The Confession of Faith: Which Was Submitted to His Imperial Majesty Charles V At the Diet of Augsburg in the Year 1530 by Philip Melancthon (1497-1560)', in *Triglot Concordia: The Symbolical Books of the Ev. Lutheran Church,* trans. F. Bente and W. H. T. Dau (St. Louis: Concordia Publishing House, 1921), https://www.iclnet.org/pub/resources/text/wittenberg/concord/web/augs-008.html

8. Martin Luther, cited in Heinrich Bornkamm, *Luther in Mid-Career, 1521-1530* (Philadelphia: Fortress Press, 1983) 681
9. Lyndal Roper, *Martin Luther: Renegade and Prophet* (London: The Bodley Head, 2016) 381
10. LW 35:209
11. Scott H. Hendrix, *Martin Luther: Visionary Reformer* (New Haven: Yale, 2015) 228
12. *Ibid.*, 265

Chapter Twelve

1. WA 6 459
2. WA 30 II 123-147: LW 46:161-205
3. Michael A. Mullett, *Martin Luther* (Abingdon: Routledge, 2015) 321
4. David M. Whitford, *Luther: A Guide for the Perplexed* (T & T Clark: London, 2011) 154
5. WA 15 741-58
6. Roland Bainton, *Here I Stand* (Oxford: Lion Publishing, 1978) 379
7. Scott H. Hendrix, *Martin Luther: Visionary Reformer* (New Haven: Yale, 2015) 277
8. Bernhard Lohse, *Martin Luther: An Introduction to His Life and Work* (Edinburgh: T & T Clark, 1986) 89
9. David M. Whitford, *Luther: A Guide for the Perplexed* (T & T Clark: London, 2011) 166
10. LW 47:137
11. Scott H. Hendrix, *Martin Luther: Visionary Reformer* (New Haven: Yale, 2015) 275
12. LW 47:268
13. *Ibid.*, 272
14. *Ibid.*, 274
15. Martin Luther, *Dr Martin Luthers Sämmtliche Schriften* ed. Johann Georg Walch (St Louis: Concordia Publishing House, 1890)
16. *Ibid.*, No. 50
17. *Ibid.*, No. 59
18. Hubert Jedin, ed., *History of the Church*, Vol. 5 (London: Burns & Oates, 1980) 286
19. Mark U. Edwards Jr, *Luther's Last Battles: Politics and Polemics 1531-1546* (Minneapolis: Fortress Press, 1983) 184
20. *Ibid.*, 185

21. WA 54 228
22. WA 54 201
23. WA 54 243
24. Scott H. Hendrix, *Martin Luther: Visionary Reformer* (New Haven: Yale, 2015) 382
25. Martin Luther, *Dr Martin Luthers Briefe, Sendschreiben und Bedenken*, Vol. 5, ed. Wilhelm Leberecht de Wette (Berlin, 1828) 727-8
26. *Ibid.*, 425-430
27. *Ibid.*, 780
28. P. F. Lyons, 'Luther's Last Sermon: In Commemoration of the 450th Anniversary of Luther's Death'. *Pro Ecclesia* 5.3 (1996): 304
29. *Ibid.*, 313
30. Scott H. Hendrix, *Martin Luther: Visionary Reformer* (New Haven: Yale, 2015) 287-8

Chapter Thirteen

1. Timothy F. Lull, trans. and ed., *Luther's Basic Theological Writings* (Minneapolis: Fortress Press, 1989) 405
2. Heiko A. Oberman, *Luther: Man Between God and the Devil* (New Haven: Yale, 1989) 12
3. Peter Stanford, *Martin Luther: Catholic Dissident* (London: Hodder & Stoughton, 2017) 396
4. James Kittelson, 'Luther and Modern Church History' in *The Cambridge Companion to Martin Luther,* ed. Donald McKim, (Cambridge: Cambridge UP, 2003) 262
5. Michael A. Mullett, *Martin Luther* (Abingdon: Routledge, 2015) 103
6. WA TR V no. 6059, 469
7. WA TR III no. 3428, 313
8. WA 47, 392; David M. Whitford, *Luther: A Guide for the Perplexed* (T & T Clark: London, 2011) 59-60
9. WA BR 2 48 ('*ego angor*')
10. Scott H. Hendrix, *Luther and the Papacy: Stages in a Reformation Conflict* (Philadelphia: Fortress, 1981) 102. Hendrix chronicles the stages of Luther's conflict with the papacy in detail.
11. LW 44:118-9
12. WA BR 2 120
13. WA 6 328
14. WA 6 37

15. LW 39:55-104
16. Oswald Bayer, *Martin Luther's Theology: A Contemporary Interpretation*, trans. Thomas Trapp (Grand Rapids: William B. Eerdmans, 2008) 331
17. WA 54 187
18. LW 39:68
19. Thomas Torrance, 'The Eschatology of Faith' in *Luther: Theologian for Catholics and Protestants*, ed. George Yule (Edinburgh: T & T Clark, 1985) 145-203; 148
20. Ibid., 149
21. WA 40 I 372.
22. Robert Jenson, 'Luther's Contemporary Theological Significance' in *The Cambridge Companion to Martin Luther*, ed. Donald McKim, (Cambridge: Cambridge UP, 2003) 281
23. WA 17/1, 438; Martin Luther, *Sermons of Martin Luther*, Vol. 8, ed. and trans. J. N. Lenker (Grand Rapids: Baker Book House, 1989) 235-6
24. WA 7 24
25. Martin Luther, *Sermons of Martin Luther*, Vol. 8, ed. and trans. J. N. Lenker (Grand Rapids: Baker Book House, 1989) 236
26. LW 48:281
27. Timothy George, *Theology of the Reformers* (Nashville: Broadman Press, 1988) 101. Despite placing Luther's life in the context of the conflict between God and the devil, Heiko Oberman does not use the same term.
28. Oswald Bayer, *Martin Luther's Theology: A Contemporary Interpretation*, trans. Thomas Trapp (Grand Rapids: William B. Eerdmans, 2008) 332
29. P. F. Lyons, 'Luther's Last Sermon: In Commemoration of the 450th Anniversary of Luther's Death'. *Pro Ecclesia* 5.3 (1996): 310
30. Mark U. Edwards Jr, *Luther's Last Battles: Politics and Polemics 1531-1546* (Minneapolis: Fortress Press, 1983) 204
31. Richard Landes, 'Millenarianism and the Dynamics of Apocalyptic Time' in *Expecting the End: Millenniasm in Social and Historical Context*, eds K. Newport and C. Gribben (Waco: Baylor UP, 2006) 4
32. Mark U. Edwards Jr, *Luther's Last Battles: Politics and Polemics 1531-1546* (Minneapolis: Fortress Press, 1983) 9
33. *Ibid.,* 10

34. WA TR 2 455-6
35. WA TR 1 87
36. Charles Taylor, *A Secular Age* (Cambridge MA: The Belknap Press, 2007) 88
37. LW 45:70
38. Martin Luther, *Luther's Basic Theological Writings,* trans. and ed. Timothy F. Lull (Minneapolis: Fortress Press, 1989) 344
39. WA 2 339. '*Pestis eram vivens, moriens ero mors tua, papa.*'
40. WA 3 279
41. WA 51 473-98
42. LW 45:108
43. LW 51:390-1
44. Elector Johann, cited in Martin Brecht, *The Preservation of the Church 1532-1546,* Vol 3., trans. J.L. Schaaf (Minnesota: Fortress Press, 1993) 377

Chapter Fourteen

1. Mike Mattes, *The Role of Justification in Contemporary Theology* (Grand Rapids: Willam B. Eerdmans, 2004)
2. Harry McSorley, 'Luther: Model or Teacher for Church Reform?' in *Luther: Theologian for both Catholics and Protestants,* ed. George Yule (London T & T Clark, 1985) 36
3. Henricus Denzinger and Adolfus Schönmetzer, *Enchiridion Symbolorum Definitionum et declarationum de rebus fide et morum, Editio XXXIV* (Freiburg: Herder, 1927) Sessio 22, Cap.8, Can. 9
4. The Fourth World Conference on Faith and Order, 'Faith and Order Paper No. 42' in *The Report from Montreal 1963,* eds P. C. Rodger and L. Vischer (London, World Council of Churches, 1964)
5. P. F. Lyons, 'Where is the Church?', *Doctrine and Life,* 51.1 (2001): 8-17
6. Cardinal Walter Kasper, *Weckrufökumene* (Freiburg: Herder, 2017) 32. Citation translated by Anshelm Barry OSB.
7. *Ibid.,* 33
8. *Ibid.,* 62-3
9. *Ibid.,* 150
10. Charles Taylor, *A Secular Age* (Cambridge MA: Harvard UP, 2007) 25

11. *Ibid.*, 530
12. *Ibid.*, 77-87
13. Carlos M. N. Eire, *Reformations: The Early Modern Word, 1450-1650* (New Haven: Yale UP, 2016) 748
14. *Ibid.*, 750
15. Joseph Ratzinger *Commentary on the Documents of Vatican II,* Vol. 5 (London: Burns & Oates, 1969) 119-123
16. Pope Francis, Homily 31st October 2016, *Pontifical Council for the Promotion of Christian Unity Information Service,* No. 148 (2016/II) 18-19, http://www.vatican.va/roman_curia/pontifical_councils/chrstuni/information_service/pdf/information_service_148_en.pdf
17. WA 40 I 372.
18. Martin Luther, *Sermons of Martin Luther,* Vol. 7, ed. and trans. J. N. Lenker (Ohio, 1884) 236
19. LW 44: 245-396
20. C.f. Saint Thomas Aquinas, *De Veritate,* Q.22 A.5; *Summa Theoligae.* I-II Q.5 A.3
21. Heiko A. Oberman, *Luther: Man Between God and the Devil* (New Haven: Yale, 1989) 219
22. Pope Francis, Homily 31st October 2016, *Pontifical Council for Promoting Christian Unity Information Service,* N. 148 (2016/II), 18-19, http://www.vatican.va/roman_curia/pontifical_councils/chrstuni/information_service/pdf/information_service_148_en.pdf

Appendix 1

1. LW 31:25-33

Appendix 2

1. Eugène Portalié, *A Guide to the Thought of Saint Augustine,* trans. R. J. Bastian (London: Burns & Oates, 1960) 109
2. Thomas Allin, *The Augustinian Revolution in Theology* (Sydney: Wentworth Press, 2007) 107
3. Roger Haight, 'Sin and Grace' in *Systematic Theology,* eds John P. Galvin and Francis Schüssler Fiorenza (Dublin: Gill & Macmillan, 1992) 403-463
4. *Ibid.*, 445

5. *Ibid.*, 446
6. Gerald Bonner, *Freedom and Necessity: St Augustine's Teaching on Divine Power and Human Freedom* (Washington DC: Catholic UP, 2007) 107
7. *Ibid.*, 110

INDEX

M